COURAGE UNDER FIRE

COURAGE
UNDER FIRE
UNDER SIEGE AND OUTNUMBERED
58 TO 1 ON JANUARY 6

STEVEN A. SUND
FORMER CHIEF OF THE UNITED STATES CAPITOL POLICE

**BLACK
STONE**
PUBLISHING

Printed in the United States of America

First edition: 2023
ISBN 979-8-200-98363-6
Biography & Autobiography / Law Enforcement

Version 1

CIP data for this book is available
from the Library of Congress

Blackstone Publishing
31 Mistletoe Rd.
Ashland, OR 97520

www.BlackstonePublishing.com

This book is dedicated to the many law enforcement officers and first responders who selflessly continue to put on the badge and vest and go to work to keep their communities safe. And to those we have lost. Your courage inspires us, your sacrifice humbles us.

There is no greater love than to lay down one's life for one's friends.

—John 15:13

CONTENTS

"10-33" AT THE CAPITOL

I was standing in the Command Center at police headquarters, surrounded by monitors, each one showing me the same story. The mob was growing, from hundreds to thousands, with even more on the way. The rioters kept assaulting my officers on the West Front of the Capitol, beating and jabbing at them with flagpoles and sticks, throwing tools and construction debris at their heads, spraying chemicals in their eyes.

I wanted to get out there myself, as I had done so many times as a cop on the street. But right now my officers needed extraordinary help, and I was the only one who could get it for them. As I made yet another frantic call for help, I watched helplessly while my greatly outnumbered officers were brutally attacked. The situation was bad and getting worse by the minute.

Inside the Capitol Building were all the members of Congress, whom I was sworn to protect, as well as the vice president and his family. I could see the rage on many faces in the crowd, and I knew that if they got into the building, they would show no mercy.

Please don't let them get inside that building, I prayed. Yet as the battle raged on, the crowd just kept getting bigger and bigger. The courageous officers fought on as hard as they could to defend every inch of ground, but the crowd kept pushing forward. My officers could not hold them back much longer.

Officers were screaming on the radio, "Ten-thirty-three! Ten-thirty-three!" When you're a cop, this is the most chilling radio call you can ever hear. It's the ultimate cry for help—a life-or-death situation. *Officer down, needs immediate assistance.*

But where would that assistance come from? Thank God the Metropolitan Police Department (MPD) had sent me reinforcements, but we needed more. Much more.

The crowd kept surging up the West Front of the building. Every available officer was running to join the fight. But then suddenly, there was a flash point on the East Front, and the mob turned instantly from agitated to violent. They were tearing down our perimeter fencing and trying to reach the rotunda steps. Many of my officers were surrounded now, some fighting their way free, while others were pulled to the ground and beaten.

Their radios were useless now. No one could hear them over the chaos, and no one was left to respond even if they could.

I called again for help, yelling into the phone. But the National Guard, fully equipped with their riot gear and standing just blocks away, was not coming to help us.

At 2:10 p.m., my watch commander announced that the rioters had begun to smash in the windows of the Capitol.

Two minutes later, he yelled across the room, "Chief, they've breached the Capitol! The Capitol has been breached!"

INTRODUCTION:
WHO'S WHO IN WASHINGTON, DC

My father was a career air force officer with the kind of larger-than-life persona you'd expect from a B-52 pilot who flew countless missions in Vietnam and over the polar ice caps during the Cold War. One of the phrases I learned from him was "SNAFU." I'm guessing you already know what this means, so you won't find it in this book's list of acronyms, but I found this term appropriate when working on the Hill. The multilayered security coordination and committee oversight on the Hill made policing very difficult, usually because issues were approached from a political perspective and not based purely on security. To a career law enforcement officer like me, the Capitol Hill security apparatus seemed alien, and with each daily reminder that I must cater to a multitude of bosses simultaneously, I came to accept that policing on the Hill can only be described as one big SNAFU.

To understand what occurred on January 6, 2021, and what I was up against on that day, you need to understand the convoluted security construct that is in place on Capitol Hill, along with all the major players in town, which together make being the chief of the Capitol Police (according to CNN) "the toughest job in America."

Before joining the USCP, I had been with the Washington, DC, municipal police force, the Metropolitan Police Department (MPD), for more than twenty-five years. During my time with the MPD, I worked in some of the most crime-ridden areas of the city, oversaw various task forces and focused mission units, managed several active-shooter incidents, and planned dozens of major events and National Special Security Events (NSSE), as well as helped shape the Department of Homeland Security's National Response Framework. At the end of 2015, I retired as commander (deputy chief) of the elite Special Operations Division, which I had commanded since 2011. It was a fast-paced division with long hours and many unpredictable situations: pulling a body out of the Potomac River, K9s searching a house for a suspect, SWAT deployment in a hostage situation, our bomb squad responding to a suspicious package—as the commander, I responded to most if not all of these scenes. I also oversaw presidential and dignitary escorts, mass demonstrations, and traffic fatalities. After five years in this position, I was ready to retire.

In my temporary "retirement," I worked in the private sector for a nonprofit providing support to the intelligence and law enforcement communities. The hours were good, and the pay was excellent. Life was simpler and slower paced, with no late-night calls for barricade situations, no more missed holidays or family gatherings due to major events in DC, no getting dressed at three in the morning to respond with lights flashing and sirens blaring. But despite all these positives, I still felt the need to return to public service. I missed being a cop.

THE US CAPITOL POLICE

In the fall of 2016, I was asked to become the assistant chief of police/ chief of operations at the United States Capitol Police Department. I was brought on board shortly before President Trump's inauguration in January 2017. Just over two years later, on June 14, 2019, I was sworn in as the tenth USCP chief of police.

The coordination of security on Capitol Hill is like no other place in the world, and the USCP is like no other police department. When I was with the MPD, the USCP had always been looked upon as the odd man out among DC's big four (MPD, US Park Police, USCP, and US Secret Service). The Capitol Police always seemed to do things their own unique way.

The USCP has an enormous responsibility for protecting the legislature and our democratic process. They protect 535 members of Congress, their staffs, and the congressional facilities so that Congress can carry out its constitutional legislative responsibilities in a safe and secure environment. Unlike the executive branch of government, which has authority over several different law enforcement agencies, including the FBI, Secret Service (USSS), DEA, ATF, and DHS Homeland Security Investigations, the USCP is the *one and only* law enforcement agency assigned to the protection and security of the legislative branch of government. The USCP cannot be given orders by any federal, state, or local authorities outside the legislative branch, and no federal, state, or local law enforcement agencies are allowed on the Hill without an invitation or permission from the legislative branch.

The US Capitol grounds, which surround the congressional facilities, are open to the public, and every day we have thousands of people walking to work, biking, jogging, or just sightseeing. Also, we host a number of free events every year that are open to the public, such as the highly attended Memorial Day and Fourth of July concerts on the West Front, and many other free events that occur in the spring and summer.

The US Capitol has also been the site of some less festive events that have literally stained the white limestone that makes up much of the floors, walls, and hardscape of this beautiful building. The British attacked and burned the Capitol in 1814. In 1954, a group of Puerto Rican nationalists opened fire on lawmakers from the House gallery, injuring five members of Congress. (Bullet holes are still visible in the House Chamber.) In 1971 and again in 1983, left-wing extremists detonated bombs in the Senate wing of the Capitol. (Both explosions caused significant damage, and the latter came very close to seriously injuring a USCP officer.) In 1998, in an incident I remember all too well, having been with the MPD at the time, USCP officer Jacob Chestnut and Detective John Gibson were killed in the line of duty on July 24 during a gun battle with a deranged man who had forced his way into an entrance at the Capitol and was trying to make his way into the House leadership offices.

Following a much-needed departmental reorganization that I had initiated in 2019, I went into that long summer of 2020 and then the events of January 6 with two assistant chiefs, each assigned to a different role within the department: Assistant Chief Chad Thomas, in charge of Uniform Operations, and Assistant Chief Yogananda Pittman, in charge of Protective and Intelligence Operations.

My total staffing was 1,843 sworn employees and 386 civilian employees, for a total of 2,229 employees. This staffing level made the USCP the twenty-fifth-largest police department in the country. People are often surprised to hear that the USCP is such a large agency, but it is a full-service police department that provides screening at building entrances, uniformed and plainclothes patrol in and around the congressional buildings, a robust K9 program, an explosives mitigation and hazardous materials program, tactical/SWAT teams, a Dignitary Protection Division, an Investigations and Threat Mitigation Division, an intelligence section, a multiagency command center, a training center, and a physical security program. We are the one-stop shop for everything law enforcement in the legislative branch. I would often tell my officials and officers that with our role protecting Congress and the legislative process, we fulfill more of a national security mission than a traditional police department function. Few people realize how different our department truly is.

While most law enforcement agencies have a chief or sheriff who reports to a single person—a mayor, city manager, or director of public safety—I had many bosses and layers of oversight, all of them in politically aligned positions. Thus, political considerations weighed heavily on their decisions involving security operations. Essentially, I had 535 bosses who could exert real influence on the department. I also had the Capitol Police Board (CPB), four oversight committees, the leadership in the House and Senate, and all of their staffs.

THE CAPITOL POLICE BOARD

As the chief, I reported directly to the Capitol Police Board, which comprises three individuals selected through three separate political processes. The chairman of the Capitol Police Board and Senate sergeant at arms

(SSAA), Michael Stenger, was nominated by Senate Majority Leader Mitch McConnell and voted in by the Senate. The House sergeant at arms (HSAA), Paul Irving, was nominated by Speaker Pelosi and voted in by the House. And the Architect of the Capitol (AOC), J. Brett Blanton, was appointed by President Donald Trump. (The Architect of the Capitol is in charge of the physical structures of the Capitol and congressional office buildings.)

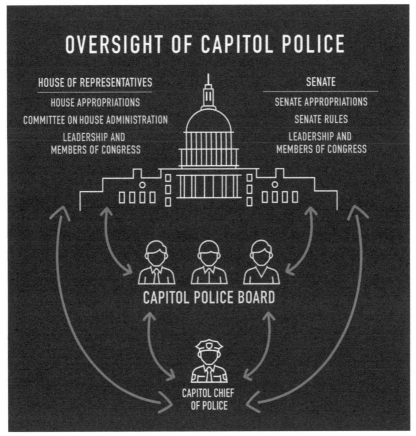

Figure 0.1. Oversight structure. Image by William McCarty. Permission granted.

Each of the three voting members of the CPB has a piece of the action in maintaining the security of a specific part of the congressional campus. Imagine the iconic view of the US Capitol from the National Mall, and picture an imaginary line running straight down the center of the dome. Everything to the right of the line, including half of the Capitol Building and the congressional office buildings, is part of the House of Representatives and falls under the authority of the House sergeant at arms. Everything to the left of the line is part of the US Senate and falls under the authority of the Senate sergeant at arms. The Architect of the Capitol is in charge of the maintenance and improvement of all the facilities, as well as the oversight of the Botanical Gardens.

At the Capitol, it is always two sides of the same building, run by two separate entities. It's important to keep this image in mind as I take you through this security conundrum. These two halves of the Capitol are completely different worlds at times, especially when you have different parties in charge of the House and the Senate, which was the case when I was chief.

Senate Sergeant at Arms Stenger served as the Senate's chief law enforcement officer, meaning that half the US Capitol Building, half the West Front, and half the East Front all fell under his purview. House Sergeant at Arms Irving was the chief law enforcement officer of the House of Representatives, and everything on the other side of the line fell under his purview. So when you think of me as the chief law enforcement officer for the Congress or the Capitol complex, think again. There are two chiefs over the chief. The SSAA and HSAA are both referred to as the "chief law enforcement officer" and are each charged with maintaining the security, rules, and regulations for their appointed house of Congress. This structure has several inherent flaws, the most important being that it doesn't allow a single person, such as the chief of police, to make the final determinations and urgent decisions regarding the security of the campus.

The final voting member of the Capitol Police Board is the Architect of the Capitol. He is on the Capitol Police Board for the role he plays in the physical security of the buildings and grounds, and the coordination of this security with the Capitol Police Board and the USCP.

As chief of the USCP, I was the final member of the Capitol Police Board, but only as a nonvoting member. In other words, the one apolitical member of the board that can provide input on security concerns and initiatives but doesn't have a vote in the final decision.

It is also important to understand that the CPB has a designated chairperson—a position that rotates annually between the House and Senate sergeants at arms. This will come into play later when we get to the events of January 6.

THE CAPITOL POLICE BOARD (CPB) ON JANUARY 6, 2021

- Michael Stenger, United States Senate sergeant at arms and chair (chair)
- Paul Irving, US House of Representatives sergeant at arms (member)
- J. Brett Blanton, Architect of the Capitol (member)
- Steven Sund, chief of police (ex officio member)

Although Stenger and Irving held identical positions in the House and the Senate, they could not have had more different personalities. While Pelosi might be seen as a sort of "godfather of the Hill" because of how she exerts her authority, Stenger personified the same character more by appearance and mannerism. He spoke slowly with a slightly raspy voice and a Jersey accent. I used to think to myself, *If Coppola is looking for an actor to do a remake of* The Godfather, *Stenger is his man.* I even had the theme music to *The Godfather* as his ringtone on my cell phone for a time.

Stenger was easier to work with than Irving. He had been a US marine before joining the United States Secret Service. He understood the ramifications that certain decisions would have on security, and he would sometimes try to stand up for me. In contrast, Irving, who also came from the Secret Service, was much more politically astute and displayed a high level of almost blind loyalty to his bosses. That's how he was able to thread the needle from a Republican Speaker to a Democrat, back to another Republican, and then back to a Democrat with apparent ease. He knew how the game is played, and was politically savvy enough to navigate the environment on the Hill. Often, when Irving was preparing to discuss an issue with leadership or oversight, he would say he was off to go do his "Kabuki dance."

CONGRESSIONAL OVERSIGHT

In addition to the Capitol Police Board, four congressional committees from the House of Representatives and Senate have statutory oversight responsibilities for the United States Capitol Police. The appropriations committees (one on the House side, the other on the Senate side) funded my agency, and the authorizing committees (again, one from each chamber) oversaw operations. The ultimate goal of these committees is to ensure that the USCP has what it needs to maintain the safety and security of Congress, the congressional facilities, the staff, and visitors on the Hill.

The type of policing we did each day was highly specialized, geared to the unique requirements of protecting Congress and the legislative process while also protecting the First Amendment rights of people coming to the Capitol to peacefully assemble and voice their grievances to Congress. The ability of people to express their First Amendment rights on Capitol grounds was very important to Congress. My oversight committee staffers would request briefings on upcoming demonstrations and would often express their concern over some aspect of our security planning. Comments and questions on why we were implementing certain security precautions were the subject of many meetings and calls. I would regularly hear complaints from staff about the "menacing look" of my officers in hard civil disturbance unit (CDU) gear. I would explain that the shields and helmets were needed for officer safety. We would often compromise and have the gear staged out of view but nearby if needed.

It was also clear that some members did not like the look of metal barricades to cordon off a section of the Capitol grounds since these barricades went against the look of an "open" campus and inhibited free passage for demonstrators.

Many members wanted to ensure that protesters were not impeded, either outside or inside the buildings (when they were open before the COVID-19 pandemic). While protesting inside a congressional building is technically against the law and violators can be subject to arrest, it occurred regularly. Many members of Congress would welcome their supporters and those with shared interests demonstrating in the buildings. Some members would even participate, sometimes helping block access to offices and hallways or participating in sit-ins in other members' offices. This would present a conundrum for the police as some members would angrily demand to know why we allowed protesters access inside the building, while other members would demand that we give the protesters unfettered public access. I would often have to explain that we can't prevent people from coming into the buildings simply on the suspicion that they *may* be there to protest. This is due to the First Amendment legal precedent of *prior restraint*, which bars the government from taking action to prohibit speech or other expression before it occurs. In other words, the buildings were open to the public, and there was no way for me to prevent a group from entering when I only *suspected* their participation in unlawful protest activity.

The effect of protests in congressional office buildings could be no more evident than during the Supreme Court nomination hearings for Brett Kavanaugh in September 2018. During these hearings, the USCP experienced significant demonstration activity on the East Plaza of the Capitol Building and in several of the congressional office buildings, resulting in the arrest of several hundred protesters. During these protests, on September 28, 2018, Senator Jeff Flake, who had been identified as a possible confirmation swing vote, was targeted by two female protesters who managed to follow Senator Flake onto an elevator, holding the door and keeping him a captive audience as media cameras captured this clearly uncomfortable moment. For four and a half minutes, the protesters prevented Senator Flake from leaving to attend the hearing as they proceeded to subject him to their accounts of being sexually assaulted, questioning his support for Kavanaugh. Following this interaction, Senator Flake proceeded to the hearing, and although he indicated his support to move Kavanaugh's nomination forward, he called for a one-week delay of the final vote to allow for a brief FBI investigation into the misconduct allegations against Kavanaugh. This protest action succeeded in its objective, delaying the final vote for cloture of his nomination until October 7, 2018.

THE INTELLIGENCE AGENCIES

Following the tragic events of September 11, 2001, the National Commission on Terrorist Attacks upon the United States, also known as the 9/11 Commission, recommended a wide range of changes to the intelligence community, as well as the establishment of a director of national intelligence. The Intelligence Reform and Terrorism Prevention Act of 2004 codified the role of the director of national intelligence (DNI).

The DNI serves as the head of the intelligence community (IC), which comprises eighteen federal organizations that are all part of the executive branch. These include the Office of the Director of National Intelligence, the CIA, the FBI, DHS, the Drug Enforcement Agency, the Department of Energy, the Department of State, and nine military intelligence agencies. According to the Intelligence Reform Act of 2004, the director of national intelligence is responsible for ensuring that national intelligence is provided to the president, the heads of departments and agencies of the executive branch, the chair of the Joint Chiefs of Staff and senior military commanders, the Senate and House of Representatives and the committees thereof, and anyone else the director of national intelligence determines to be appropriate. The act further states, "Such national intelligence should be timely, objective, independent of political considerations, and based upon all sources available to the intelligence community and other appropriate entities."

It is important to understand that *all* the agencies of the IC are part of the executive branch. As previously noted, the legislative branch has only one law enforcement agency, the USCP, and we are not part of the IC, which is why the law specifically includes the requirement for the DNI to report national intelligence to Congress, to ensure the connection between the executive and legislative branches of government in the sharing of intelligence.

Within the USCP, I also had my own intelligence unit, the Intelligence and Interagency Coordination Division (IICD), which serves as the principal point of contact for the USCP within the intelligence community and is responsible for identifying potential threats to the legislative branch from domestic and foreign entities and briefing the USCP, the Capitol Police Board, and others on emerging threats.

THE US MILITARY AND THE NATIONAL GUARD

The DC National Guard has over 2,700 soldiers, who live and work mainly in Washington and the surrounding suburbs of northern Virginia and Maryland. The motto of the DC National Guard, embroidered on its patch and embossed on its challenge coins above an image of the US Capitol dome, is "Capital Guardians."

The history of the DC National Guard dates back to 1801, when Washington, DC, was designated the capital of the United States. The District of Columbia was put under the control of Congress and not a governor since it was a federal territory and the seat of the federal government.[1] In 1802, Thomas Jefferson (the first president to spend his term in DC) was witnessing a deep political divide between the two major political parties that was threatening to tear the country apart. With the Virginia militia on one side of the city and the Maryland militia on the other, the District of Columbia was surrounded by military forces under the control of generals who belonged to Jefferson's rival political party. Jefferson was concerned that the will of a military leader could affect the ability of the legislative branch to carry out the will of the people, so in 1802, he swore in the first members of the DC National Guard, whose mission was to protect the new capital city.

Unlike in the states, where the National Guard reports to the

---

1. "History," District of Columbia National Guard (official website), US Department of Defense, accessed October 17, 2022, https://dc.ng.mil/About-Us/Heritage/History/.

governor, in DC the National Guard reports to the president of the United States. In 1949, by executive order, the president delegated this authority over the DC National Guard to the secretary of defense (SECDEF). That same year, the secretary of defense issued an official memorandum delegating the authority over ground forces of the DC National Guard to the secretary of the army, and the air component to the secretary of the air force. These delegations remain to this day.

On January 6, 2021, the acting SECDEF was Christopher Miller, the secretary of the army was Ryan McCarthy, and the secretary of the air force was Barbara Barrett.

The US military's support to domestic civil authorities during times of crisis is nothing new. The military is often called in to assist with relief work during natural disasters such as hurricanes, big fires, and pandemics. Support has also been made available to civil authorities during man-made crises such as terrorist attacks and instances of civil unrest. In the past, the military also provided support in DC for incidents and events such as the 2004 World War II Memorial dedication, the 2009 H1N1 flu pandemic, state funerals, and presidential inaugurations. In 2020, during the pandemic, significant military support was provided around the country to assist with the COVID-19 response.

There are basically three ways in which the DoD can provide support to civil authorities. The first and most common method is through an official request for assistance (RFA), submitted in advance of an event or situation in which the DoD's assistance may be requested. This is the type of military support request that would occur before a planned major event such as the Super Bowl or the presidential inauguration, when there is significant time to plan and coordinate support with the Department of Defense.

There are also two methods for the DoD to provide rapid response in the event of a serious emergency. These two processes are called *immediate response authority* and *emergency authority*. The main difference is that immediate response is not an exception to the Posse Comitatus Act (PCA) and does not allow the US military to be used in a domestic law enforcement capacity, whereas emergency authority is an exception to the Posse Comitatus Act and can permit the US military to participate in domestic law enforcement activities, though seeking it requires presidential approval.

When I was with the MPD, I deployed the National Guard and its quick reaction force (QRF) in a civil disturbance response capacity on numerous occasions. The QRF was a forty-soldier team trained and equipped to handle violent protesters. I would activate the assistance of the National Guard for events such as the International Monetary Fund and World Bank annual meetings and for every presidential inauguration. Often, I would keep the National Guard's QRF out of view, placing them in a room near the IMF/World Bank headquarters or in a government building off the inaugural parade route, only to be rapidly "uncloaked" and deployed on the line if things went south. I knew their training, equipment, and capabilities. They were a great resource to have in my pocket.

For January 6, the mayor of the District of Columbia had submitted an RFA well in advance for unarmed DC National Guard to assist with crowd and traffic control around the city. The DC National Guard conducted a mission analysis of the request that had been submitted to the secretary of defense. Then, as a result of this analysis, they prepared a tasking for 340 National Guard troops. This staffing included a forty-person quick reaction force and twenty soldiers assigned to the civil support team. The QRF was fully outfitted with riot gear and staged at Joint Base Andrews, a military base about twenty minutes outside Washington, DC.

As chief of the USCP, the rules for me were very different because two specific statutes within the US Code (2 USC § 1974 and 2 USC § 1970) restricted my ability to obtain the needed support for my officers.[2] These two statutes prohibited me from calling in the National Guard or

---

2. "2 U.S. Code § 1974 - Capitol Police Special Officers," Legal Information Institute, Cornell Law School, February 20, 2003, www.law.cornell.edu/uscode/text/2/1974; "2 U.S. Code § 1970 - Assistance by Executive Departments and Agencies," Legal Information Institute, Cornell Law School, January 10, 2002, www.law.cornell.edu/uscode/text/2/1970.

federal law enforcement support in advance of an event unless the Capitol Police Board had enacted a declaration of emergency *and* obtained the approval of congressional leadership.

But one statute provides that in an *emergency situation*, I need only secure the approval of the House *or* Senate SAA to be able to request help from executive-branch agencies such as the National Guard on their behalf. While this sounds sufficient to address critical emergency situations such as the events of January 6, there is a major issue. The statute further stipulates that in these emergency situations, the chief can request assistance on matters related to that SAA's specific chamber, and the request must be in writing. In other words, during an emergency, the House or Senate sergeant at arms can authorize support from an executive-branch agency, but *only* for that particular side of the Capitol. Think about this for a moment. If the chief is facing an emergency on the Hill that urgently needs outside support, the issue is most likely not going to affect only half the Capitol. So while there *seems* to be a streamlined approval process for requesting assistance in an emergency situation, the chief still must obtain approval from both the House and Senate SAAs to request support across the Hill.

This wouldn't be a who's who without a few words about three of the most powerful people in Washington, DC:

SPEAKER NANCY PELOSI

In the time I spent leading the USCP, I felt that I had developed a good relationship with the Speaker of the House, Nancy Pelosi. We would occasionally have non-work-related conversations, and she could be quite personable. My extended family lives in San Francisco, and the Speaker and I would sometimes compare our favorite parts of the city and Napa Valley.

In March 2020, my daughter and I attended the Gershwin Awards, an annual event celebrating musicians sponsored by the Library of Congress. We were standing in the VIP area, and Pelosi was there as well. When I introduced my daughter to her, Pelosi asked her, "Have you met Garth Brooks?" Then she took my daughter by the hand and led her across the room and introduced her to him.

The next day, I ran into the Speaker on the Hill, and she made a point to ask me how my daughter was doing, and mentioned how happy she had been to meet her.

When the great photographer Annie Leibovitz came to the Capitol to photograph the Speaker, the session coincided with the annual memorial service for fallen US Capitol Police officers. The Speaker was going to give a tribute and ask for a moment of silence for the fallen officers during the opening of the session. She had authorized me, in full uniform, to escort the widow of Officer Chestnut into the gallery. (Uniforms are not authorized in the galleries without the Speaker's approval.)

I had been friends with Mrs. Wen-Ling Chestnut before this event, and I felt honored to be able to escort her to the memorial service. Ms. Leibovitz captured a beautiful image of Mrs. Chestnut holding on to my arm as we both bowed our heads for the moment of silence. I was gifted with a copy of the photo and will always be grateful for the opportunity the Speaker gave me that day.

PRESIDENT DONALD TRUMP

During my time with the USCP, I had the opportunity to meet President Trump on several occasions. The first time I met him was less than six months after I joined the department. On June 14, 2017, James Hodgkinson opened fire with a rifle on members of the Republican congressional baseball team, critically injuring Representative Stephen "Steve" Scalise. I was the assistant chief and in charge of operations at that time, and Andy Maybo, one of my K9 officers, called to advise me that the United States Park Police helicopter (Eagle One) would be transporting Scalise to MedStar Washington Hospital Center. Officer Maybo also told me that one of our Dignitary Protection Division

(DPD) agents, Crystal Griner, was seriously wounded and would also be going to MedStar and that her partner, David Bailey, was less seriously wounded, having taken fragments to his knee. I went to the hospital to establish a security detail and prepared for the family and close friends of both Scalise and Griner to visit them. Bailey had already been taken to another hospital and arrived on crutches to check on his partner, still wearing his bloodied pants.

That evening, President Trump and the First Lady arrived at the hospital to check on Scalise and my two officers. I met the motorcade as it arrived at the back of the hospital, and then walked with them and their security detail down the long hallway. The president looked at me in my uniform with the stars on my shoulder and said, "They have the big boss man here."

We shook hands, and he asked how my two officers were doing. Both the president and the First Lady expressed sincere concern and appreciation for what the officers had been through and wanted to thank them for their heroic actions that "undoubtedly saved numerous lives." I escorted them to the recovery room where Griner was sitting up in bed. The president and the First Lady went in and met with Griner and some of her family.

When they came back out of the room about a half hour later, I asked the president if some of my officers could take a picture with him.

"Absolutely," he said, smiling. When I stood back to line up the shot with my cell phone, he said, "No, wait, you need to be in the picture. We can't have a picture without the big boss man in it."

I handed my phone to a member of his entourage, and he took the photo.

The president stayed at the hospital for about ninety minutes, going down to visit Congressman Scalise and thanking all the hospital staff along the way. Later that evening, I learned that June 14 was the president's birthday and that he had left the White House during a celebration to check on the officers and Scalise. His visit and genuine concern for my officers were much appreciated.

The next day, Vice President Pence and the Second Lady also came to visit Griner and Scalise. As I was briefing them on the latest developments, someone on Pence's detail snapped a picture of us and posted it on Pence's Twitter page.

PRESIDENT JOE BIDEN

As a command official with the MPD, I supported numerous USSS security details for the Obama-Biden administration. From when I worked as one of the lead planners for the January 20, 2009, inauguration until I retired from the MPD at the end of 2015, the president and vice president rarely moved in Washington, DC, without my unit's support. Seeing the POTUS and VPOTUS was a regular occurrence for me. I remember that on his way to the motorcade or at the airport, Biden would regularly stop and chat with officers from various agencies and ask how they were doing, and he was always willing to take photos with the officers. When I was retiring from the MPD, Vice President Biden graciously provided a photo opportunity for me. We met outside his residence at the Naval Observatory in DC. During our meeting, Biden was very surprised that I was considering retiring, and tried to talk me into reconsidering. He said, "You're far too young to retire. Law enforcement needs good people like you."

Little did I know that a year after retirement, I would be back in uniform in Washington, DC, or that four years later, I would be the chief of Capitol Police and the man coordinating a massive law enforcement response to allow Biden's presidential election certification to proceed.

Sean Gallagher, my deputy chief in charge of the Protective Services Bureau, grew up in Scranton, Pennsylvania, the same town as Joe Biden. Gallagher used to tell a story of some of his family having lived in Biden's childhood home on North Washington Avenue in Scranton. One day shortly after the election, Gallagher's young son dressed up like Biden for a school event. He wore a dark suit and tie and had his hair styled just like the president-elect's. But more importantly, he sported a pair of aviator sunglasses just like the ones Biden had made famous.

Gallagher shared the story and the photos of his son with some Secret Service agents who were working with him on various protection details. A few days later, Gallagher's wife received a call from Biden himself. Biden had called to tell Gallagher's son how proud he was to have been chosen as an influential figure to represent at school. He also thanked him for doing such a good job and for looking so handsome. Gestures like this from Biden really meant a lot to those who worked around him.

————

With these personal stories about the Speaker of the House and the two presidents, I'm not trying to name-drop, but rather to establish right here at the beginning of this book that I had a friendly working relationship with all three individuals.

Everything you are about to read in the rest of this book comes not from a Republican, not from a Democrat, but from an impartial, apolitical police chief. It is vital that you understand I'm about to tell you what really happened on January 6, uncolored by any political viewpoint.

CHAPTER 1:

THE GATHERING STORM

*We must learn to live together as brothers or
perish as fools.*
　　　　　　　　　　　—Martin Luther King Jr.

Many forces were at work leading up to and during the terrible attack on
the US Capitol on January 6, 2021—forces that had been brewing in our
country for years, tearing at the very foundations of our society. Forces that
pitted American against American, politician against politician, government
branch against government branch, and society and media against law enforcement. On January 6, all these forces converged at the US Capitol.

On January 6, we became our own worst enemy.

A COUNTRY ALREADY DIVIDED

Even before Trump's 2016 election win, America's social fabric was beginning to strain at the seams. A lack of confidence in elected officials,
the emergence of extreme media outlets, and an ever-growing level of
divisiveness after a tightly contested 2016 election threatened to split
the country in half. Moral and social issues such as equality, diversity,
and racial justice; constitutional issues such as voting rights and the

Second Amendment; immigration issues, reproductive rights, and religious issues such as abortion; not to mention the future makeup of the Supreme Court—all contributed to heightened social tensions. I was seeing these issues manifest in the skyrocketing number of threats against members of Congress, going from just below two thousand in 2015 to over nine thousand in 2020.

The stressors of a deadly global pandemic, combined with nightly reporting of violent antipolice, antigovernment demonstrations around the country, added to the general sense of insecurity. From Los Angeles to Atlanta, Portland to New York City, Seattle to Washington, DC, the nightly news and social media were filled with images of buildings being burned; statues being toppled; and police officers being pelted with rocks, hit with bats, and attacked with lasers to the eyes, and their vehicles and buildings firebombed.

The frequency and intensity of antipolice and antigovernment demonstrations in the United States began to increase after the 2014 shooting death of Michael Brown in Ferguson, Missouri. Several days of violent protests occurred in Ferguson as well as in cities around the country. It was during these protests that we began to see the involvement of the Black Lives Matter movement, which first appeared on the national scene after the 2012 shooting death of Trayvon Martin in Sanford, Florida. Protests around the country were becoming far more violent than anything we had ever experienced—worse than the violent Seattle World Trade Organization (WTO) protests in 1999 or the DC inaugurations and IMF/World Bank protests in the early 2000s.

Between 2015 and 2020, many of these antipolice and antigovernment demonstrations followed high-profile use-of-force incidents, such as the deaths of Freddie Gray in Baltimore on April 12, 2015, Breonna Taylor in Louisville on March 13, 2020, and George Floyd in Minneapolis on May 25, 2020. As an official at the MPD, I had firsthand knowledge and experience with protests and riots, which was why I was deployed to Baltimore, Maryland, during the 2015 riots that followed the death of Freddie Gray. Gray had died while in police custody after being arrested for possession of a knife. I was commander of the Special Operations Division for the

Metropolitan Police Department in Washington, DC, at the time, and my chief, Cathy Lanier, sent me to Baltimore with two civil disturbance unit (CDU) platoons and members of our Domestic Security Operations Unit to help support a multiagency response to quell the violence.

After the death of George Floyd, violent protests sprang up once again in many cities around the country, including nightly protests in Portland, Oregon. In DC at the end of May and the beginning of June 2020, the White House and Lafayette Square became the center of Black Lives Matter and antipolice protests, with a number of violent clashes between law enforcement and protesters. On Friday, May 29, 2020, these violent clashes were reaching a breaking point near the White House. The US Park Police (USPP), the Secret Service (USSS), and a handful of other federal agencies were doing their best to keep the protesters off Pennsylvania Avenue and away from the north side of the White House. They attempted to maintain a perimeter with metal crowd-control barricades in parts of Lafayette Square, which is under National Park Service jurisdiction. The clashes went on for hours and became extremely violent. Protesters were throwing rocks, bricks, sticks, and frozen bottles of water at the officers trying to hold the line.

For the next three days, these violent clashes would continue right outside the White House, with the USSS Uniformed Division taking the brunt of the beating. As the violent clashes progressed, rioters began to use incendiary devices. They set a large bathroom structure in Lafayette Square on fire. The rioters also tried to torch construction scaffolding on the side of the occupied Hay-Adams Hotel, a beautiful historic building directly across the street from Lafayette Square and the White House.

A lot of USSS special agents and Uniformed Division officers were injured in the protests, some with serious head injuries. In my Capitol Police Command Center just down Pennsylvania Avenue, I could see many officers on video being led away from the police lines with bloodied faces. It got so bad at one point that the Secret Service evacuated the president and his family to the White House bunker. But as violent and intense as the protests became, the MPD, the largest and primary municipal police department in Washington, DC, was not allowed to help protect the White House, having been directed not to go onto federal property, including the White House grounds, to engage protesters.

Although MPD could provide the USSS officers with a public address system, some chemical defensive spray, and some basic protective gear, such as helmets and shields, it was not permitted to deploy personnel onto the federal property. I spoke to a ranking MPD official, who told me that they could stage on the adjacent DC streets and engage only those protesters who happened to confront the MPD while on DC property. They were not allowed to respond to the numerous calls for help from the USSS. As the head of security for one of the largest federal facilities in DC, this created a lot of concern for me. What if I needed the city's municipal police department to come to the aid of my officers? This prompted my call to the chief of the MPD, Peter Newsham.

Pete and I had known each other well throughout our careers at MPD. We had been officers together at the Sixth District in the early 1990s. I was assigned as a patrol officer, and Pete often worked in a plainclothes unit. We were both promoted to the rank of sergeant around 1996, and the two of us were assigned to the Seventh District. We worked evenings and would sometimes ride together. Pete always liked to drive, and when I rode with him, I always held on tight.

One evening, we were riding together when a call went out for multiple gunshots in a liquor store parking lot on Minnesota Avenue SE. It was a dark, wet autumn night as we responded quickly to the location. Pete pulled up, and we jumped out to quickly assess the scene. We found multiple victims and several weapons strewn throughout the parking lot. As additional MPD units arrived and we secured the scene, I started working on one of the victims who looked to have the best chance of survival. But he was in really bad shape. I cut off his shirt and discovered a bullet wound in his torso. It was a sucking chest wound. I could clearly see the hole, which was gurgling blood with every breath he took. I discovered an entry and exit wound right through his torso. I grabbed my gloves, rolled him on his side, flattened the gloves, put one on each wound, and applied pressure to seal them until the ambulance arrived. He survived, and I later learned he was an off-duty police officer from the Fifth District.

Pete and I were promoted together to the rank of lieutenant, at which point our career paths diverged somewhat, but we still saw each other regularly at meetings and events. Although Pete and I would share in many adventures during our careers, it was the critical incidents like what we experienced in that liquor store parking lot that would leave an indelible mark on us and build the strong bond between us.

I called him on his cell phone: "Pete, I'm seeing Secret Service having problems at the White House, and MPD is not responding. If we need help here on the Hill, can I rely on you?"

"MPD will be there if needed," Pete replied.

It was obvious from this conversation that the stand-down order had come not from him, but from someone higher up. I knew that Pete would have assisted Secret Service with the full force of the department had he been allowed. A few weeks later, I spoke to a few of my former MPD officers who were positioned just outside the White House on Seventeenth Street during the protests. As they described the scene to me, I could tell they were still deeply traumatized by what they had seen.

"It was just so fucked up," one officer said. "DC Fire and EMS had staged ambulances right near us for the injured officers at the White House complex. We would see them walking out bloodied Secret Service officers, one after another, to the ambulances, and we weren't allowed to do shit." He shook his head and took a deep breath. "All we could do was give them our shields and helmets and stand by and watch them get the shit beat out of them."

It was clear to me, not for the first or last time, that politics had overtaken the concern for public and officer safety.

The inability of the MPD to assist the USSS outside the White House that day prompted the Department of Justice to discuss federalizing the DC police force. During a meeting around the same time, Attorney General William Barr, who styles himself as a stalwart supporter of police, unleashed his anger and frustration with the MPD by chastising Newsham in front of the attendees. Barr then began coordinating law enforcement support for DC and the White House, calling in the National Guard to offset the lack of MPD assistance. This would result in some highly questionable tactics on June 1, a day that would begin with a Trump press conference in the White House Rose Garden. After two consecutive nights of nationwide violent demonstrations, the president vowed to support law and order, while also praising and encouraging law enforcement with this statement:

> New York's finest have been hit in the face with bricks . . . A police precinct station has been overrun. Here in the nation's capital, the Lincoln Memorial and the World War II Memorial have been vandalized. One of our most historic churches was set ablaze. A federal officer in California, an African American enforcement hero, was shot and killed. These are not acts of peaceful protest. These are acts of domestic terror. The destruction of innocent life and the spilling of innocent blood is an offense to humanity and a crime against God . . . I am also taking swift and decisive action to protect our great capital, Washington, DC. What happened in this city last night was a total disgrace. As we speak, I am dispatching thousands and thousands of heavily armed soldiers, military personnel, and law enforcement officers to stop the rioting, looting, vandalism, assaults, and the wanton destruction of property . . . We must never give in to anger or hatred. If malice or violence reigns, then none of us is free. I take these actions today with firm resolve and with a true and passionate love for our country.[1]

Following this statement, an entourage of advisors and military officials escorted the president to St. John's Church for the now infamous Bible-wielding photo opportunity after federal law enforcement had cleared Lafayette Square. The entourage included AG Bill Barr, General

---

1. Donald Trump, "Statement by the President," Trump White House Archives (website), June 1, 2020, https://trumpwhitehouse.archives.gov/briefings-statements/statement-by-the-president-39/.

Milley, and SECDEF Mark Esper, among others. (The USCP was not involved in this action.)

The televised clearing of Lafayette Square by federal law enforcement brought significant pushback from the mayor's office. Only days later, on June 6, Mayor Bowser participated in a protest in the city, calling on the Trump administration to remove all out-of-state National Guard from the city. She wanted it to be clear that DC was not a place for "the feds to stage attacks on peaceful protesters."[2]

Two weeks later, on June 19, the MPD would escort a group of "peaceful protesters" to a small patch of federal property right outside MPD headquarters at Third and D Streets NW, where the statue of Confederate General Albert Pike stood. The MPD officers stood by and watched, apparently under another stand-down order, as the protesters tore down the statue and tried to set it on fire. DC officials had been trying to remove the statue for decades, but because it was on federal property, the federal government would not authorize its removal. What the DC municipal government had not been able to accomplish since 1992, a crowd managed to do in minutes, all while the MPD stood by and watched.

Later, in October 2020, some of these same groups would turn their anger on the MPD, attacking police outside the Fourth Police District headquarters on Georgia Avenue following the death of an individual riding a motor scooter, who was hit by a car while evading police. These protests would result in significant damage to the police station and numerous injuries to law enforcement personnel, including serious injuries to an MPD lieutenant after someone in the crowd threw a large firework mortar.

During what became nightly protests in DC, I would either be stationed in our Command Center at USCP headquarters watching the various news and video feeds from the downtown protests, or jump into my police car and head into the field. Often, when I decided to go out, I would take one or both of my assistant chiefs with me. We had deployed

2. Julie Bykowicz, "D.C. Mayor Bowser Battles Trump over George Floyd Protests," *Wall Street Journal*, June 10, 2020, www.wsj.com/articles/d-c-mayor-bowser-battles-trump-over-george-floyd-protests-11591792859.

significant civil disturbance unit (CDU) resources in anticipation of the violent protests coming to the Capitol, and I liked to make the rounds and talk to the officers on post and on CDU details. I loved this part of the job because I've always enjoyed talking to my officers. Even on regular days, I would stop and chat because I wanted to know more about them and what they were dealing with in their daily interactions. Not only was this feel for the field and connection with the workforce important to me, but I felt it was imperative to my objective of moving the agency forward as a strong, unified body that respects its leadership.

Occasionally, I would also drive outside our territory, often taking my assistant chiefs to the downtown area to show them some of the security preparations the other agencies were implementing, as well as to introduce them to the on-site officials, many of whom I knew well from my years with the MPD. I felt it was important for my officials to take the time to check on the troops and make first-person assessments of what was going on in the field. This way, the information they were evaluating, such as the actions and demeanor of the crowds, the actions of the officers, and the overall feel of the demonstration, would be unfiltered. Also, it allowed my somewhat sheltered assistant chiefs to meet the key players who held more operational roles. And I knew that exposing my officials to other agencies would help build their relationships and expand their knowledge base. Outside of special events, USCP officials did not have a lot of multijurisdictional operational experience with our partner agencies.

Finally, I've always felt it is important for officers to see their officials out in the field with them. USCP officers work hard and need to know that the command staff is working these late-night events right alongside them.

Relationships among law enforcement agencies are particularly important in Washington, a city with so many jurisdictions so close to one another. When leading special-event courses, here's how I would break it down to officials from outside DC: The 900 block of Pennsylvania Avenue NW is one of the major roadways in Washington and is literally a straight line from the US Capitol, in the center of the city, to the White House, at 1600 Pennsylvania Avenue. The 900 block of Pennsylvania Avenue sits almost directly between the two. On the south side of the block is the headquarters for the United States Department of Justice, and on the north is the headquarters of the FBI. The DOJ is under federal jurisdiction, protected by its own security force and the Federal Protective Service. The sidewalk outside the DOJ Building belongs to the National Park Service and is under the jurisdiction of the US Park Police (USPP). Pennsylvania Avenue itself is MPD jurisdiction. The north sidewalk is USPP jurisdiction, and the FBI building is protected by the FBI Police. In a single block, you can traverse five police jurisdictions just by crossing the street! And beyond that, at one end of that long Pennsylvania Avenue, you have the US Secret Service at the White House, and at the opposite end, you have the USCP.

Even now, when I drive down the streets of Washington, DC, memories from a lifetime in law enforcement come back to me. In September 2001, I was a lieutenant in the Special Operations Division at the MPD, assigned to the Special Events Branch, where I helped coordinate all the major events and demonstrations in DC. The headquarters was located on L Street NW, just off Washington Circle and six blocks from the White House. This was the same facility where the Watergate "plumbers" were taken after being arrested for breaking into the Democratic National Committee headquarters at the Watergate Hotel in 1972. Shortly before 9:00 a.m. on September 11, 2001, as I walked into my planning office, I saw a special report on the television showing video of one of the World Trade Center towers burning. My planning sergeant yelled, "Lieutenant Sund, the White House is on the phone for you!"

I picked up the phone, and USSS Special Agent Steve Woodard asked, "Steve, you see what's going on in New York?" Woodard had been involved in the investigation of the 1993 World Trade Center bombing.

"I don't know, Steve," I said. "I'm concerned it may not be an accident."

He echoed my concern, and at 9:03 a.m., as we were talking, a second plane crashed into the WTC on live television. At that point, Woodard abruptly stated, "We are calling an emergency meeting at the White House. I need you to come down to the Emergency Operations Center ASAP."

Shortly after the second plane hit the South Tower on September 11, we began to implement emergency security protocols for the city, and I was just about to head to the Emergency Operations Center at the White House. But then I felt a tremor rippling through Special Operations Division and heard the old windows rattling in their frames. That was the third plane, hitting the Pentagon, which was less than two miles away. I ran to my car and drove code one—emergency lights flashing and siren blaring—six blocks to the White House, just in time to see dozens of people running outside, screaming for everyone else to get away from the building.

That was Tuesday. It would be Friday before I made it home. Even while the Pentagon was still smoldering, I handled the security detail for President Bush's motorcade to the Pentagon. Along with his national security advisor, Condoleezza Rice, and his secretary of defense, Donald Rumsfeld, he went there to observe the recovery efforts and to show his support for the first responders. I will never forget the burning smell, the sight of the devastation at the Pentagon, and the president himself walking in front of the collapsed portion of the building with the American flag that the firefighters had just unfurled over the side.

I'm relating my story of 9/11 to illustrate just how important relationships are in law enforcement, especially in a town like Washington, DC.

When I was finally returning home several days later, while stopped at a traffic light in my marked police car, a group of pedestrians began clapping and shouting, "Thank you!" I knew many other officers and first responders who experienced similar displays of appreciation in the days after 9/11. As exhausted and emotionally spent as I was, I will never forget this show of support.

But in the summer of 2020, right here in the same city where I was now serving as chief of the United States Capitol Police, those days felt like something from a different lifetime as the protests grew more and more violent. Protesters were fighting with the police and throwing projectiles, fireworks, and Molotov cocktails at them. They were smashing storefront windows and looting businesses. Many of the high-end retail stores in the downtown and CityCenter retail areas were targeted by protesters. At one point, while watching a live-stream video feed in our Command Center, I saw a white male in dark clothing with his face covered, trying to break through the glass door of a retail shop with a ball-peen hammer. The store appeared to be a jewelry store with windows of some sort of security glass. I deduced this while observing the protester struggling to break through the window with numerous strikes from the hammer. Of course, *protester* is probably not the right word to describe this individual, who was clearly breaking into this building for other reasons than to express his grievance regarding the police's use-of-force policy. As he was trying to break through the glass, a white female protester with long brown hair jumped in front of him and the glass storefront and held her hand out, trying to dissuade the looter from breaking the window. Without even skipping a beat, the guy grabbed her by the hair and threw her violently to the ground, then continued his assault on the window. I found the assailant's determination and ready violence against a fellow protester, especially an unarmed female, terribly disturbing. And it was representative of the type of people running unimpeded on DC streets.

Over two thousand law enforcement officers were injured that summer, and over a billion dollars' worth of property damage occurred nationwide.[3] The USCP had seen limited skirmishes and vandalism on Capitol grounds, but given the situation other police agencies were facing, we thought it prudent to be ready for similar incidents on the Hill. We activated several platoons of our civil disobedience units, which were outfitted with specialized hardened and padded uniforms and riot helmets—or, as we call it, *turtle gear*. But the sight of the Capitol Police in riot gear bothered some members of Congress, my oversight committees, and their staffs, and I would hear about how they didn't like seeing my officers looking "menacing" and "aggressive."

That summer, after many began to label police departments nationwide as excessively heavy-handed, I had to work even harder to strike a delicate balance between protecting my officers and appeasing

---

3. POL staff, "More than 2,000 Officers Injured in Summer's Protests and Riots," *POLICE*, December 3, 2020, www.policemag.com/585160/more-than-2-000-officers -injured-in-summers-protests-and-riots.

the bosses. While I fully understood and appreciated the de-escalation benefit of taking a soft approach at demonstrations when the crowd's demeanor allowed it, there were times when it was just not appropriate for my CDU officers to go out without their hard gear.

On several occasions that summer, violent demonstrators would leave the White House and march to the Capitol. The MPD would notify us that a group was headed our way, and they'd let us know if the group was being violent with police. We would ready the force and wait for the chanting group to cross into Capitol jurisdiction. Usually, after an hour or so on Capitol grounds, the groups would disperse, often heading back to the White House and Black Lives Matter Plaza. As a result, the USCP made only six arrests and deployed no chemical munitions during these protests. This scenario repeated itself a dozen times over the summer of 2020. A couple of times, I watched the groups march to our grounds from the White House, only to stop in their tracks, have an intense discussion or disagreement, and then turn around and march off. I found it odd at first. Why didn't they seem interested in repeating their antipolice assault on us? I could only guess that perhaps they felt they had a sympathetic ear in Congress and didn't want to disrespect its turf.

To protect against vandalism and other destructive actions we had seen across the country, we erected metal barricades around many of our statues. We also implemented twenty-four-hour surveillance on many of them. Several members of Congress had requested meetings with me to ensure that I was keeping safe the artifacts of the United States Capitol, many of which had gone through significant refurbishment at substantial cost. Ironically, the only statue that suffered significant damage was the Peace Monument, located on Capitol grounds at First Street and Pennsylvania Avenue NW, just off the West Front of the Capitol.

The memorial is a monument to the members of the Navy who died during the Civil War, and one evening, a large group of hundreds of protesters surrounded the statue. We had CDU and plainclothes officers in the area watching the group. At one point, we saw an individual start to climb onto the statue and begin spray-painting the pedestal. Due to the size of the crowd, my officers could not safely move in to apprehend the suspect. The officers watched as the individual climbed down from the statue and moved to the periphery of the crowd. That is when my officers moved in and collared him, finding a number of cans of spray paint in his backpack. The crowd immediately turned hostile and tried to forcibly "unarrest" the suspect. In this case, it didn't work, and we quickly transported the suspect from the scene.

The next morning, I went down to view the Peace Memorial and was disgusted by what I saw. "ALL COPS MUST DIE. DEATH TO COPS" was written in large blue letters on the white marble pedestal. I was hurt to see such words written about a profession I had dedicated my life to. A profession that had provided birthday parties to less-fortunate kids on Ridge Road. A profession that had filled the trunk of my police cruiser with Christmas gifts to drop off to kids in some of the most poverty-stricken parts of DC. A profession that would see me helping distribute Thanksgiving dinners to families on Central Avenue SE, and on random days buy lunch for homeless people and Popsicles for little kids outside the market on Forty-Second Street in the Sixth District. How could these protesters write such words about people they obviously knew so little about?

Although I was saddened, these words only solidified my steadfast resolve to continue being the best police officer I could be. I had the Command Center call the office of the Architect of the Capitol to get the memorial cleaned, but it took a number of attempts to remove the graffiti. Some of it is still faintly visible.

Sometimes, I would walk the police lines that summer to reassure the officers and occasionally talk to the demonstrators. Assistant Chief Pittman would often volunteer to come along. During one of the large protests on the East Front of the Capitol, several of the protesters called on officers to take a knee to show solidarity and support for their cause. I have been in policing for almost thirty years, much of that time involved in handling and managing First Amendment assemblies, and I have always prided myself in taking a strictly unbiased and apolitical approach. All the agencies I have worked for, including the USCP, share this philosophy. Regardless of the message or my personal views, our job as police officers is to protect everyone's right to peacefully assemble and voice their grievances, as provided by the First Amendment. We must remain unbiased in our application of this constitutional right and in our protection of those expressing their views within it.

During this protest, we did have several officers and officials of varying demographics take a knee. This resulted in jeers and ridicule from the protesters toward those who remained standing. As I saw this happening and heard officers voicing their concerns, I knew this had to be addressed. Many of my officers were young, and the social pressures associated with the demonstrations weighed heavily on them. I understood that, but after the demonstration, I called together all the available workforce and members of our labor union in Emancipation Hall in the United States Capitol Visitor Center to discuss our role in handling First Amendment demonstrations. That's where I explained my philosophy and the importance of an unbiased approach and application. "We handle hundreds of protests on Capitol grounds every year," I said. "We must treat all of them the same. From the application and review process to how we provide operational support and security, every group must be treated the same."

The address was well received. I had many officers, officials, and police union members of various demographics come up to thank me. Only days later, Speaker Nancy Pelosi would lead Senator Schumer and House and Senate Democrats in silent tribute to George Floyd for eight minutes and forty-six seconds in the very room where I had addressed my officers about being apolitical.

(Let me be clear: I do NOT support the actions of the officer who knelt on Floyd's neck. I just think that the Democratic leadership could have gone about this in a better way. By appearing to condemn *all* law enforcement at the same time, tarring all of them with the same oversize brush, this very public action helped put US law enforcement officers in increased danger.)

The increasingly violent protests in the past few years have not been confined to left-wing activists. We all have seen many right-wing groups participating in protests around the country, many turning violent with the police and counterprotesters. The Unite the Right rally in Charlottesville, Virginia, on August 11–12, 2017, turned especially violent, with numerous injuries on the first day of the rally after right-wing groups clashed with counterprotesters. On the following day, more violent clashes between the various right-wing groups, counterprotesters, and the police occurred before a state of emergency was declared and the Virginia State Police shut down the rally around noon. At about 1:45 p.m., just four blocks from the rally location, James Alex Fields Jr., a Nazi sympathizer, drove his car into a group of counterprotesters, killing Heather Heyer and seriously injuring many others.

In addition to the demonstrations, many attacks and ambushes on police officers occurred that summer, further exacerbating America's concern for its own security. FBI data shows an increase in killings of police officers whenever there have been significant instances of civil unrest in the country.[4] During a Black Lives Matter protest in Dallas on July 7, 2016, a suspect named Micah Xavier Johnson opened fire on police from a nearby building, killing five Dallas police officers and wounding nine others. In September 2020, two Los Angeles sheriff's deputies were shot at point-blank range while sitting in a marked vehicle. Miraculously, neither officer was killed. On May 29, 2020, during an antipolice protest in Oakland, California, an active-duty air force police officer named Steven Carrillo, a proclaimed member of the far-right group the Boogaloo Boys, shot and killed a federal officer protecting a government building. A week later, Carrillo shot and killed Santa Cruz County Sheriff's Deputy Sgt. Damon Gutzwiller when police tried to take him into custody.

While there may once have been a consensus among the media and public that the police were a positive force in society, in recent years this positive perception has shifted considerably. During my own time in law enforcement, I have never seen police officers as a group vilified as

4. Bill Hutchinson, "Police Officers Killed Surge 28% This Year and Some Point to Civil Unrest and Those Looking to Exploit It," ABC News, July 22, 2020, https://abcnews.go.com/US/police-officers-killed-surge-28-year-point-civil/story?id=71773405.

much as they were in 2020. They were ambushed, attacked, had their vehicles set on fire with themselves inside, and were killed in record numbers. According to data from the National Law Enforcement Officers Memorial, over 260 federal, state, military, tribal, and local law enforcement officers died in the line of duty in 2020—a 96 percent increase from the 135 officers killed the year before.[5]

Police officers were also refused service at restaurants, had their food and drinks tampered with, and were even asked to leave establishments because they made other patrons feel "unsafe." But despite this vilification of law enforcement, police officers continued to answer the 911 calls without bias, no matter who needed the assistance. They risked their lives daily to help complete strangers. They coordinated coat and school-supply drives for the less fortunate, bought homeless people food, and made sure families had holiday dinners and presents. Why? Because that is what police officers do. The vast majority of people who join the profession do it for the right reasons, with good intent and the desire to leave the world a better place. Sadly, by 2021 we were already seeing a record number of police officers resigning or retiring, primarily due to how they were being treated—both on the streets and by their elected officials.

Perhaps some of that divisiveness we were seeing on the streets and at protests reflected the division that many were seeing within our own government. Infighting within the legislative branch, not to mention tensions with the executive branch, was regularly showcased in the news and in real time around the world via social media. No longer were members of Congress seen as being able to reach and work across the aisle. Shaming and bashing those with opposing political views was the new norm, a trend that angered and alienated many people watching it happen. On top of that, repeated occurrences of politicians seen not adhering to their own COVID-19 mandates irritated the public with their perceived "Good for thee, but not for me" attitude.

5. National Law Enforcement Memorial and Museum, *2020 Law Enforcement Officers Fatalities Report*, 2021, www.nleomf.org/wp-content/uploads/2021/01/2020 -LE-Officers-Fatalities-Report-opt.pdf.

This sentiment permeated the state and local governments as well, often mimicking what was happening on the federal level. Many who had looked to politicians to help bring the country together during these tumultuous times now viewed them as instigators of the division in our society. Whether it was President Trump going on an early-morning Twitter rant, or Speaker Pelosi tearing up President Trump's State of the Union speech on national television, many Americans were becoming disheartened by the childish antics of their elected officials.

Threats against members of Congress rose dramatically. Since I started with the USCP in January 2017, several violent attacks and plots were focused on political figures. These included the aforementioned June 14, 2017, shooting attack on members of the Republican congressional baseball team, which critically injured Representative Scalise, USCP Special Agent Crystal Griner, and lobbyist Matt Mika, as well as injuring another team member and USCP Special Agent David Bailey. The shooter, James Hodgkinson, was later found to harbor strong anti-Republican views and was angry at the results of the 2016 presidential election.[6]

In November 2018, Cesar A. Sayoc Jr., a staunch supporter of President Trump, manufactured and mailed sixteen improvised explosive devices to people he identified as opposing Trump. The devices were sent to high-profile individuals and media outlets, including Senator Kamala Harris, Senator Cory Booker, and Representative Maxine Waters. None of the devices exploded or caused any injuries, but their mass mailing caused widespread fear and panic across the country. The big break in the case came when one of the devices, which had been addressed to Representative Maxine Waters, arrived at the House of Representatives mail facility. My bomb squad managed to recover the device intact, and from it investigators managed to obtain a single fingerprint that

6. Bryan L. Porter, *Use of Force Investigation and Analysis*, Office of the Commonwealth's Attorney - City of Alexandria, October 6, 2017, https://media. alexandriava.gov/docs-archives/commattorney/info/17-001---simpson-field-shooting ---final-10.06.17.pdf.

led us to Sayoc. I was tremendously impressed with our bomb squad's capabilities and very proud of them for this recovery. In 2019, Sayoc pleaded guilty to sixty-five felony charges associated with the mailing of the pipe bombs.

Not coincidentally, Americans' trust in the mass media and major news outlets had also been consistently low over the past decade.[7] Further adding to this distrust of the media was the nightly reporting of "mostly peaceful" protests that included firebombing and physical violence toward law enforcement. Just as with the polarization of politics, America also began to experience a polarization of media outlets and news sources.

During the Trump presidency, many Republicans turned to Fox News and a number of other outlets, such as Newsmax and the One America News Network, while Democrats turned to MSNBC, CNN, the *New York Times*, and National Public Radio.[8] Whatever your political affiliation, the media was telling you how to feel and why you should be enraged with the other side of any given issue. The twenty-four-hour news cycle and various social media outlets further angered and divided the population.[9]

Online conspiracy organizations, such as QAnon, and social media conspiracy groups on Facebook, Twitter, 4chan, and 8chan readily provided many alternative narratives that were consumed by a growing audience. Online groups pushed conspiracy theories such as the one that led to the "Pizzagate" hoax during the 2016 presidential campaign. Online postings offered a variety of now-invalidated information indicating that the Comet pizzeria in Northwest Washington, DC, housed a

7. Megan Brenan, "Americans Remain Distrustful of Mass Media," Gallup, September 30, 2020, https://news.gallup.com/poll/321116/americans-remain-distrustful -mass-media.aspx.

8. Elizabeth Grieco, "Americans' Main Sources for Political News Vary by Party and Age," Pew Research Center, April 1, 2020, www.pewresearch.org/fact-tank/2020/04/01 /americans-main-sources-for-political-news-vary-by-party-and-age/.

9. Sophia Moskalenko, "Why Social Media Makes Us Angrier—and More Extreme," Psychology Today, July 6, 2018, www.psychologytoday.com/us/blog/friction/201807 /why-social-media-makes-us-angrier-and-more-extreme.

sex-trafficking ring. The pizzeria received numerous inquiries and threats regarding the allegations, and on December 4, 2016, Edgar Maddison Welch entered the pizzeria, firing shots from a high-powered rifle in an effort to investigate and free children he believed were being held in the (nonexistent) basement.

Further adding to concerns over the divisions within the country has been the proliferation of violent extremist organizations. Groups such as the Proud Boys, Antifa, Sons of Liberty New Jersey, Oath Keepers, Boogaloo Boys, the Base, and the Three Percenters have all been involved in violent rallies and incidents around the country. In 2020, suspected members of Antifa tried to seal a police station's doors with quick-drying cement to trap officers inside as they lit fires next to the building.

I've already cited the numerous right-wing extremist groups who participated in the Unite the Right rally in Charlottesville, Virginia, in 2017. In 2020, the FBI foiled a plot by another right-wing extremist group, the Wolverine Watchmen, to kidnap Michigan's Democratic governor, Gretchen Whitmer. According to the FBI, the militia group had also discussed a plan to storm the Michigan state capitol. The group had conducted reconnaissance missions and had begun planning and training in advance of its mission before being stopped by law enforcement.

As we saw in this foiled attempt to kidnap a sitting governor, the group had targeted Whitmer because they felt she had exerted too much authority and control over the citizens of Michigan during the COVID-19 pandemic. A societal backlash against pandemic mandates and restrictions is not new. Groups opposed to government mask-wearing mandates appeared during the 1918 flu pandemic, forming large organizations that participated in demonstrations and an attempted bombing of a public official.[10] Over a century later, the threat of extremist violence has only been made worse by the psychological effects of a deadly

10. Gary Ackerman and Hayley Peterson, "Terrorism and COVID-19: Actual and Potential Impacts," *Perspectives on Terrorism* 14, no. 3 (June 2020): 15, www.universiteitleiden.nl/binaries/content/assets/customsites/perspectives-on -terrorism/2020/issue-3/ackerman-and-peterson.pdf.

global pandemic that increased susceptibility to recruitment, radical-ization, and conspiracy theories.

The COVID-19 pandemic had changed everyone's life. People lost their jobs, kids stopped going to school, travel was greatly curtailed, care-givers stopped showing up, and entire communities were thrown into lockdown. Countless people experienced the loss of loved ones, friends, and coworkers as a result of COVID-19. Daily routines changed, and people began to experience high levels of anxiety and depression due to the uncertainty and isolation. Because of the travel restrictions, people began spending more time online and, thanks in part to the psycho-logical impact of the pandemic on their personal lives, became more susceptible to radicalization from extreme messages and conspiracy the-ories on social media and websites.[11]

Social media platforms such as Telegram had seen significant in-creases in online traffic, especially channels associated with right-wing and white-supremacist ideology. The pandemic helped create a path-way to radicalization, and the associated isolation and lack of social interaction had reduced the chance that a person's change in behavior may be detected by friends and coworkers. Many physicians and thera-pists stopped in-person appointments, opting instead to conduct video consultations, further reducing the chance that concerning changes in people's behavior would be detected and appropriately addressed.

During the COVID-19 pandemic, we saw many cases of people being pushed to acts of violence due to the pandemic and conspiracy theories. On April 1, 2020, Eduardo Moreno tried to attack the United States Navy hospital ship *Mercy*, which was docked at the Port of Los An-geles to provide COVID-19 hospital services. Moreno, who was a train operator at the port, deliberately drove a locomotive at full speed and derailed it in an effort to hit the hospital ship. Moreno had subscribed to an online conspiracy that the USNS *Mercy* was not actually a hospi-tal ship but was instead associated with some kind of new world order.

---

11. Ackerman and Peterson, "Terrorism and COVID-19," 15.

America was becoming a divided nation on edge. The usual outlets for people to decompress and blow off steam were not available to them for most of the year. Beaches were closed, amusement parks shuttered, and gyms and yoga studios not allowed to open. People on both sides of the elections felt a very strong personal sense of attachment and often developed a belief that there was a moral, religious, and constitutional imperative to get their nominee across the finish line. Anything else would mean the end of the country as they knew it.

ELECTION DAY: NOVEMBER 3, 2020

To understand everything that went into the USCP's planning for the joint session of Congress, as well as for all the demonstrations that would take place leading up to and including January 6, it's important to understand the process that we undertake when planning for any public event, and the role that the various units within the department play in this combined effort. Like any other law enforcement agency, the USCP plans for events based on the available intelligence. Considerations such as staffing, perimeters, permits for First Amendment activity, enhancing the protection for members of Congress, and activating civil disturbance units are all based on this intelligence. The more accurate the intelligence, the better the planning and the event's security will be.

It is also important to understand that due to the number of law enforcement agencies in DC and the various jurisdictions in the downtown area, few large events occur in the city without extensive coordination among all our partner agencies. All the major law enforcement agencies in DC—MPD, USPP, USSS, and USCP—were deeply experienced in major-event planning, especially in coordinating some of the most complex security events: National Special Security Events (NSSE). Only the most important events that are deemed to have significant national relevance or give rise to a significant threat may be designated by the secretary of the DHS as an NSSE. The designation places the United States Secret Service in charge of the event security planning and automatically brings an array of federal resources, including the National

Guard, to the planning table. A testament to the experience of these agencies in DC is the fact that well over half the events designated as NSSEs have occurred in the District of Columbia. No other city in the country comes close. During my time in Washington, DC, I was involved in the planning of almost thirty NSSEs.

As election night 2020 approached, we were already anticipating the possibility of acts of civil disobedience in the city and possibly on Capitol Hill. Although the Democratic National Convention, held in Milwaukee, and the Republican National Convention, held in Charlotte, went off without any major protests, we did experience some issues during the final event at the White House. That final RNC event was President Trump's nomination acceptance speech on August 27 and included a variety of speeches, musical entertainment, and a large fireworks display on the National Mall near the Washington Monument.

Several members of Congress attended the event at the White House. It was marred by some violent altercations between guests leaving the event and anti-Trump and antipolice protesters positioned outside. Law enforcement had to intervene, physically separating the groups. The MPD assisted in escorting Senator Rand Paul to his hotel after he was surrounded by an angry mob as he and his wife left the event.

Coming into the elections, tensions were already high. Both the Senate and the House had gone out of session for the election, allowing the members to go back to their home districts for one last campaign push. The Speaker had adjourned the House on Monday, November 2, and they were expected to be back in session on the fifth. The Senate had been meeting regarding the confirmation of Amy Coney Barrett to the Supreme Court. On October 26, the Senate approved Judge Barrett's nomination to the Supreme Court and then went into a mix of pro forma sessions and recess until after the election. A pro forma session occurs when the Senate is in session in form only. It is usually a very short session, lasting only a few minutes and often attended only by the presiding senator and the Senate parliamentarian. Calling the Senate into a pro forma session is a way to get an official proceeding of the Senate on the calendar in order to ensure that the chamber is abiding by the "three-day rule" in Article I of the US Constitution. The three-day rule prohibits either chamber of Congress from *not* meeting for more than three consecutive calendar days during a congressional session without approval from the other chamber. It is a way for the Senate to be marked as working when, in fact, it really isn't. (I am waiting for my son to learn this trick with school. It's bound to happen.)

On October 27, 2020, the Intelligence and Interagency Coordination Division (IICD) produced an eight-page information paper regarding the 2020 election. Although the report indicated there was no credible intelligence of a specific terrorist plot relating to the 2020 election, it assessed the three greatest areas of concern for the election to be cyberattacks, politically motivated terrorism, and civil unrest. Along with the possibility of terrorism associated with Election Day, the IICD paper also assessed the likelihood of increased election-associated threats from domestic violent extremists.

The elevated concern over terrorist activity from domestic violent extremists stemmed from the foiled plot to kidnap Michigan governor Whitmer. The IICD paper went on to assess the possibility of large-scale demonstrations, depending on the outcome of the election results. Several groups planned to protest in Washington, DC, on Election Day, some with plans to target various critical intersections around the city in order to create gridlock.

Over the summer, there had already been several attacks on members of law enforcement, and the IICD was concerned that individuals could use the cover of the large protests to facilitate further attacks on police officers.[12] The FBI and DHS also produced a joint intelligence bulletin about the election, citing potential cyberattacks. In addition, the FBI Washington Field Office hosted an executive-level meeting to discuss concerns associated with the 2020 election. I attended this meeting along with many of the other police chiefs from agencies around the National Capital Region.

---

12. Intelligence and Interagency Coordination Division (IICD), "21-A-0147 Threats to the 2020 Presidential Election," IICD Information Paper (internal restricted document), updated October 27, 2020.

We had seen the violent demonstrations that the MPD had dealt with over the summer, with the antipolice and anti-Trump protests occurring downtown and at the White House. Violent protesters were smashing storefront windows, lighting fires, fighting with the police, pelting them with rocks and bottles, and shining lasers in officers' eyes—which not only can cause significant ocular damage but also leaves officers vulnerable to subsequent physical attacks. In this case, the protesters would throw frozen bottles of water, rocks, bricks, and even cans of food at the officers once they were blinded by the lasers. This tactic worried me, and I immediately reached out to the MPD to see what they were using to provide laser eye protection for their officers. With their specifications, I began working with my chief administrative officer Richard Braddock and Tom Madigan of our Property Asset Management Division to procure the eye protection for members of our four hard CDU platoons.

As Election Day neared, we continued to develop a civil disturbance unit plan in the event that we must respond to demonstrations on Capitol grounds. Businesses in DC had seen damage caused by violent protests over the summer and were not taking any chances. Throughout the downtown area, I saw street after street of boarded-up buildings. It looked like preparations for a hurricane. I took a drive with Pittman through the city to look at the boarded-up buildings and the security precautions being put in place. Many had put up signs or painted slogans and murals on the boarded storefronts showing their support for groups such as Black Lives Matter, or socially responsible messages such as VOTE. Some businesses even posted messages on the plywood asking protesters to please spare their store.

The USCP Command Center was fully operational, and I had USCP officials assigned to several of our partner agencies' emergency operations centers, including MPD, DC's Homeland Security and Emergency Management Agency, and DHS's National Operations Center. As is the usual course of business for the chief of police, I had briefed the Capitol Police Board and my oversight committees on our security planning. As the day progressed, I was in the USCP Command Center, monitoring events on the Hill and downtown. I would regularly reach out and talk to Jeff Carroll and Robert Glover at MPD for updates. All seemed to be going well in the city.

We had anticipated about six major protests to occur in the District of Columbia on election night. Some of these we had experienced before, such as the regular Saturday evening "Fuck the Police," or FTP, march. It was anticipated that if Trump was projected to win, we would see significant violent demonstrations in the city, similar to what we had seen over the summer. The White House had been surrounded by a mile of seven-foot-high antiscale fencing and concrete Jersey barriers. On election night, the weather was clear and mild. From a police officer's standpoint, if you're expecting large demonstrations, this is not the weather you wish for.

We began seeing groups form early on Election Day, with about two hundred people at Black Lives Matter Plaza around 4:00 p.m. The number of protesters around the White House and at BLM Plaza and other locations grew steadily throughout the night. There were a couple of minor skirmishes in which the MPD made arrests. Gallagher, was providing regular email updates to the USCP command staff and the sergeants at arms.

As the election results started coming in, Biden began to show a lead. Things remained calm in the city as people watched the numbers trickle in, many watching on large television screens at Black Lives Matter Plaza. About 10:30 p.m., Fox News called the state of Arizona for Biden. Arizona had gone to Trump in 2016 and was a key state to flip. Trump was furious at Fox for making this early prediction, but within a few hours, both New Mexico and Minnesota were also called for Biden. As more election results came in, Trump refused to concede and tweeted that he had won the election "by a lot," and began to increase the rhetoric and tenor of a stolen and fraudulent election. But ultimately, election night itself concluded without any major incidents. On Capitol Hill, we didn't have any demonstrations or arrests associated with the election.

MAGA I: NOVEMBER 14, 2020

Following the election, the Trump campaign staff maintained that he was still very much in the race. Trump himself had already been waving the "fraudulent election" flag for months, constantly warning his rallygoers of shady dealings involving mail-in ballots. When images surfaced of election workers covering up windows, and observers being barred from standing near the ballots, coupled with videos of supposed late-night deliveries of ballot boxes, Trump's supporters were not surprised at all. In fact, their suspicions were turning into the reality the president had been warning them about for months. With the impeachment and the constant negative press, it was evident to them that the mainstream "fake news" media and political left were just trying to remove Trump from office by any means necessary.

Grounded in this belief, many Trump supporters came to feel the idea of the Left orchestrating a fraudulent election to unseat Trump was practically a given. In their view, there was simply no other way that Biden could win the election. In their perception, he had barely campaigned, and his crowds were modest—not due to the pandemic, but because of his obvious lack of popularity.

So when the election results did not go in Trump's favor, he and his supporters cried foul. The legal team Trump put together promised indisputable resounding evidence proving their claims, arguing that the voting machines had been tampered with and had switched votes from Trump to Biden and that many Democrat-led cities had created many fake ballots. Some even claimed that US military intelligence had intercepted the proof of international meddling in the vote tabulation and had flown it from Europe to the United States, where it was being analyzed in Quantico.

The claims of fraud would continue for weeks, and when Trump's team began their losing streak in courts around the country, his supporters naturally believed it was because Democrat or "never Trump" Republican judges and legislators were not allowing the process to go forward. Trump's legal team kept promising they would "release the Kraken," raising as much as $200 million to support the fight. But the resounding proof and significant evidence would never materialize.

Compounding the frustration of those who believed that the election had been rigged were the dismissive and derogatory comments from

Democratic leaders and much of the media. The concerns of Clinton voters over the integrity of the 2016 election had been openly addressed at the highest levels of government, and widely covered by the media. But now the concerns of Trump voters regarding a potentially fraudulent election were being blatantly ignored and openly mocked. This sense of dismissal and abandonment only served to energize them, and as the days passed and every new promise from the Trump team went unfulfilled, they set their sights on one last chance to undo the results of the election.

In September 2020, CNN's Fareed Zakaria aired a segment on how Trump could lose the general election but still win through a legal process involving sending the election results back to the states and having the governors vote in the next president. Since there were more Republican governors, Trump would be declared the winner. Trump himself seemed to endorse this long-shot strategy in his public addresses, setting up an unprecedented test of wills between one branch of the government and another, and even between the president and his own vice president.

Within days of the election, Trump supporters reached out to the National Park Service in Washington, DC, and began inquiring about obtaining a First Amendment permit for areas in the downtown area to hold a pro-Trump rally. The group focused on a Park Service location called Freedom Plaza, about two blocks east of the White House. The group began organizing a pro-Trump Million MAGA March in support of the president, and a march to the Supreme Court to protest the election results and to encourage the court's intervention. Several pro-Trump groups began affiliating themselves with the MAGA rally, forming under a variety of names such as the March for Trump and Stop the Steal DC, and identifying various areas around the White House, such as the Washington Monument grounds, to hold their rallies.

On November 11, IICD published an information paper regarding the Million MAGA March event scheduled for November 14. The paper indicated that five main groups would be organizing events associated with the MAGA march from various locations, including Freedom Plaza, the White House, and the Washington Monument grounds. It was anticipated that most of these groups would combine as they proceeded toward the Supreme Court. Various prominent attendees were expected to attend, including Alex Jones, Mike Cernovich, Scott Presler, and Nick Fuentes. We also anticipated that several members of Congress would be speaking at Freedom Plaza as part of this event, including Representatives Louie Gohmert, Paul Gosar, and Mike Kelly and member-elect Marjorie Taylor Greene from Georgia.

It was expected that members of the Proud Boys would attend with their leader, Enrique Tarrio. Other militia groups were expected to attend as well, including the Oath Keepers and the Three Percenters. From our discussions with MPD, we knew there had been a spike in hotel occupancy rates for this weekend, and we expected several thousand pro-Trump supporters to attend. I reached out to Jeff Lundy, the director of security at the Grand Hyatt in DC, who advised that he, too, was seeing a spike in the reservations at his hotel for the weekend. We also anticipated that a number of counterprotest groups, such as the They/Them Collective, Refuse Fascism DC, and Antifa-type protesters, would also be there.

On November 12, the IICD published a daily intelligence report providing an assessment of all the groups expected to be demonstrating in the city during the upcoming weekend. The Million MAGA March and the They/Them Collective were rated at roughly even odds for the possibility of civil disobedience and arrests. All other groups were assessed as either "remote" or "improbable" for civil disobedience. We started developing an operational plan for what we began to call "MAGA I" based on the available information and intelligence. Again, as on election night, neither the House nor the Senate was scheduled to be in session on Saturday, November 14. This made staffing the CDU detail much easier since I would have fewer doors, vehicle entry points, and other posts in the congressional buildings to staff.

The Operational Services Bureau (OSB) developed the CDU plan under the guidance of Assistant Chief Thomas and Deputy Chief Eric Waldow. Knowing that I had experience in this area, they often would consult with me regarding specifics such as CDU staffing and the perimeter. Waldow was assigned as the incident commander for all the associated demonstration activity. The plan would also assign an OSB captain—usually the individual who wrote the CDU plan— as the mobile field force commander. For this event, that commander was Captain Neysha Mendoza. The mobile field force commander is in charge of all CDU deployment activity, including protective actions such as putting on helmets or other protective gear and shields. As is now standard practice after a series of vehicle ramming attacks around the world, Waldow included a plan to protect the march route against the possibility of a ramming by a vehicle.

The CDU plan activated a total of four hard CDU platoons for this event. A USCP CDU platoon comprises about forty officers divided into squads of ten, each fully equipped with special helmets and body protectors and specifically trained in crowd management. We activated four hard CDU platoons because this is the maximum number of hard platoons that the department could sustain with equipment and train- ing. Also, historically, four hard CDU platoons had sufficed for the demonstrations that we had faced thus far on the Hill.

The plan also activated a less lethal grenadier team for this event. The term *less lethal* refers to a weapons system that, when properly em- ployed, is not designed to inflict a lethal injury. Less lethal systems used by the USCP included the PepperBall weapon systems, the FN 303 less lethal launcher, the 40mm foam impact round, and the beanbag system. Over the summer, Thomas had recommended a temporary suspension in deploying the larger 40mm impact round after several injuries were reported following use of the round by the United States Marshals during some of the violent protests in other states. For the MAGA I event, the less lethal grenadier teams deployed the PepperBall weapon system and the FN 303 less lethal launcher. Both these systems fire a highly accu- rate small-impact round that also contains a chemical irritant and/or a marking round. The marking round is used to mark suspects with a very visible paint so they can be apprehended at a later time.

I had reviewed the initial steel crowd-control barrier plan established by OSB and was concerned that it did not provide a method to help

separate the protesters and counterprotesters in the area of the Supreme
Court. I discussed this concern with Pittman and Thomas and advised
them that I wanted to go into the field and see firsthand where they were
putting the fence. After the Veterans Day holiday, I drove the proposed
march route and met with Deputy Chief Waldow and Captain Mendoza to discuss the current metal crowd-control barrier plan. I parked on
First Street between the Capitol and the Supreme Court and walked the
proposed fence line with the two of them. We discussed some options
to help maintain a chute for the marchers, establishing a fence line on
the north and south sides of First Street by the Supreme Court. While
on-site, we also met with Chief Smith of the US Supreme Court Police.
I wanted to make sure everyone was on board with the updated barrier
placement. Waldow worked with Pittman's Security Services Bureau to
obtain additional bike racks and to reconfigure the barrier placement.

Eric Waldow was a good cop. Just under six feet tall and built like
an ox, he was one of the kindest people I ever met. One of the things
I really liked about Waldow was his ability to talk to protesters and
look for a peaceful outcome. Not every cop would bother trying to establish these lines of communication with protesters, but I felt that it
was important to our job. When my wife and kids would come to the
Capitol, Waldow was often the one who would escort them to their
seats or show them around. He would introduce them to the various
actors and performers, who all knew him. Waldow was a big sci-fi fan
and always got a kick out of talking to my family about all things Star
Wars. My kids loved his signature directive: "Now, remember, if there's
any problem at all, you just ask any officer here, 'Where's Waldow?' and
I'll come find you."

Coinciding with the MAGA I march was the New Member Orientation taking place on the Hill. New Member Orientation is a program
to get the newly elected members of the House of Representatives
acquainted and up to speed on how things work on the Hill and in
Washington, DC. The Protective Services Bureau is in charge of security
planning for the New Member Orientation, and it developed an operations plan for the several-day event. The orientation program covers

everything from getting your office space and hiring staff to using congressional franked mailing privileges and computer security. The chief of the USCP is usually invited to speak. He gives an overview of the department and talks about crime on the Hill and in DC, coordinating activities with the USCP, and handling threats. I had been invited to speak at the New Member Orientation on Friday, November 13, at 10:00 a.m. in the auditorium at the Capitol Visitor Center (CVC). This was the first time I can recall using this auditorium for the New Member Orientation. It's a modern-looking two-level auditorium that holds about five hundred people, and I knew it well, having administered the oath of office there to many graduating recruit officers. It was selected for this event because it provided adequate social-distancing space for the new members in attendance.

For the New Member Orientation, I was presenting along with Kim Campbell, the assistant House sergeant at arms, and Randy Vickers, the chief information security officer for the House of Representatives. When I came into the auditorium to prepare for my presentation, it was already filled with dozens of House members-elect, who were just completing a break between sessions. In the middle of the auditorium, I noticed a group of members near the center aisle, deep in conversation. I noticed them because none of them were wearing masks, and the House was very particular about masks and social distancing. They were standing huddled close together, and it looked like a very animated discussion. They were smiling and laughing. And why wouldn't they be? They were newly elected members of Congress. I recognized two of them as Marjorie Taylor Greene and Lauren Boebert because they had garnered a lot of media attention as they were coming to Washington. I didn't recognize the third member.

I sat in the middle of a three-person table at the front of the room, with Kim and Randy on either side of me. I presented last, and then the moderator opened the floor for questions. One member asked about how to handle threatening or concerning phone calls coming into her office. It was a question I regularly got, and I had a quick, easy answer. The next question came from Lauren Boebert, the newly elected member from

Colorado and a fervent Second Amendment supporter. Boebert wanted to make it clear she planned to carry a firearm while she was in the city and while working on the Hill. She wanted to know the rules regarding her ability to carry in the Capitol and congressional office buildings.

From her media coverage, I wasn't surprised by the question, and I was prepared to answer it. I explained to Ms. Boebert that members of Congress are afforded certain privileges regarding possessing firearms and having them in their offices on Capitol Hill, but with certain restrictions. I referred her to House Sergeant at Arms Paul Irving for more specifics since his office coordinates with House members on such matters. I also provided a general overview of the District of Columbia's laws regarding firearm ownership, registration, and the process to obtain a concealed-carry permit.

Boebert then began to engage me in the constitutionality of the District's gun laws and why she should be able to carry a concealed weapon. I calmly and respectfully advised her this was something I could not help her with since I was not with the Metropolitan Police Department or the DC government. Boebert then flipped back to the topic of guns at the Capitol. She stated that she was aware she was prohibited from carrying her firearm onto the House floor, and wanted to know where she could lock up her gun. I explained that all safety and security equipment are provided by the House sergeant at arms and that since that is who purchases and installs these items, she should ask the HSAA.

She began to accuse me of deliberately evading her questions. "Why is the chief of police refusing to answer my questions?" she asked. "Where are you going to put a lockbox so I can lock up my weapon while I'm on the House floor?"

"Ma'am, I am unable to provide you with a lockbox," I answered. "You need to ask the SAA. His office handles these types of issues."

As the other junior members of Congress looked on, the conversation began to reach an uncomfortable tenor as I repeatedly had to keep referring her to the House sergeant at arms. It felt as if time stood still, and I looked for support from anyone from the House SAA's office who was in attendance. I saw one of the general counsels from the Sergeant at Arms Office quickly duck out the back of the auditorium. I could also feel Kim slowly sinking into her chair beside me. It was clear that no one would be making any immediate efforts to come to my rescue.

I took a breath and again referred Ms. Boebert to the sergeant at arms. Just as she was ready to reengage me for one more round, the moderator stepped in and concluded the session. Irving contacted me shortly after the presentation and complimented me on how I handled the situation. News travels fast. It was apparent that Ms. Boebert, like many others, was not aware of the hierarchal structure on the Hill. As the chief, I was not at the top of the pyramid. I was at the bottom.

It was also a regular practice for me to brief certain members and committees before major events and demonstrations that could affect the congressional community. I would brief the staff of my oversight committees, usually the Committee on House Administration (CHA) and the Senate Rules Committee, about upcoming demonstrations. Because the MAGA I march coincided with the New Member Orientation, the CHA wanted to be certain there would be no delays or disruptions. I briefed them on the expectations for the day and on the preparations the department had undertaken to secure the event. Other than the CHA, there were no specific concerns or requests for personal briefings from any members of Congress, but I still sent an email to all my oversight committees advising them of any upcoming special events or major demonstrations.

MAGA I happened on a cool and clear day. There was to be a rally on Freedom Plaza, then a march to the Supreme Court. I stayed in contact with our partner agencies, often reaching out to the MPD, the USPP, and Chief Sullivan over at the USSS. As expected, the event was well attended, with tens of thousands present. I was watching the event on the video screens in the USCP Command Center, and I could see that Freedom Plaza and the surrounding streets were packed with people.

At the beginning of the rally, in a highly unusual maneuver, President Trump had the USSS drive his motorcade through the thick crowd of supporters gathered around Freedom Plaza. I can only imagine the "pucker factor" that the Secret Service agents were experiencing as they made this drive and as the motorcade was being rushed and surrounded by hundreds of unscreened individuals. I have no doubt this detour was against the collective better judgment of his security detail. Trump then headed out to play golf in Northern Virginia. As the event at Freedom Plaza began to conclude and participants began to march toward the Supreme Court, large masses of people began funneling down Thirteenth and Fourteenth Streets toward Freedom Plaza and onto the march route. They were coming out of Metros and buses, joining the marchers. It was wall-to-wall people. I called Carroll over at MPD and asked him about this massive influx of people.

"I don't know where all these people came from," Jeff said. "They just keep coming!"

I was looking all the way down Pennsylvania Avenue from the Capitol toward the White House, and the street was filled with people. The organizer had set up a podium in front of the Supreme Court for several designated speakers to address the crowd. One of the speakers was the radio-talk-show host Alex Jones. I remember hearing over the police radio that members of the Proud Boys were escorting Jones through the crowd on the East Front of the Capitol, toward the podium at the Supreme Court. I directed the Command Center personnel operating our camera system to see if they could find them. They quickly located the group of about twenty Proud Boys walking along the sidewalk by the Senate grassy area on the East Front. As we watched the group make its way through the crowd, I saw members of the Proud Boys pushing what appeared to be fellow Trump supporters out of the way. I was surprised to see how they treated fellow marchers. I remained in the Command Center, monitoring the march along with Pittman and Thomas.

As the march continued past the Supreme Court, a group of about forty Antifa-type counterprotesters marched onto Maryland Avenue from the back side of the Supreme Court. They began advancing down Maryland Avenue toward the Trump supporters. We had officers deployed along the fence line on First Street at Maryland Avenue, but some of the pro-Trump marchers had inadvertently marched on the wrong side of the barrier and were now beginning to intermingle with the counterprotesters.

Quite a few verbal altercations and fights erupted between marchers and counterprotesters. My officers were caught in the middle of the two groups on the north side of First Street, next to the Supreme Court. Lines of USCP officers tried to keep the two groups separated. We deployed CDU officers from the hard platoons in protective gear to assist. My less lethal team responded, moving to the steps of a building next to Maryland Avenue in the event they needed to be deployed. There were several physical altercations between the groups and police, but less lethal capabilities proved unnecessary. The MPD had some CDU units come in from the back of the Supreme Court on Maryland Avenue to assist us. We managed to get control and separate both groups, but not before a few officers and the CDU captain were roughed up in the altercations.

As the MAGA I march was concluding, we had a number of fights occur as protesters and counterprotesters were leaving the event and walking off Capitol grounds. In one case, we had a counterprotester throw frozen water bottles at some Trump supporters, and we had another individual spraying people with pepper spray. This individual was arrested.

The USCP Intelligence and Interagency Coordination Division (IICD) intelligence had proved accurate. The MPD arrested twenty-one persons for criminal charges, including four for firearm violations, two for simple assault, one for assault on a police officer, and two for disorderly conduct. The MPD recovered seven firearms, and two MPD officers were injured.

Following the MAGA I event, we conducted an after-action report (AAR) to identify any lessons learned. Captain Mendoza completed the AAR and identified several issues. One of the big takeaways was that the MAGA I activities on Capitol grounds had started sooner than expected, and it became difficult to get some of our CDU platoons through the crowds to their assigned areas. After MAGA I, civil disturbance unit commanders would be directed to deploy their personnel to their assigned locations immediately after roll call. In addition, hard platoons would be outfitted in their hard gear and prestaged, ready to respond wherever civil disobedience was expected. Another recommendation from the AAR was to have the riot shields staged closer to the CDU officers' hard platoons.

MAGA II: DECEMBER 12, 2020

On November 20, we learned that Women for America First was submitting First Amendment demonstration permits to the National Park Service for the weekend of December 11–13, 2020. Like MAGA I, the event would be held at Freedom Plaza and would include a march to the Supreme Court. The main event would be on Saturday, December 12. On November 23, the USCP began receiving permit applications for events on Capitol grounds for groups in support of the Women for America First rally—what we would call MAGA II.

On November 30, the USCP IICD published an intelligence information paper regarding the MAGA II event. The same group that had organized MAGA I was planning this second rally. Besides the events at Freedom Plaza and John Marshall Park, the group was also looking to demonstrate on Capitol grounds in area 15—Union Square, the grassy area west of the Capitol Reflecting Pool near Third Street. The IICD information paper indicated that the event would be similar to MAGA I, with speeches and a rally in support of President Donald Trump. The department was receiving additional permit requests from other pro-Trump organizations for events on Capitol grounds. The report also indicated that at least three groups would be conducting counter-protests to the MAGA II event: the They/Them Collective, the Fuck the MAGA rally, and the Fuck the Police march.

On December 7, IICD produced a second information report related to the MAGA II event. The information paper reiterated the previous information and added that some high-profile speakers would attend. The information paper also predicted that the crowds would be smaller than at MAGA I and that the event would be held even if President Trump conceded. Groups expected to attend included the Proud Boys,

Oath Keepers, and Three Percenters, and MAGA II participants were encouraged to come armed.

On December 11, IICD published an information paper regarding the planned protests expected to take place in the District of Columbia and on Capitol grounds the weekend of December 12–13.[13] Of the five demonstrations on the report listed as "demonstrations of concern," civil disobedience was anticipated only from the counterprotest groups.

Based on this intelligence, we again developed a CDU operations plan for the event. As during the event in November, Congress would not be in session on Saturday, December 12, and no other official congressional events were scheduled. Therefore, we had routine Saturday staffing for the congressional buildings, which again made staffing a CDU plan considerably easier.

Waldow prepared a plan that activated four hard CDU platoons for the march. I met with Pittman and Thomas to discuss the perimeter plan and deployment of the steel crowd-control barriers. As a result of the clashes between the marchers and counterprotesters in the area of Maryland Avenue and East Capitol Street during the MAGA I march, I knew we had to reconfigure the placement of the steel crowd-control barriers to create better separation between opposing groups. For the MAGA II march, we set up the metal racks around the march routes to create one-block "no-man zones" on each of the streets leading to the march route. Thomas and Waldow assigned CDU personnel to the various fence lines in support to the established no-man zones. This would help keep the marchers and counterprotesters separate. The metal crowd-control barriers were deployed by Pittman's Security Services Bureau and checked by Waldow and Mendoza before the march. This configuration of the perimeter would prove very effective during the march.

On Friday evening before the march, the MPD had to deal with several clashes between the Proud Boys and other Trump supporters

13. Intelligence and Interagency Coordination Division (IICD), "21-A-0469 Planned Protests in Washington DC - December 12-13, 2020," IICD Information Paper (internal restricted document), December 11, 2020..

fighting with counterprotesters in the area of Black Lives Matter Plaza just north of the White House. These clashes continued throughout the night, with quite a few protesters and officers injured.

On Saturday, December 12, the weather in Washington was unseasonably warm and mild. It was about sixty degrees and partly cloudy. Again, perfect weather for demonstrations. On my way into the office in the morning, I called in to the USCP Command Center to see how things were going. There were some marchers walking around the Capitol Hill area, but nothing of concern. The watch commander advised that they had been monitoring Freedom Plaza and it didn't appear very busy down there. A stage was set up on the plaza, and people were starting to show up. I arrived in the office around 8:00 a.m. and did a quick check-in with the Command Center.

The official events started on Freedom Plaza at 11:00 a.m. with a number of speakers: Boris Epshteyn, Michael Flynn, Sebastian Gorka, Congressman Vernon Jones, Congressman-elect Bob Good, and others. Several thousand spectators attended, and a couple of thousand more were on the National Mall. I could see that the crowds were significantly less than at the MAGA I event, but they were still sizable. While I was in the Command Center, I monitored the march, regularly asking my camera operators to monitor our outer perimeter. We observed several groups of counterprotesters trying to access some of the streets leading to the marchers, but they were stopped by CDU officers and the metal barrier configuration. Although we had a handful of counterprotesters make it onto the march route and get into some verbal altercations with the pro-Trump marchers, we managed to prevent any physical altercations.

Shortly after 1:00 p.m., I got word from the USSS that Trump was considering doing a flyover of the event. We had seen one of the big Sikorsky helicopters fly into the area and land on the south grounds of the White House. Sure enough, in true Trump showmanship fashion, the president paid tribute to his supporters by flying over the event. At 1:34 p.m., two Marine Sikorsky helicopters (the one carrying Trump designated *Marine One*) took flight from the south grounds of the White

House. The crowds on the plaza could clearly see the helicopters as they cleared the tree line. The two massive aircraft slowly passed over Freedom Plaza, eliciting loud cheers from the crowd. They flew in tight formation around the Capitol and the Supreme Court, making several passes over the energized crowd.

The events on Capitol Hill concluded without any major issues or arrests, although one matter drew the ire of a prominent staffer on one of my oversight committees. During the event, a group of marchers had made their way over to the Senate side of the East Front, which was open to the public. The marchers were able to hang a large Trump banner over the wall above the north entrance to the Capitol Visitor Center. The images of the Trump banner hanging off part of the Capitol deeply aggravated Kelly Fado of the Senate Rules Committee staff. She called me and made her displeasure very clear. She gave me the impression that she felt we were sympathetic toward Trump, and suggested that the officers condoned the hanging of the banner and therefore didn't take it down immediately. This could not be further from the truth. This action was not condoned, and we addressed it as soon as officers were available and had the resources to remove it.

I wasn't overly surprised by Kelly's assumptions. She would often tell me that she felt that USCP leadership watched too much Fox News. To be clear, we have multiple news outlets playing at USCP and do not favor one over the other. USCP officials on the Hill know that the Capitol and the congressional office buildings must remain neutral and should not show support for any political or commercial messages. In fact, after seeing protesters use high-powered projectors to shine political messages on federal buildings, we took steps to outlaw the projection of messages onto any building on Capitol Hill.

I was apparently not the only one who heard from Fado about the banner. After MAGA II, all Waldow's operations plans included personnel assigned to be on the lookout for banner drops. This is a good example of the degree of influence the committee staff had on my operations.

Although this event ended without any major incidents on the Hill, the MPD was not so lucky. Following the march, a group of Proud Boys and others made their way downtown to Black Lives Matter Plaza, and numerous fights broke out with groups like Antifa and Black Lives Matter. During the evening, at least four people were stabbed north of Black Lives Matter Plaza. The MPD arrested thirty-three people, two of whom were identified as being involved in the stabbings. Members of the Proud Boys also removed a Black Lives Matter banner from a church and set it on fire in the street. The theft and destruction of this banner would result in an arrest warrant being issued for Enrique Tarrio, the leader of the Proud Boys. That evening, eight officers were injured, one receiving multiple fractures and a laceration to his face.

Overall, we had successfully planned and developed the MAGA I and MAGA II event operations plans based on intelligence. We had deployed our crowd-control barriers to prevent the anticipated problems between opposing groups. We had expected and planned for armed protesters, which were encountered off Capitol grounds and dealt with by the MPD. We had limited arrests and injuries to our officers, just as the intel showed we would. Our plans and expectations were guided by our intel, and our intel turned out to be correct again. I had no reason to doubt our intelligence and planning process going forward.

PLANNING FOR MAGA III: JANUARY 6, 2021

On Monday, December 14, immediately following the MAGA II weekend, we learned that another MAGA event was being planned in the city to coincide with the January 6 joint session of Congress to certify the Electoral College votes. We had received information through the National Park Service and other partner agencies that an organizer had submitted a permit to hold an event on the Ellipse, just south of the White House. Unlike previous demonstrations that occurred on Saturdays when Congress wasn't in session, this event would occur on a Wednesday and during the joint session of Congress. This meant that both the House and the Senate would be in session, and the vice president of the United States would be in attendance.

On the afternoon of December 14, Deputy Chief Gallagher sent an email to Pittman and Thomas indicating that he would have an assessment of the January 6 event the next day. He also indicated that some representatives might try to challenge the vote and that this could bring some demonstrations to the Hill. Pittman forwarded a copy of the email to me that evening. I responded that we had already started discussing civil disturbance units and that I was considering a "significant deployment."

Over the next twenty days, IICD would produce four intelligence assessments that guided planning and preparation, not only for the USCP but also for the members of the Capitol Police Board (CPB). The first, Special Event Assessment 21-A-0468, was a four-page document dated December 16, 2020. It started with a bottom-line-up-front, or BLUF, section. BLUF is a method in which the key information (i.e., the bottom line) is listed first. It noted, "The certification of the electoral votes will take place on January 6, that some Republican representatives may attempt to challenge the certification against the advice of Senator McConnell."

The assessment noted that the IICD was tracking two protests scheduled to take place on Capitol grounds—one pro-Trump, the other pro-Biden. It then provided an overview of the joint session and said that the vice president of the United States would be attending. In referencing the certification process, it noted, "The president and vice president must achieve a majority of electoral votes (i.e., at least 270 votes) to be elected. In the absence of a majority, the House selects the president, and the Senate selects the vice president."

The assessment then provided an overview of the threats to congressional leadership for the 116th Congress, and investigations thereof. The report indicated that in reference to organizational or group threats, there was no information to indicate that any type of violence or civil unrest would be associated with the joint session of Congress. The IICD's overall analysis indicated that they had "no information to indicate there would be acts of civil disobedience targeting this function." The assessment further stated that "due to the tense political environment, threats of disruption or violence cannot be ruled out."

It concluded that with the possibility of some members of Congress objecting to the certification, we should anticipate that the certification could very well run into the morning hours, possibly until sunrise. We immediately began working to develop a staffing plan to provide around-the-clock coverage until the certification concluded.

A week later, on December 23, the IICD produced the second assessment. Special Event Assessment 21-A-0468 v.2 was a seven-page document. The BLUF section read almost identically to the first assessment, with the addition that "some protesters have indicated that they planned to attend the demonstrations armed." The assessment further provided an overview of the expected protests, indicating that the demonstrations were "expected to be similar to the previous Million MAGA March rallies in November and December 2020" and that members of the Proud Boys, Antifa, and other extremist groups would be present. The assessment provided an overview of the various known pro-Trump and pro-Biden demonstration groups expected. Organizers of one main pro-Trump protest group said that they planned to be on the Capitol lawn and steps to show support for senators planning to object to the certification. The MPD had indicated that hotel occupancy rates were high, so we anticipated a well-attended event. The assessment also included social media references encouraging protesters to come armed. Again, the December 23 overall IICD analysis of the joint session of Congress indicated that there was "no information regarding specific disruptions or civil disobedience targeting this event."

On December 23, I received an email from the MPD's Intelligence Division regarding a website called wildprotest.com, which contained information about groups expecting to protest on January 6. When I received the email, I immediately forwarded a copy to Pittman and Gallagher for the IICD's awareness and for inclusion in future intelligence products. Gallagher immediately responded to me that the IICD was aware of the website and its contents and was tracking it.

As already noted, the MAGA I and MAGA II events had a couple of major differences that we needed to address. Since the previous MAGA events had occurred when Congress was not in session, I'd had far fewer required posts to staff, because the office buildings were closed, the chambers and the galleries did not require full staffing, and fewer pedestrian and vehicle access points required officers. As a result, I had more officers available to help staff the event and the civil disturbance units without having to hold people over for very long. With the House and Senate both in session and planning to hold an all-night joint session of Congress with the VP attending, we would be subjected to the greatest staffing demands on our already limited resources. This would make pulling together the staffing for a large CDU detail even more difficult. Both sergeants at arms and my oversight committees were well aware of these staffing requirements and my existing personnel shortages.

I began meeting with my two assistant chiefs, Thomas and Pittman, almost immediately to start planning for January 6. I directed that we activate the greatest number of hard CDU platoons, and Thomas advised that Waldow would handle the CDU plan. Four hard platoons were the largest number of fully outfitted CDU officers we could deploy. I directed that the department be put into an all-hands-on-deck (AHOD) staffing posture, meaning that all available personnel would need to be at work on January 6. This was a staffing term I had brought from my time at the MPD, where Chief Ramsey and Chief Lanier would implement AHODs for citywide crime initiatives and major events. The week of January 3, we canceled rotating anyone out into the COVID Ready Reserve posture. No one was to be working remotely, and no one was to take January 6 as a day off.

I did not take the step to cancel leave for the limited number of officers who had already been approved for various reasons. None of the intelligence I was seeing during the planning mandated taking this step. And in my experience, canceling leave rarely achieves the full staffing results you might expect, especially when trying to cancel it around the holidays and during the last pay period of the year. This would have been a move that caused significant concern with my labor unions as well. Nevertheless, if the intelligence had indicated a significant likelihood of violence and attacks on law enforcement, I absolutely would have taken this action.

On December 29, Waldow developed a draft plan for civil disturbance units and submitted it for review. The plan activated four hard CDU platoons and less lethal capabilities. Waldow was designated the incident commander, and an Operational Services Bureau captain was assigned as the field force commander in charge of CDU resources for the event.[14] The plan included the assignment of two less lethal grenadiers to each CDU platoon—one with an FN 303 less lethal projectile weapon, and another with the PepperBall launcher. As is standard when preparing a plan for a large demonstration, Waldow activated a tactical team from our Containment and Emergency Response Team (CERT) to provide a tactical response and overwatch. CERT is the specially trained and equipped SWAT team for the USCP.

The plan also established a perimeter around part of the East Front of the Capitol and around part of the West Front, the Reflecting Pool, and Union Square near Third Street. Upon review of the draft plan, I knew that I wanted to make some adjustments to the perimeter fencing layout Waldow had suggested. Any changes I was going to make to the perimeter would have to be approved in advance by the House and Senate sergeants at arms, but I wanted to find a way to better control the groups with permits on the East Front and also to provide a better perimeter on the West Front. As Waldow was completing the draft, I added the all-hands-on-deck staffing for January 6 and increased the CDU staffing requirements for January 6, based on the additional available personnel.

On December 30, IICD published a third special event assessment for the joint session of Congress, which was numbered 21-A-0468 v.2. (It was mistakenly titled "v.2," just like the December 23 assessment.) This version was a nine-page document with the BLUF section reading almost verbatim with the December 23 assessment. The assessment indicated that much of the previous violence occurred between pro-Trump and

14. Chris Marquette, "Capitol Police Riot Control Unit Did Not Plan for the Violence of Jan. 6," Roll Call, June 8, 2021, www.rollcall.com/2021/06/08/capitol -police-riot-control-unit-did-not-plan-for-violence-on-jan-6/.

opposing groups, often after the march concluded. The assessment again provided an overview of the various known pro-Trump and pro-Biden groups of demonstrators expected on January 6, and reported, "No group is expected to march and all are planning to stay in their designated areas."

This assessment forecast the January 6 event to be well attended, due to high hotel occupancy rates. The assessment also indicated, "IICD found no information regarding specific disruptions or acts of civil disobedience targeting this function."

As I mentioned, when we had a major event or a large demonstration planned on Capitol Hill, I would get briefing requests from my oversight committees and certain members of Congress regarding our intelligence and preparations for the event. The members who were briefed in advance of January 6 included Chairman Blunt, Chairperson Lofgren, Chairman Ryan, Representative Davis, and, oddly, Representative Waters. The first four of these representatives were on my oversight committees. However, Representative Maxine Waters made a random request for a briefing, and House Sergeant at Arms Irving directed me to provide it, which is a story in itself.

On December 31 at 11:00 a.m., I was at home with my family when I received a call from Representative Maxine Waters's chief of staff. It was highly unusual for Waters to request a personal briefing. I had never briefed her in the past, and she was not on any of my oversight committees. Nevertheless, we had a phone call for more than thirty minutes, during which we discussed the expectation of protests at the Capitol and security preparations for the event. The overview was the same that I would give anyone else. I discussed the events that were scheduled downtown and the fact that we expected a large march to culminate at the Capitol. When I told her that members of the Proud Boys and other right-wing militias were expected to attend, she interrupted and said, "These people are dangerous. What are you going to do to protect us?"

A reasonable question. I began to explain about the CDU plan we had in place to secure the Capitol and that the East Plaza would be restricted to members of Congress and other authorized personnel.

She wanted to know what we would do if protesters decided to block access to the building. Blocking entrances was a tactic various groups had used on the Hill before, so this was another reasonable question. I recommended that members use the underground system to get to the Capitol from the office buildings. I also advised that we had contingency plans in place if a member of Congress was unable to access the Capitol complex. I was prepared to send a marked police car out to pick them up and bring them in.

Representative Waters then asked what seemed like the most random question: What were we going to do "to prevent protesters from climbing on top of the Capitol"?

She's concerned about people climbing on the building? I asked myself. We had never had protesters climb on top of the Capitol. Where was this coming from? I told her that we would have USCP officers on the buildings and looking out for unusual activity.

When I mentioned that we had received six permit applications for groups to conduct First Amendment demonstrations on Capitol grounds, Representative Waters got very upset, and this topic dominated the remainder of our call. She kept asking me detailed questions about the permitting process and specifics of who had applied for permits. I explained that I didn't have information on the applicants but that I knew the names of the organizations and where they would be demonstrating. I clarified that our process to obtain a First Amendment assembly permit at the USCP is almost identical to the process used by the MPD and the Park Police and that our process to obtain a First Amendment permit is a transparent first-come, first-served process and that the directions for requesting a permit are available online.

She wanted to know whether the message or grievance of the group should play a part in denying permits. In fact, she appeared to be angry that some groups would be issued permits on Capitol grounds. I explained that the USCP must remain content-neutral and that to expressly deny a permit based on the message or grievance being portrayed would be inappropriate.

She was concerned that these people could be dangerous and that violence could erupt. I explained that denying the right to a First Amendment assembly solely on the suspicion that violence may erupt would be construed as a form of censorship or prior restraint in the eyes of the law.

She then asked another odd question. She wanted to know if we considered the demographics of the groups applying for permits. I explained that we absolutely do not take into account a person's or group's demographics when considering approving a First Amendment permit. In fact, demographics information is not even a question on the application. She explained that she was concerned we could be putting protesters of different demographics next to each other in the First Amendment assembly areas. I again explained to her that while we do not take demographics into consideration, we try not to put groups with opposing viewpoints together. I also explained that we would have personnel near the demonstration area to help prevent any physical altercations.

Waters then wanted to know how someone who wanted a permit and didn't have backing from big organizations or corporations would be granted a permit. I explained that First Amendment permits are very easy to obtain and that anyone can apply and be granted a permit. I further reiterated that we do not consider the message, demographics, corporate or financial backing, political affiliation, or any other personal traits of the applicant when evaluating the First Amendment permit application. I told her once more that the information about the permit process is available to everyone online and that the process is first come, first served, and that it is the same process used by our partner agencies. I found myself bewildered by her line of questioning regarding First Amendment activities, even as it was obvious she was getting more and more agitated and upset with me.

She was still angry about the permit process and said, "Well, we are going to have to look further into this. You will be hearing from me."

The call ended. *That was a very interesting conversation*, I thought. I was confident in my knowledge of the First Amendment permitting process and restrictions, which had been upheld by the Supreme Court. Race and the grievance of the applicant are not two of those restrictions.

The very next day, January 1, at 10:00 a.m., I got on a call with

Chairman Roy Blunt and some staff from the Senate Rules Committee. Fitzhugh Elder, staff director for the Senate Rules Committee, had contacted me a few days earlier to request the briefing. I had made Stenger aware of the scheduled call, but he was happy to let me handle it without his assistance.

I had regularly briefed this group in the past, so I felt fairly comfortable with the call. I gave them an overview of the expected events and our preparations, much as I had done with Maxine Waters. Chairman Blunt was concerned about members of Congress being able to get through the protests and wanted to make sure they could access the East Plaza. I told him that the plaza would be closed to the public and recommended that members access the Capitol through the office buildings. Since Blunt was the chairman of the Joint Congressional Committee on Inaugural Ceremonies, he was responsible for the inaugural platform on the West Front. After months of construction, the structure was almost completed. Blunt wanted to make sure I wasn't going to let anything happen to the platform. I knew how he felt about all the work that had gone into it. This was his baby.

I told him, "Sir, I will not let anything happen to the platform. We will have it barricaded off and officers assigned to it." This got me thinking about adjusting the perimeter to better secure the West Front. I told them we were staying in close contact with our partner agencies and keeping an eye on intelligence and would advise them should anything change.

As was customary with Blunt, he concluded the meeting by asking if the department needed any assistance from him or the Rules Committee. "So what do you need from us?" he asked. He was always very kind with his offers of assistance.

I thanked him and said, "We are good at this point."

On Saturday, January 2, I learned that my good friend Robert Contee had been named acting chief of police for the Metropolitan Police Department. I had known Bob for decades and had the pleasure of working with him during my time with the MPD. I had always known he would make an outstanding chief there. He knew his community and his officers and would be good for both. I called Bob on January 2 to congratulate him, but I also called him to ask a very important question. It was the same thing I had asked Chief Newsham after some of the protests at the White House. At the time, Newsham had assured me that the MPD would be there to assist the USCP if needed. Knowing that there was a new person in the chief's position, I thought it important to ask Contee the same question, especially in advance of January 6 and the presidential inauguration.

"Absolutely," Contee replied. "MPD will always have your back." I felt comforted by his response and by the support I knew I could count on from an experienced agency like the MPD.

As January 6 approached, I knew that this was going to be a well-attended event and that the perimeter would be my biggest issue. My staffing was already overextended since both the House and the Senate would be in session. The staffing needs of an extended joint session of Congress, even with the AHOD directive, would leave me few extra personnel to help support my perimeter and CDU operations. SAAs Stenger and Irving were both aware of these issues. I felt I needed some additional support to help staff the perimeter and maintain its integrity. We had used unarmed National Guard soldiers on the Hill during major events like presidential inaugurations before, and I believed this would be an appropriate request. However, for me to request the National Guard in advance, according to federal law, I would first have to get the approval of the CPB and congressional leadership. I had to get the support of the two chief law enforcement officials for the House and the Senate to move forward. Without their support, there was no way I could get the National Guard.

My initial request for the National Guard occurred on the first day of the 117th Congress, Sunday, January 3, 2021. The first day of Congress is usually a very busy day, with all the members and their spouses and children in attendance, but the inaugural day of the 117th Congress appeared a little subdued this time due to COVID-19. At 9:00 a.m., the campus didn't seem overly busy. It seemed odd that the first day fell on a Sunday. I decided to go over to Irving's office in person to make my request.

I drove over to the Capitol from USCP HQ, going through the

north barricade off Constitution Avenue. This was the barricade where I would usually see Officer Billy Evans, Officer Singh, and others who manned the barricade. They were always very pleasant, and I would often comment on the garden gnome they had in the planter in front of the barricade. I parked on the Senate side of the plaza and walked under the carriage overhang and through the north carriage door, shaking the hands (due to COVID-19, more of a knuckle bump than a handshake) of the officers who manned the door. This was my way of showing my respect and appreciation for all they do. They were good officers, professional and courteous.

I personally went to meet with the sergeants at arms because I knew this would be a sensitive issue for them and for leadership. I walked down the empty halls of the Capitol to H-124, the office of the House sergeant at arms, arriving at 9:24 a.m. I know this because after my testimony at the Senate hearing, the USCP did a video review and found the video of me walking into the office. Irving's office was just to the left of the House carriage entrance on the east side of the Capitol. His office was a beautiful light yellow and very ornate, with a fireplace in the outer office and one in his office as well. I had been surprised to learn that the fireplaces in the Capitol work and are regularly used in the winter.

As I walked into his office, I was greeted by Bob Dohr, chief operating officer for the House sergeant at arms. I then said a quick hello to Tim Blodgett, Irving's deputy SAA, before walking into Paul's office.

As usual, Irving was up on his feet in the office, wearing slacks, a long-sleeved dress shirt, and a tie. He was a very energetic person, always walking and talking fast. He greeted me with his usual "Gooood morning, Chief."

I skipped any small talk and went right for the ask: "Sir, I've been thinking a lot about Wednesday and our perimeter, and I would like to request the assistance of the National Guard."

I could immediately tell this did not sit well with him. He straightened up, clenched his teeth, and drew back a flat smile as he inhaled loudly. "I don't like the optics of that," he said, shaking his head slowly. Then he added, "Besides, I don't think the intelligence supports it."

I responded by telling him we knew the event was going to be well attended and that I could use the support on the perimeter. He told me to go talk to Stenger to see what he thought of the idea. Stenger was the current chairman of the Capitol Police Board, so that made sense to me. *Maybe I'll have better luck with him*, I thought, so I said okay.

Irving grabbed his coat, and we left his office, walking fast through the halls toward the center of the Capitol. As we walked, he talked about the swearing-in ceremony for the 117th Congress, which would be taking place in a couple of hours. We went through the crypt below the rotunda and into the Senate side of the Capitol, at which point I separated from Irving to head toward Stenger's office. "Let's catch up later," Irving said.

Minutes later, I walked into S-150 in the Capitol. This was the office of the Senate sergeant at arms. Stenger's lavish Wedgwood-blue office was located on the west side of the Capitol and looked out onto the Senate side of the upper West Terrace, with an amazing view of the West Front that extended all the way to the National Mall and the Washington Monument. The door to his office was open, and I walked right in, but no one was there, not even his secretary or Jennifer Hemingway, his deputy sergeant at arms. I left his office and went back to headquarters.

I returned to Stenger's office later that morning, at 11:53 a.m. As I walked in, he was grabbing his suit jacket, about to go to the Old Senate Chamber for the swearing-in. I started to ask him about getting the National Guard's support for January 6, but before I could even finish the question, Stenger stopped me and asked, "Do you know anyone at the DC National Guard?"

"Yes, sir," I said. "I'm good friends with the commanding officer, General William Walker."

Stenger then asked if I could unofficially inquire with Walker about what assistance the National Guard could provide if we needed them on January 6. He wanted me to find out how many soldiers they could provide if we needed them and how quickly they could send support.

I told Stenger that I would call Walker that evening and ask him. But I could already tell by this response from Stenger that my request to have the Guard predeployed on the perimeter was dead on arrival.

Stenger then threw on his jacket, and we walked out the door heading to the swearing-in ceremony just down the hall. But I couldn't shake the feeling that Stenger's idea for me to call General Walker had come to him much too quickly. I suspected that Irving must have warned him that I was coming to ask for the National Guard's support. And I was right. Several weeks after January 6, I had the chance to ask Stenger if he had been given a heads-up that I was coming to request the Guard, and he told me that Irving had called him and said, "Sund just came to my office asking for National Guard assistance. We need to come up with another plan. I will never get this by Pelosi."

At 11:00 a.m. on Sunday, Gallagher gave Irving and his staff an updated intelligence brief regarding January 6. This was less than an hour after Irving had denied my request for support from the National Guard. Gallagher's briefing provided no new concerning intelligence and raised no concerns.

Around noon, I had left my meeting with Stenger and was back at USCP headquarters. I was on the seventh floor, walking down the hallway past the two assistant chiefs' offices, and ran into Gallagher outside Pittman's office. He said he had received a call from Carol Corbin, program director at the United States Department of Defense, and she wanted to know if we would be requesting the National Guard to assist us on Wednesday. I knew Carol well. She was the DoD representative who would usually assist agencies in developing their requests for military support, and she had been in almost every National Special Security Event (NSSE) meeting I ever attended. It was apparent she was just trying to button up any outstanding requests for military support that might be coming. The offer for the National Guard assistance from Corbin did not come with any concerns regarding intelligence or threats to the Capitol.

What timing, I thought. I told Gallagher that I had just been over to the SSAA's office to request the National Guard and had been denied. So I asked Gallagher to please tell Corbin, "Thank you, but at this time we will not be requesting the National Guard."

Later that day, I contacted both Irving and Stenger and told them about the call from Carol and the inquiry from DoD. Both Irving and

Stenger knew Carol—especially Irving, who had attended meetings with her in the past. I told them both that based on their instruction to me, I had asked Gallagher to inform Carol that the USCP would not be requesting the National Guard. I also reiterated that I was still planning to call General Walker that evening and would advise them of the outcome.

That evening, as I was driving home in my gray unmarked Ford police SUV, I called General Walker of the DC National Guard. It was 6:14 p.m. Walker was a longtime friend, and I hoped he wouldn't mind my calling on a Sunday evening. He picked up the phone almost immediately and said, "Chief Sund, how can I help you?"

I could hear a television in the background, and Walker asked if I could hold for a minute. Things got muffled and I could hear him talking to someone in the background, and then the television was turned down. Walker came back on the line, now unmuffled, and asked how I was doing. I told him that I appreciated his taking my call and apologized for calling at this time of night on a Sunday.

"It's no problem at all," he said. "I was just having dinner with my wife and watching *The Untouchables*." This sticks in my memory because my father-in-law also enjoyed watching that show.

"I went to request the assistance of the National Guard from Irving and Stenger for January 6," I told him, "but they wouldn't give me the approval to formally request that Guard. They asked that I call you and unofficially ask that if we needed the Guard on the sixth, how many troops could you send us and how quickly?"

"I have about a hundred and twenty-five troops assisting DC with COVID relief, and if needed I could repurpose them fairly quickly," he said. "I'd have to get them back to the DC armory to get their gear and then over to you." He reminded me that I would need to have a USCP official available to swear them in as special police officers, and he would have to get approval from the secretary of the army. Again he reassured me this could happen fairly quickly once we made the official request. He then said he would give the secretary of the army a heads-up about our call.

I told General Walker that I did not have an approved Declaration of Emergency from the Capitol Police Board to make the request and that I was specifically asked to inquire unofficially so that he could "lean forward" on the request to expedite it more quickly. I knew that if word got back to congressional leadership that I was coordinating National Guard assistance without their approval, there would be hell to pay. General Walker said he understood, and we concluded the call.

That same evening, the final intelligence assessment from the IICD was published. IICD Special Event Assessment 21-A-0468 v.3, dated January 3, 2020, was distributed shortly before 11:00 p.m. to a limited audience to include myself and the HSAA. This one was also mistakenly titled with the wrong date.

This report was distributed two more times by the IICD on January 4, the first at 10:59 a.m. and limited to both assistant chiefs, all deputy chiefs, and all division commanders. Almost eight and a half hours later, at 7:24 p.m., IICD distributed the report a second time, this time to all department officials, all the CDU lieutenants and several sergeants, the chief administrative officer, and the Office of the General Counsel. According to the IICD report, the information provided in the final assessment was current as of January 3 at 1500 hours (3:00 p.m.).

The fifteen-page assessment provided a more detailed description of the various demonstrations expected to occur both downtown by the White House and on Capitol grounds. The BLUF, the most critical section of the report, included four points:

On Wednesday, January 6, 2021, the 117th United States Congress will gather for a joint session in the chamber of the House of Representatives to certify the counting of the electoral votes.

There are some representatives and senators who plan to challenge the votes during this session, which will allow the objection to move forward.

The Intelligence and Interagency Coordination Division is currently tracking several protests slated to take place on Capitol grounds and elsewhere in Washington, DC, on January 5, 2021, and January 6, 2021, and some protesters have indicated they plan to be armed. There is also indication that white supremacist groups may be attending the protests.

Detailed information concerning potential counterprotest activity is limited.

The final IICD intelligence assessment once again indicated that the January 6 protests and rallies were "expected to be similar to the previous Million MAGA March rallies in November and December 2020, which drew tens of thousands of participants." The assessment also stated, "No groups are expected to march and all are planning to stay in their designated areas."

The assessment stated that members of the Proud Boys and other white-supremacist groups, Antifa, and other extremist groups were expected to participate in the January 6 event. (That same statement was found in the previous November and December events.) The MPD reported that hotels in the DC area were noting a significant increase in bookings around January 6. According to the report, several social media posts were encouraging protesters to be armed. The assessment also referenced the arrest of Moses Geri in Arlington, Virginia, in the early morning hours of January 1. Geri was found in possession of a rifle, a shotgun, and a pistol, along with a large quantity of ammunition and marijuana, and he was charged with firing two rounds just outside a hotel. According to the police report, Geri had traveled to Washington, DC, "to protect Donald Trump" on January 6. The assessment also indicated that some armed militia members were looking to march into DC on January 5.

At the end of the fifteen-page document, after several pages of traffic closures in the city, the last paragraph provided the IICD's overall analysis of the event:

Due to the tense political environment following the 2020 election, the threat of disruptive actions or violence cannot be ruled out. Supporters of the current president see January 6, 2021, as the last opportunity to overturn the results of the presidential election. This sense of desperation and disappointment may lead to more of an incentive to become violent. Unlike previous post-election protests, the targets of the pro-Trump supporters are not necessarily the counter-protesters as they were previously, but rather Congress itself is the target on the 6th. As outlined above, there has been a worrisome call for protesters to come to these events armed and there is the possibility that protesters may be inclined to become violent. Further, unlike the events on November 14, 2020, and December 12, 2020, there were several more protests scheduled on January 6, 2021, and the majority of them will be on Capitol grounds. The two protests expected to be the largest of the day—the Women for America First protest at the Ellipse and the Stop the Steal protest in Areas 8 and 9—may draw thousands of participants and both have been promoted by President Trump himself. The Stop the Steal protest in particular does not have a permit, but several high profile speakers, including Members of Congress are expected to speak at the event. This combined with Stop the Steal's propensity to attract white supremacists, militia members, and others who actively promote violence, may lead to a significantly dangerous situation for law enforcement and the general public alike.

Many have focused on this final paragraph as damning, specifically because it indicated that "Unlike previous post-election protests, the targets of the pro-Trump supporters are not necessarily the counter-protesters as they were previously, but rather Congress itself is the target on the 6th." It is critical to understand that the target of every protest that occurs on Capitol Hill is Congress. That is why groups come to Capitol Hill to protest. People have read this paragraph and construed the term *target* to mean the target of some type of violence. When considered in the context of the intelligence we were receiving, we were anticipating a large First Amendment demonstration, so these words alone didn't raise any red flags.

It is also important to note that even though the IICD report states, "The targets of the pro-Trump supporters are not necessarily the counter-protesters as they were previously," this section of the assessment was incorrect. While a small percentage of the participants in the previous MAGA rallies may have engaged in physical altercations with counterprotesters, the focus of the event organizers, speakers, and Trump supporters was the Supreme Court, not counterprotesters.

Even Assistant Chief Pittman acknowledged this in her written statement to the House Appropriations Committee when she stated, "The first and second 'MAGA marches' were intended to put public pressure on states where vote counting was ongoing and on the Supreme Court to intervene in the election. This event was different because all judicial remedies for opposing election results had been exhausted and the only way for their candidate to win was for Congress to reject the Electoral College results. Thus, the scheduled demonstrations were intended to pressure Congress."[15]

When interpreting the intelligence that IICD was distributing to the department in advance of January 6, it is important to consider this.

In reading the rest of the final paragraph, no new or alarming intelligence was provided. We had anticipated that some protesters might be armed. The presence of armed participants had already occurred during the previous MAGA marches and had been dealt with effectively by law enforcement. We had developed a contingency plan in case we had to deal with armed protesters on Capitol Hill. During the previous MAGA events, people had expressed a sense of desperation over the elections, and we had seen altercations with counterprotesters and between Trump supporters and law enforcement. We anticipated that this could occur on January 6 as well. This was one of the reasons why I had been pushing for expedited delivery of the riot helmets we ordered back in September.

Coinciding with the distribution of the final intelligence assessment

15. Yogananda D. Pittman, *Statement of Acting Chief of Police Yogananda D. Pittman, United States Capitol Police*, U.S. House of Representatives Document Repository, https://docs.house.gov/meetings/AP/AP24/20210225/111235/HHRG -117-AP24-Wstate-PittmanY-20210225.pdf.

on January 4 was a second document from the IICD, the daily intelligence report (DIR), also dated January 4. This was a detailed twenty-seven-page report that provided an individual summary assessment of every group expected to demonstrate on January 6, especially regarding "the level of probability of acts of civil disobedience/arrests occurring based on current intelligence information." It is important to note that for all the groups expected to demonstrate on Wednesday, January 6, the report assessed the probability of acts of civil disobedience/arrests as "remote" to "improbable." Even the two demonstrations specifically referenced in the last paragraph of the IICD's final intelligence assessment—the Women for America First and the Stop the Steal demonstrations—were now assessed as "remote" and "highly improbable" regarding possible acts of civil disobedience or arrests.

The DIR also stated, "The Secretary of Homeland Security has not issued an elevated or imminent alert at this time . . ." indicating that DHS and the intelligence community did not possess any information showing that a coordinated attack might occur on January 6. I received this report from the IICD at 10:06 a.m. on Monday, January 4. This DIR was distributed again, almost verbatim, on January 5 and January 6. It was also distributed to the offices of the sergeants at arms.

On Monday morning, my chief administrative officer, Richard Braddock, advised me that some of the riot helmets that had been ordered back in September were finally arriving. Although we had originally wanted them sometime before the inauguration, with this large demonstration coming up, I had asked Richard back in December to see if we could expedite delivery and get them by January 6. Richard had worked out a deal to have the company fly in a pallet of about a hundred helmets as soon as they were manufactured. The original delivery had been postponed for months due to COVID-induced manufacturing delays.

Although I was glad they were coming in, I hated to rush the distribution of new equipment without giving the officers the opportunity to try it on and get used to it. Since coming on board with the USCP in 2017, I had been pushing for better personal protective equipment for every officer on the force. I thought every officer in a major police department should have basic equipment such as a helmet, riot baton, and air-purifying respirator, especially in an agency like the USCP. Frankly, I was baffled that an agency that had been the target of two biological-agent attacks—anthrax in 2001 and ricin in 2013—did not already issue air-purifying respirators to all its workforce. Since 2017, I had been working with Braddock and his Property Asset Management Division to identify ways to fund these items. But it wasn't until September 2020 that Braddock could finally identify funding to purchase helmets for every sworn member of the department who didn't have one.

In the days leading up to January 6, I briefed several members of Congress who had requested an advance briefing on our security plan and the permitted demonstration activity scheduled for January 6, 2021. Speaker Pelosi did not request a briefing from me, but that was not unusual since Irving personally briefed her on everything. I developed a briefing sheet with input from my two assistant chiefs to ensure that I was providing consistent, up-to-date information.

The intelligence provided for the briefing sheet said there would be six permitted demonstrations on Capitol grounds and two large events downtown, including the March for Trump. The two major events on the Ellipse promoted by Trump, the March for Trump and Stop the Steal, were expected to draw thousands, and include a speech from President Trump himself. The six demonstrations on Capitol Hill anticipated that several members of Congress would address the group at areas 8 and 9. The briefing information also indicated that some of the events might tend to attract white supremacists, militia members, and others who promote violence, and that the USCP was tracking social media sites for posts encouraging protesters to come armed. None of the information provided by the two assistant chiefs for the briefing sheet indicated that January 6 might lead to a significantly dangerous situation for law enforcement.

Between welcoming in a new Congress, running a large agency, and preparing for January 6, it was a very busy time for me. I felt I had developed a good team, and I placed a lot of trust in them. I met regularly with them during the planning, and I trusted that they were preparing and handling everything that needed to be addressed within their lanes. This trust and autonomy were essential to my ability to run the department and move other critical initiatives forward.

An ongoing concern of mine was members' protection. I had been working with Pittman and Gallagher on ways to address the concerning increase in the number of *directions of interest* (in which a private citizen exhibits an alarming degree of interest in a public figure, though without any behaviors that rise to the level of a crime) as well as outright threats against members of Congress. I had recently obtained approval through the CPB and my oversight committees to pursue the staffing of five regional field offices, to assist with threat investigations, and to enhance member security across the country.

The other area we had been working on was members' security when traveling on commercial airlines. On January 4, I wrote a memo to Serge Potapov, the assistant supervisory air marshal in charge of the Federal Air Marshal Service (FAMS) Washington Field Office, to coordinate awareness and support for members of Congress traveling on commercial air carriers. This was interagency support I had successfully coordinated on several previous occasions with Potapov. But now, with the increased threat activity since the election, I wanted to formalize the information exchange and increase security coordination with the FAMS for the foreseeable future. This would allow both Potapov and me to hand off this initiative to those in our organizations better suited to sustain it day in and day out.

I worked on the memo with Salley Wood, Pittman, and Gallagher during the day and emailed it to Potapov at 4:48 p.m. on January 4. Potapov acknowledged receipt and said that since this request would require resources beyond those of the FAMS Washington Field Office and his command, the request would be forwarded to leadership at the FAMS headquarters Field Operations Division.

The next morning, when Potapov inquired about the status of my request through his local chain of command, the assistant administrator of the FAMS Field Operations Division, instead of approving the request or requesting additional information, had Potapov counseled for having direct communications with the head of the USCP. This response was unexpected and unwarranted since I had previously engaged with the FAMS and recently hosted Potapov and his staff at USCP headquarters to collaborate on several threat-reduction initiatives. This was doubly frustrating because my request was put aside without any further action taken or anticipated, during one of the tensest weeks in the history of the USCP.

The very next day, Senator Mitt Romney would be harassed in an airport in Salt Lake City and again on his flight to Washington, DC. The altercation on the airplane became very heated between some of the passengers and the hecklers to the point that some passengers were yelling to the flight attendants that they were "threatening to kill us." Unfortunately, the federal air marshals would not have any advance visibility on this type of action that could jeopardize the safety of the passengers and crew on the plane because my letter was simply put aside and not acted on. Trump would later comment on the harassment Romney encountered on his flight: "I wonder if he enjoyed his flight in last night." Needless to say, comments like this from a sitting president only embolden people to become more aggressive. Politicians need to be very cautious about the effects their words can have. Whether it's Trump's comments calling for people to "fight like hell," or Kamala Harris's reference to the often-violent protests of 2020 stating, "They're not going to stop. And everyone beware, because they're not going to stop. They're not going to stop before Election Day in November, and they're not going to stop after Election Day . . . they're not going to let up, and they should not, and we should not."[16] Politicians need to be aware of how their words are construed and how they put law enforcement in the middle.

The intelligence assessments indicated that a number of websites were advocating that demonstrators come armed to Washington. On

16. Ali Swenson, "Kamala Harris Said Protests Should Continue, Not Riots," AP News, October 8, 2020, https://apnews.com/article/fact-checking-afs:Content:9579800331.

January 4, Assistant Chief Thomas returned to work after being off the prior week. I met with him to work on our plan to deal with the possibility of armed protesters. As already noted, we had dealt with armed protesters in the city during the MAGA I and MAGA II events, and we were already anticipating that on the sixth there would be some people in the crowd with guns, but I wanted to make sure we had a coordinated plan and that individual officers wouldn't try to take action on their own.

We discussed various resources that could be used, including officials, civil disturbance units, our tactical CERT team, and plainclothes assets. Thomas met with his team and finalized a plan. A few hours later, I ran into him in the hallway outside his office, and he briefed me. It was a good plan that needed only minor tweaks. I explained to him that for a plan like this to be effective, everyone involved must clearly understand their role. I asked him if all the involved units had been briefed on their responsibilities, and Thomas said that he thought so. That response didn't sit well with me, especially on a plan as serious as this one. I told him to go back and make sure that all the involved units had been briefed and to let me know when that was completed. Later that day, he informed me that all involved units had been briefed and the plan was good to go.

Following the distribution of the final intelligence assessment on January 4, the IICD scheduled a 1:00 p.m. intel briefing. The call was scheduled by the Protective Services Bureau, to be provided by IICD Director John Donohue. It would also be an opportunity for those on the call to ask any clarifying questions before the event on Wednesday. During my time with the USCP, I had participated in numerous intelligence briefings, usually in person but some by telephone. I always found the briefings beneficial and usually found myself asking most of the questions, wanting to gather as much information as possible. But due to carelessness, oversight, or perhaps some other reason, I was not invited to participate in this intel conference call. I would later learn from those participating in the call that no new or concerning intelligence was provided at the briefing and that the briefing did not portray a high level of concern about violence toward law enforcement or a threat to the Capitol.

On January 4, I sat down to go over the final planning with Pittman and Thomas. Gallagher gave us an update on the current intelligence, advising that there was still the possibility of armed protesters and extremist groups attending. He also advised that a large number of Proud Boys might be attending and that they would not be wearing the traditional yellow-and-black garb. We continued to see a significant uptick in occupancy being reported by DC-area hotels, and Airbnb was reporting 50 percent booked rentals in the area. He also mentioned the arrest of Geri on a weapons violation outside an Arlington, Virginia, hotel on January 1.

Other pre-event planning that we discussed included

- deploying civil disturbance units;
- the sergeants at arms publishing a "Dear Colleague" letter to the congressional community, advising members to arrive early for the joint session and to use the parking garages and underground tunnels;
- Special Operations Division providing marked police cars to escort members if they should get stuck off campus;
- restrictions on the East Plaza (to members of Congress and other authorized personnel only);
- increased visibility of uniformed officers at the barricades;
- a team inside the Capitol Building to escort the senators when they were traversing the Capitol; and
- increased security for leadership teams.

Earlier on Monday, Speaker Pelosi had issued a "Dear Colleague" letter to all members of the House of Representatives, reiterating the need for social distancing and reminding members that if they were asked by staff to leave the floor, it was not merely a suggestion.

This unusual and public chastising of members occurred after an incident on the House floor on Sunday evening when Representative

Chip Roy called for the members-elect from six states with contested election results to refrain from taking the oath of office with the other members. Following this move, a vote was called regarding the oath, which resulted in various members of Congress flooding the floor despite several attempts by the Speaker to clear it. Irving and some of his staff were summoned to the House floor to assist. It was clear that the Speaker was not happy with the conduct of many in her new House.

Irving was called to a meeting in the Speaker's office on Monday afternoon at two thirty to discuss added security for the electoral count. Following this meeting, Irving contacted Gallagher to discuss additional security measures he wanted in place for January 6. Gallagher briefed us on the additional requests that appeared to have come from the Speaker's office. Some of these security enhancements included having additional plainclothes USCP officers on the House floor. Irving specifically wanted Dignitary Protection Division special agents to staff these additional posts.

It was not unusual for Irving to go directly to Deputy Chief Gallagher on this type of request; nor was it unusual for him to prefer DPD agents. Perhaps it was his Secret Service experience, but Irving always felt that these agents had more experience and finesse when working closely with the members of Congress. It was clear that Irving believed these qualities could help prevent encounters with members from escalating into something worse.

But what I found peculiar was that Irving also wanted the DPD agents to have access to hand-wand metal detectors. I had never heard of the USCP being asked to be ready to screen members of Congress on the House floor. This was an unprecedented request, and I can only suspect that it was implemented because members were suspected of having prohibited items when they were on the House floor. (This may have been a precursor to the walk-through metal detectors the Speaker had installed immediately after January 6.)

Further compounding the oddity of the hand-wand metal detector request was the fact that Irving and Gallagher had also determined a specific route that officers would take through the labyrinthine corridors of the Capitol in the event that a member had to be arrested or taken into custody. They had developed this to enable them to move undetected with the detained member through the Capitol and off the Hill without being subjected to additional media attention.

After checking with the events unit and determining that no group had applied for a demonstration permit on the West Front, I reached out to both sergeants at arms and discussed adjusting the perimeter on both the East and West Fronts. Traditionally, if we establish a perimeter on the East Front, we barricade off the hard surface area (roughly half the space). On the West Front, we usually have protest groups on the grassy lower area and barricade off the lower West Terrace. Since we had the inaugural platform on the West Front and no one had a permit for area 1, I wanted to completely bike-rack in the west side of the Capitol. This time, Irving was immediately in favor of my idea, but he wanted to see and approve the final plan. Stenger thought about it for a minute and then said, "We want that too."

On the East Front, I wanted to tie in the perimeter from the West Front on the north, as well as on the south side of the Capitol, up to the south barricade. This would provide a large area for protesters to leave in an emergency and still maintain a barrier between the permitted demonstration areas on the East Front and the plaza. Initially, Thomas had discussed completely fencing in the East Front, which would have included fencing in the groups who had been issued permits to demonstrate there. I explained to him that you always must keep a path for demonstrators to be able to leave in an emergency or after an order to disperse. Thomas discussed some options, and we sketched out some plans. I recommended that we drive the perimeter so that everyone would be comfortable with it and so that Pittman would know what to tell her Security Services Bureau.

At 3:00 p.m. on Monday, January 4, the USCP Special Events Section also participated in a weekly conference call hosted by the Metropolitan Police Department. This call usually occurred on Mondays and was attended by representatives from many different law enforcement agencies, including

- MPD,
- United States Park Police (USPP),
- USCP,
- Washington Metropolitan Area Transit Authority (WMATA),
- FBI,
- United States Supreme Court Police,
- USSS, and
- DC Fire and Emergency Medical Services.

Having all the partners on this call was an excellent way to make sure all agencies were on the same page regarding planning and intelligence. I participated in this call on January 4, and it included an overview of the schedule of events and agency preparations. No other agencies provided any new or alarming intelligence on this final call. In addition to the Special Events Section, the IICD was also invited to this call, but notably, no one from IICD participated.

The Proud Boys were expected to be at the demonstrations on Wednesday, and based on previous rallies, we anticipated some issues with them, especially involving counterprotesters. In the past, most of the issues involving this group occurred after the organized events and usually took place in the downtown areas, near their hotels. The MPD usually bore the brunt of the clashes with the Proud Boys, having to step in and break up numerous physical altercations. Following the burning of the BLM banner after the December MAGA rally, the MPD had obtained a destruction-of-property arrest warrant for the leader of the Proud Boys, Enrique Tarrio. On Monday, as Tarrio arrived in Washington, DC, in a rideshare vehicle, he was stopped in the Third Street tunnel and arrested by the MPD. In addition to the destruction-of-property warrant, Tarrio was also charged with possession of a high-capacity feeding device, which is against the law in the District of Columbia. Allegedly, he had been found with two high-capacity firearm magazines. Tarrio was released from custody the following day and ordered to stay out of DC until his pending trial.

A total of six First Amendment demonstration permits were issued for groups to demonstrate on Capitol grounds on January 6. Each permit was issued for a group of fifty or fewer demonstrators due to the COVID-19 restrictions on mass gatherings that were in place at the time. Most of the requests were for demonstrations on the East Front of the Capitol, with two exceptions: one group had received a permit for area 7, which is two blocks north of the Capitol, near Union Station, and a second group had been granted a permit for area 15, which is on the west side of the Capitol between the Reflecting Pool and Third Street.

I signed off on the permits, approving them by proxy on behalf of the Capitol Police Board, but not before they went through a thorough review process. In preparing the permit packages for final approval, the IICD provided an assessment of the likelihood of arrests or acts of civil disobedience from each group seeking a permit. The six applications for permits to demonstrate on Capitol grounds on January 6 got these assessments:

Group	Location	IICD Assessment
One Nation Under God	Area 8	Highly Improbable
Bryan Lewis	Area 9	Remote
Jesus Lives	Area 15	Remote
Rock Ministries International	Area 11	Remote
Virginia Freedom Keepers	Area 7	Remote
Women for a Great America	Area 10	Highly Improbable

As part of the approval process, the applications were reviewed and endorsed by the commander of the Protective Services Bureau (Gallagher), along with my two assistant chiefs. This endorsement included their recommendation on whether the permit should be approved or disapproved. All six permit applications were endorsed by each of the reviewers, who recommended approving them all, most of the endorsements occurring after the final IICD Special Event Assessment had been published. Once the application proceeded through the review process, it came to me for final approval and signature. Based on the recommendations and the information available to me at the time, I approved all the permits.

On Monday evening, both Paul Irving and Mike Stenger sent out a notice to their congressional communities providing their guidance regarding January 6. This was a usual course of action before a big event such as a joint session of Congress or any event on the Hill where members' or employees' access or daily activities may be affected. These "Dear Colleague" letters are sent to every employee of the Senate and the House of Representatives, including every member of Congress and their staff. Irving and Stenger would always coordinate together in advance to ensure they were providing similar guidance and sending them at roughly the same time. The last thing they wanted was for members or staff to complain that the other side got information before they did or received different information altogether. Since these messages were going out to such a large audience, I am sure that the wording was approved by leadership or their senior staff.

Irving was the first to distribute his "Dear Colleague" letter, at 5:29 p.m. on January 4. The notice was titled "Security Information – Wednesday, January 6 Joint Session" and provided an overview of expectations for the day, along with recommended parking and access points for the congressional buildings. The letter began, "As a result of the January 6 joint session of Congress, members and staff should expect demonstration activity and street closures to impact access to the US Capitol complex. The following information is being provided to assist your office in planning accordingly." This was followed by a safety and security section recommending that everyone arrive early and consider using parking garages. An overview was provided showing the street closures being put in place by the Metropolitan Police Department, as well as access to the Capitol and House office buildings.

Less than two hours later, at 7:12 p.m., Stenger sent his notice to the Senate. It was virtually identical to Irving's. And like Irving's, Stenger's notice went on to say, "In addition, on Tuesday, January 5, 2021, beginning at 6:00 a.m., through Thursday, January 7, 2021, there will be several First Amendment activities that will take place throughout the District of Columbia. The US Capitol Police and the sergeant at arms are aware of these First Amendment activities and will continue to monitor impacts to the congressional activities."

The notices concluded by providing contact information to report emergencies or to obtain additional information. It was apparent that both sergeants at arms, two well-seasoned career law enforcement officers, had interpreted the intelligence assessments and briefings the same as my officials and I had. Come Wednesday, we were anticipating First Amendment demonstrations on the Hill that would be similar to the previous MAGA marches in November and December.

Late Monday evening, Gallagher contacted me about a threat relayed by the FBI. The Federal Aviation Administration had picked up a transmission overheard on a general aviation radio frequency by air traffic control in New York. The message stated, "We are going to fly a plane into the Capitol on Wednesday. Soleimani will be avenged." (This was a reference to the death of a high-ranking Iranian military officer killed in a US drone strike.) We received an audio excerpt of this radio communication along with the notification from the Bureau.

I listened to the communication, and it was evident that it was a digitized voice, but that made it no less concerning. The same message was played a second time over the FAA frequency the next day. The USCP worked with the FBI to investigate and determine the validity of the threat, and I provided notification of the threat to the CPB. Also, since it appeared that this threat was going to make it into the media, I also notified my oversight committees regarding the threat. The last thing I wanted was to have my oversight blindsided by an inquiry into an incident they knew nothing about.

On January 5, I drove around the Capitol with Thomas and Pittman to finalize the perimeter plan. Then we sent a copy of the final plan to the sergeants at arms, and they both approved it. Pittman then worked with her Security Services Bureau to reconfigure the metal barricades to the latest design. Irving was quick to restrict and close the House East Plaza to prevent any protesters from getting to the areas where representatives might park on January 6. He clearly had the support of the House for this move, but he wanted to approve it once it was finalized.

Stenger, on the other hand, didn't want to give the impression that the Senate East Plaza was closed to protesters. I got the impression he felt that Senate leadership would not favor this approach. We came to an agreement that the Senate Plaza would be open on January 6 until the demonstrations began. But I knew these would start early, so in essence, the Senate Plaza would be closed, and we bike-racked it in.

Waldow had been completing the CDU plan for the past several days, and once we had a final perimeter on January 5, he published the final version. The CDU plan provided an overview of the event and expected protests, and a threat analysis based on the final special event assessment produced by IICD on January 3, 2021. The "Expected Protests Overview" section of Waldow's CDU plan was cut directly from the IICD assessment. It read: "The protests/rallies are expected to be similar to the previous Million MAGA March rallies in November and December 2020, which drew tens of thousands of participants. It is also expected that members of the Proud Boys (who intend to wear plainclothes and not their traditional yellow and black clothing), white supremacist groups, Antifa, and other extremist groups will rally on January 6, 2021."

This section also indicated that at the previous rallies, multiple arrests had been made for assaults between pro-Trump protesters and counterprotesters and that multiple arrests had been made for weapon violations, assault, destruction of property, and assaults on police officers. The expected protests section concluded by stating, "Many of the confrontations occurred after the rallies concluded."

The "Threat Analysis" section of Waldow's CDU plan contained a single sentence: "At this time there are no specific known threats related to the Joint Session of Congress Electoral College Vote Certification."

It is important to note that this final CDU plan was published the day after the IICD conducted its final intelligence briefing, and Waldow's assessment was based on the contents of that briefing (which he participated in) and IICD's final assessment.

The CDU plan listed Waldow as the incident commander and an OSB captain as the field force commander. The field force commander would be in charge of all CDU operations and protective actions and would have the primary responsibility to authorize less than lethal options. With the additional staffing made available by activating the all-hands-on-deck order, the CDU plan now had eight platoons—four hard platoons with all the protective gear and four soft platoons to assist in supporting operations and maintaining the perimeter. However, not all the platoons were completely staffed with forty personnel. This was due to some people being out sick, on quarantine, or pulled to support the joint session. One soft platoon, for instance, comprising about ten officers, had to assist Inspector Loyd with the joint session at the Capitol Division.

The plan established a civil disturbance unit support-staff structure to assist the field force commander and activated two less lethal grenadiers with the FN 303 and the PepperBall gun for each of the four hard CDU platoons. In total, the plan activated 251 officers and officials to support CDU operations. The CDU plan also activated a CERT tactical component and contained an intelligence note that numerous social media posts had been requesting that protesters come armed, and indicated that plainclothes officers would be on the lookout for weapons violations.

For major events like a joint session, we implement many routine measures to help secure the complex, including

- restricting access to the East Plaza;
- restricting access to the Capitol and admitting only staff with offices in the building;
- placing additional officers at the underground walkways, tunnels, and Capitol entrances to *challenge and validate* visitors and credentials to ensure they were authorized;
- deploying additional assets from CERT and our Hazardous Device Section;
- increasing interior patrols;
- deploying metal crowd-control barriers;
- posting officers at vehicle barricades to facilitate access for authorized personnel;

- posting additional officers at building entrances and on exterior patrols;
- enhancing leadership details;
- instituting twenty-four-hour intelligence;
- placing USCP officials in operations centers of partner agencies such as the MPD and DC Homeland Security and Emergency Management; and
- hosting partner law enforcement agencies in our command center.

Although many believed that these enhancements came in response to specific intelligence or to the January 3 assessment, this was not the case. These enhancements are a regular order of business for major events at the Capitol. The USCP was well experienced and had a very robust process of planning for major events at the Capitol. We host the presidential inauguration every four years and the State of the Union annually. And the pope always makes a visit to Congress when he is in town (perhaps to personally absolve them of their sins).

At 10:00 a.m. on Tuesday, January 5, Irving and I briefed Chairperson Zoe Lofgren and Jamie Fleet from the Committee on House Administration. Before handling the call, I advised Irving of my call to General Walker on Sunday. I told Irving that Walker had assured me the National Guard would be prepared to repurpose 125 troops and send them our way once Walker notified the secretary of the army. We would just need to send someone over to the armory to swear them in. Irving seemed satisfied with this level of support and thanked me for following up with General Walker.

We then did our video call with Lofgren, and I used the briefing sheet we had developed the day before. I advised the chairperson about the two large pro-Trump events downtown, including the March for Trump, and told her there might be four counterprotests. We discussed the six demonstrations permitted on Capitol grounds and informed her that members of the Proud Boys, white supremacists, and various militia members might be in attendance. I also told her the USCP was tracking several social media sites that were encouraging protesters to be armed.

Chairperson Lofgren expressed an obvious and natural concern for the security of the Capitol and the members of Congress. I told her we had activated a large CDU contingent, were monitoring events, and were in contact with our law enforcement partners. I gave her an overview of the MPD's preparation and the support the National Guard would provide them with crowd and traffic control. When Irving blurted out that he had me reach out to the National Guard, Lofgren asked me if that was correct.

"Yes, ma'am," I said. "I talked to the National Guard, and they will be ready to assist if necessary."

Chairperson Lofgren seemed satisfied with this, and we concluded the call. Irving left me a voice mail soon after, confirming that we would handle the 4:00 p.m. call with Tim Ryan the same way. But I found it interesting that Irving, who had been one of the biggest obstacles to my bringing in the National Guard before January 6, was so quick to advise our oversight that I had reached out to coordinate the Guard's support if needed.

Around 11:30 a.m. on January 5, I was preparing to host a call with some of our law enforcement partners, along with Pittman and Thomas. Because we were tied up on the call, Deputy Chief Gallagher went over to the Rayburn House Office Building to brief Representative Rodney Davis and his deputy staff director, Tim Monahan, regarding January 6.

At 11:48 a.m. on January 5, I sent an email to all my primary points of contact on the four committees with oversight of the USCP. This was my usual course of business before a major event or a protest on Capitol Hill. The email stated:

> As you are likely aware, significant demonstration activity is expected to occur this week. Starting today Tuesday, January 5, through Wednesday, January 6, multiple organizations are planning to congregate in various locations in Washington, DC, including permitted areas on Capitol grounds. Information gathered by the department indicates that the majority of this week's demonstration activity is scheduled to occur on

Wednesday, January 6, concurrent with a joint session of Congress to certify the electoral count.

As was the case during the November 14 and December 12 demonstrations, we expect these events to be widely attended and to present a possibility of civil disobedience.

I closed by saying that we were working closely with the House and Senate sergeants at arms, as well as with our law enforcement partners, to monitor these demonstrations and to protect the Capitol complex.

Shortly before noon on Tuesday, Stenger came over to my office to participate in the video call I had scheduled with our partner law enforcement agencies. When he arrived, I told him about my conversation with General Walker on Sunday evening. He seemed satisfied with the National Guard's ability to provide 125 troops if necessary and thanked me for making that call. Then we sat down at my conference table for the video call.

The purpose of this call was to have a final discussion about January 6 and the upcoming presidential inauguration and also to introduce three new people in key positions. On this call were the who's who of security in our nation's Capitol. I had the director of the USSS Washington Field Office; the director of the FBI Washington Field Office; the chiefs of the Metropolitan Police Department, the United States Park Police, Metro Transit Police, Amtrak Police, and the USSS Uniformed Division; and the top generals from the DC National Guard and the Army's Military District of Washington—all the key people responsible for securing the city against domestic or international attacks. I also had all the members of the Capitol Police Board on the call, including Irving and AOC Blanton, who had logged in from their offices. With me in my conference room were Stenger, Pittman, Thomas, and Inspector John Erickson. Thomas had brought Erickson to provide a brief on the inaugural planning.

I opened the call by introducing three new key people in critical positions, welcoming Robert Contee as the new chief of the Metropolitan Police Department, Samuel Dotson, the new chief of the Amtrak Police Department, and Steven D'Antuono, the new director of the FBI's Washington Field Office. I then introduced the Capitol Police Board and offered them the opportunity to make some opening remarks. Both Mike and Paul congratulated the new chiefs and directors on their positions. Paul kept it very high-level and formal. Mike, on the other hand, always liked talking to fellow law enforcement and made it more personal. Then AOC Blanton thanked everyone for participating and said he was looking forward to a safe event the next day and at the presidential inauguration.

When it was my turn to speak, I gave an overview of our preparations, specifically that we were all hands on deck as far as staffing and that we had activated eight CDU platoons, four of which would be hard platoons. I discussed our expectations for the event and the fact that we had issued six First Amendment demonstration permits for Capitol grounds. We anticipated that the event would be well attended and that we had heard that hotel occupancy was high through the sixth. We anticipated groups such as the Proud Boys and other militia groups to attend. We also expected possible skirmishes between Trump supporters and counterprotesters, as well as with the police.

I introduced my team, going around the table, starting with Pittman. She briefly stated her role as the head of Protective and Intelligence Operations in the newly reorganized department. Pittman reiterated our expectations for the event. Thomas went next, saying that "the chief pretty much already covered everything." Thomas added that the certification was expected to go until the early morning hours on January 7. He also mentioned that our command center would be fully activated and open if anyone wanted to send a representative.

Then, since we had some new people in command, we had all the participants introduce themselves and provide an update on their plans, along with any new intel. As we went around the room, everyone gave an update on their planning for the event. At no time did any of the other officials on the call indicate any concerns or provide any alarming new intelligence. All the information was very similar to what we had seen in the three previous special event assessments from the IICD.

As we were concluding the call, I asked everyone one last time, "Does anyone have anything to add?"

If anyone at the meeting thought that I or any of the partner agencies were lacking proper intel, now was the time to speak up. But no one said a word.

"Good luck, everyone," I said. "If anyone needs or hears anything, please reach out." Then I gave everyone my cell phone number. As the call ended, I felt we all were confident that we knew what to expect on January 6.

PARTICIPANTS OF THE JANUARY 5 VIRTUAL MEETING:

- Paul D. Irving, House sergeant at arms
- Michael C. Stenger, Senate sergeant at arms
- J. Brett Blanton, Architect of the Capitol
- Chief Steven Sund, United States Capitol Police
- Assistant Chief Chad Thomas, United States Capitol Police
- Assistant Chief Yogananda Pittman, United States Capitol Police
- Inspector John Erickson, United States Capitol Police
- Special Agent in Charge Matthew Miller, United States Secret Service
- Chief Thomas Sullivan, United States Secret Service Uniformed Division
- Assistant Chief Alfonso Dyson, United States Secret Service Uniformed Division
- Assistant Director in Charge Steven D'Antuono, FBI Washington Field Office
- Acting Chief Robert Contee, Metropolitan Police Department
- Assistant Chief Jeffery Carroll, Metropolitan Police Department
- Acting Chief Pamela Smith, United States Park Police
- Chief Ron Pavlik, Metro Transit Police
- Assistant Chief Michael Anzallo, Metro Transit Police
- Chief D. Samuel Dotson, Amtrak Police
- Assistant Chief James Cook, Amtrak Police
- General William Walker, Commander, DC National Guard

- Major General Omar Jones, US Army, Military District of Washington
- Mr. Egon Hawrylak, US Army, Military District of Washington

At 4:00 p.m. on January 5, Irving and I handled the final congressional briefing with Representative Tim Ryan, the chairman of the Legislative Branch Appropriations Subcommittee. The Appropriations Committee was one of my four oversight committees and authorized my funding for the House of Representatives side of Congress. We handled the briefing exactly the same way that we did for Lofgren, covering the same issues and topics. I found myself doing most of the talking, with Irving jumping in occasionally. As in the Lofgren briefing, Irving mentioned that I had reached out to the National Guard in case they were needed. Ryan concluded the briefing by thanking us for our efforts and asking if there was anything we needed.

At 4:47 p.m., within minutes of our completing this briefing, Steve Marchese, a high-level staffer on Ryan's Appropriations Subcommittee, sent Irving an email raising an issue regarding the National Guard's proximity to the Capitol. The email started by thanking Paul for taking the time to brief the chairman, then went on to state, in part: "I had one question regarding the placement of the National Guard with regard to the traffic control. Do you know how close they will be to the Capitol Complex? I only ask to be ahead of any member who might question a photo or live TV shot that shows the National Guard with the Capitol dome in the backdrop."

It appeared they too were concerned about the *optics* of the National Guard near the Capitol.

About 5:00 p.m., Pittman sent me an email asking if I would be available to discuss some information she had received about the tunnels leading from the congressional office buildings to the Capitol, along with intel that some protest groups were talking about trying to surround the Capitol. A short time later, Pittman and Gallagher came into my office and briefed Chad and me on this new information. The IICD had been contacted by an individual who operated a website featuring historical information on the Washington, DC, tunnel systems, including the pedestrian tunnels beneath the Capitol. The operator of this site had reported seeing an increase in the number of visitors accessing information about the Capitol tunnels. Also, IICD had discovered that protest groups on another website were discussing surrounding the Capitol to prevent members of Congress from being able to attend the joint session. We had experienced protest groups trying to surround the Capitol in the past, and this information was described as "rhetoric" and "aspirational" at best.

We discussed the preparations we had already put in place, such as additional officers both at the building entrances and in the tunnels to the Capitol to validate the credentials of people using them. We also discussed our plans for getting members of Congress into the Capitol in the event they were blocked by protesters. We didn't feel that we had the ability to bring in our CDU platoons any earlier, and neither Gallagher nor Pittman expressed an urgent need to do so.

We had planned to hold over our midnight officers until the CDU was in place the next morning, and Gallagher advised that he would have some Protective Services Bureau officers in the field to monitor for such activity in the morning and keep the Command Center informed. Everyone felt that this effectively addressed the concerns raised by Pittman and Gallagher. I asked them if they were going to notify the sergeants at arms of this information, and Gallagher said that he would.

A few hours later, at 8:55 p.m., Gallagher sent an email to the deputy House SAA and several of the HSAA staffers and cc'd Pittman. The email stated, "Meant to send this earlier today, but got tied up. We are running this out . . ." He went on to describe the information reported on the tunnels and discussions of surrounding the building on the website TheDonald.win. He didn't express any high level of concern about the information and concluded the email by stating, "It is unknown if the groups will actually mobilize as early as 0600, but tomorrow is an all-hands-on-deck for USCP and we will have additional assets to deal with any blocking of the barricades/entrances/etc. ID [Investigation Division] will continue to run out the investigation side of this and IICD is actively monitoring the information via Open Source."

Having worked for the MPD handling major events for years, I knew the importance of advance coordination for major events. At 5:29

p.m. on January 5, I reached out to MPD Assistant Chief Jeff Carroll to exchange information on our designated incident commanders for the anticipated march and demonstrations. In my email, I designated USCP Deputy Chief Eric Waldow as our exterior IC and provided Waldow's contact information as well. I also included Waldow and Thomas in the email. Carroll responded that Inspector Robert Glover would be their incident commander. I already had Glover's contact information, and I made sure Waldow had it as well. I felt it was important that we exchange this information in advance to establish a unified command in the event we needed assistance from MPD.

I already knew that the MPD had activated the support of the National Guard for January 6, using the added support in the same manner as they had for the two previous MAGA marches: to assist with traffic control and to "box out" the demonstration and march route. Following the vehicle ramming incidents that had occurred at major public gatherings around the world over the past decade and in Charlottesville, Virginia, in 2017, law enforcement was concerned about another vehicle attack. The MPD and Glover had been proactive regarding this threat and had worked extensively to close the areas around large rallies or marches to vehicular traffic. Glover would use traffic closures and blocking vehicles to "box out" a buffer area around the event, where vehicles could not easily gain access. On Capitol Hill, we did the same using our in-street mounted retractable steel barriers and a limited number of blocking vehicles.

I felt that using the National Guard for traffic control and to "box out" the route was a very smart use of those troops. However, after the events over the summer and the use of federal law enforcement and the Guard at some of the demonstrations, Mayor Bowser wanted to ensure that the DOJ was not going to bring in any additional federal resources on January 6 without first coordinating with the city and the MPD. On January 5, Mayor Bowser wrote a letter to Acting Attorney General Rosen, Secretary of the Army McCarthy, and Acting Secretary of Defense Miller to clarify that the District of Columbia was not requesting any additional federal support and that she wanted to be notified immediately if additional federal resources were going to be deployed in the city.[17]

Having been a cop for many years and having worked more major events than I could count, I knew how important it was for officers to get the best possible information on the day's events. I did not doubt that officers were already seeing news reports on the joint session of Congress and the MAGA rally downtown, and I wanted them to have the same information I had as they came out of roll call the next morning. The last thing I wanted was to have a member of Congress ask my officers what they were anticipating for the day or ask them about the report that someone had threatened to fly a plane into the Capitol on January 6, and for the officer to respond, "I don't know; nobody tells us anything."

So one of the last steps I took on Tuesday night at ten was to send an email out to my assistant chiefs, Thomas and Pittman, as well as to all my deputy chiefs, directing that all officers be briefed during the next day's morning roll calls on the day's expectations for the demonstrations and the joint session of Congress. I also directed them to ensure that the officers were aware of the aviation threat and of the investigation into the incident by the USCP and our federal partners. I would even follow up on the morning of January 6 in an email to all my officials, requesting confirmation of their briefings. They would all confirm that the officers had been briefed.

As I pulled out of the parking lot of USCP headquarters that evening and drove down Constitution Avenue toward the Ellipse and the White House, I could see that large crowds of Trump supporters were already in the city. Cars and trucks were driving around town with Trump flags, and large groups were walking along the sidewalks and on the National Mall. It was not unusual to see this type of activity and to feel the tempo of the city pick up before a large event. Tonight was no different.

---

17. Muriel Bowser (@MayorBowser), "To be clear, the District of Columbia is not requesting other federal law enforcement personnel and discourages any additional deployment without immediate . . . ," Twitter, January 5, 2021, https://twitter.com /mayorbowser/status/1346530358674792466.

I knew that tomorrow would be a busy day, but I thought we had put together a good plan for it, based on the intelligence we had. I thought we had covered all the bases and had checked all the boxes.

I thought we were ready.

What I didn't know as I drove home that night was that many of these people who were filling up the city had already been in continuous communication with each other, saying things like this: "Be ready to fight. Congress needs to hear glass breaking, doors being kicked in, and blood from their BLM and Pantifa slave soldiers being spilled. Get violent, stop calling this a march, or rally, or a protest. Go there ready for war. We get our President or we die. NOTHING else will achieve this goal."

And this: "Deploy Capitol Police to restrict movement. Anyone going armed needs to be mentally prepared to draw down on LEOs. Let them shoot first, but make sure they know what happens if they do."

And this: "Get into Capitol Building, stand outside Congress. Be in the room next to them. They won't have time to run if they play dumb."

And this: "You might have to kill the palace guards. Are you ok with that?"

I didn't know any of this that night, but the thing that will haunt me for the rest of my life is that many others in the intelligence community *did* know. This intelligence had been gathered by the FBI, the Department of Homeland Security, and the military. Hell, this intelligence was even available to the IICD—the intelligence division of my own USCP! Intelligence that had been known for weeks before January 6.

All this intelligence was out there, sitting on desks and laptops all over town, much of it known by many of the very agencies that had been represented at my video call just hours earlier. Attended by agency leaders either unaware of, or unwilling to share, the intelligence their agencies possessed.

No one said a word about this DEFCON 1, flashing-red-alert, this-changes-everything intelligence. And now, as I was driving home on the evening of January 5, I had no idea that my life and the lives of so many others were about to be altered forever.

CHAPTER 2:
JANUARY 6, 2021, MINUTE BY MINUTE

January 6 has arrived. After almost three decades of policing, a morning like this always feels different. Whether it's a presidential inauguration, a papal visit, the International Monetary Fund/World Bank demonstrations, a marathon, or a joint session of Congress, these are the mornings that stand apart. From the moment I open my eyes, I feel the anticipation and stress about what the day will bring. As I go downstairs, my two dogs follow me. They don't know that today is any different. They just want to go outside. I let them out and grab my first cup of coffee. I start running through the timeline in my head, thinking of any possible last-minute issues. And then finally I remind myself that in twenty-four hours, God willing, I'll be having another cup of coffee, this one stress-free, with the event behind me.

I always prep my uniform the night before. My wife bought me a valet stand years ago to help keep my uniform and gear in one place. It stands next to my dresser on my side of the room. Dressing for work is always a production, and I try to do it as quietly as I can so I don't wake my wife. But inevitably, between cinching the Velcro on my bullet-resistant vest and fastening the heavy badge, the shirt stays, and the brass nameplate on my uniform shirt, I usually manage to bang the corner of at least one piece of furniture. This morning, it's the snap of the radio clipping onto my belt, then the distinctive sound of my firearm sliding into the holster, followed by the snap of the retention clip. The snap wakes her up, but maybe that's exactly what I want. I always enjoy seeing her look over at me with her head still on the pillow, that cheeky smile as she says some variation of "I love watching you put on your uniform."

Maria has been with me since shortly after I graduated from the police academy, and she knows what I'm like before big events. She has always provided nothing but unconditional support. Today, I remind her that we're expecting the certification of the electoral votes to go well into the early hours of tomorrow because of the anticipated objections from Republican lawmakers. I tell her that I have a couple of meetings planned for tomorrow morning but that I expect to be on my way home by early afternoon. I grab my blue Samsonite duffel bag, which is stuffed with sheets and a pillow in the unlikely event I'll be able to catch an hour or two of sleep in the next twenty-four hours, and then head downstairs to brew one more cup of coffee for the road. Then I grab my computer bag and quietly slip out the front door.

Driving to work, I take a moment to say a prayer, as I do every day, asking for God's blessings on the day ahead. I have been in policing long enough and have seen too many days go bad to take *any* day for granted. Usually, I say this prayer as I cross over the Theodore Roosevelt Memorial Bridge. It's a beautiful location overlooking the Potomac River with the Kennedy Center on the left, the Lincoln Memorial on the right, and the Capitol dome barely visible in the distance. But I know that today, the MPD and Park Police have already closed Constitution Avenue because of the MAGA event on the Ellipse, so I divert toward the Pentagon and go into the city on the Fourteenth Street Bridge.

I have already designated Assistant Chief Pittman as the early official and Assistant Chief Thomas as the late official to ensure executive-team coverage throughout the long day. I will be there for the duration. But even as I drive into Washington from Virginia, I have no idea that the president has already started a series of tweets regarding the certification of the Electoral College results.

6:00 a.m. President Trump sends out his first tweet of the day, stating,

Donald J. Trump ✓
@realDonaldTrump

If Vice President @Mike_Pence comes through for us, we will win the Presidency. Many States want to decertify the mistake they made in certifying incorrect & even fraudulent numbers in a process NOT approved by their State Legislatures (which it must be). Mike can send it back!

JAN 6, 2021

Figure 2.1. President Trump's first tweet on January 6

7:15 a.m. As I am driving down Route 110 in Arlington, Virginia, toward the Pentagon, I decide to call Robert Glover at the Metropolitan Police Department. At this time, Bob is an inspector with the Special Operations Division. I worked extensively with Bob when I ran the SOD at MPD. When I became the commander of SOD in 2011, Bob was a lieutenant on the Emergency Response Team (ERT). ERT is the MPD's SWAT team, and Glover was the official in charge. Bob is a very competent official, with an intense personality and a deep devotion to the job. He's a go-getter who cares for his officers, and he's not afraid to get his hands dirty or do the hard work. Even as the official in charge of SWAT, Glover would often join in the ERT "stack," or lineup, of officers making an entry into a location on a warrant or at a criminal barricade. Bob and I would often talk about his family and work and how to balance both. I would mentor him on being the best official he could be, and more than once I'd have to remind him that this might mean having to pull himself out of the action and provide leadership from a higher level.

During my time at the SOD, Bob displayed a great aptitude for managing special events like today. After some discussion and maybe some arm twisting, Bob transferred from the ERT over to the Special

Events Branch, where he took over the job I once held for seven years, planning and preparing for all the major events and demonstrations in the city. In recent years, his intense no-nonsense personality, drive, and methodical handling of special events have earned him the nickname "the Glovernator."

This morning, I'm calling to ask him for an assessment of the crowds at the Ellipse. Bob is in his police vehicle, not far from the entrance to the event. He tells me there are already a couple of thousand people in line at the gates.

"How's the demeanor of the crowd?" I ask. "You seeing or expecting any issues?"

Bob says it appears to be an older crowd, with a lot of "moms and pops" in line. He isn't seeing anything that would cause him to anticipate trouble. I'm relieved to hear it because I trust his professional opinion. We've been through many DC events and barricades together.

"Sounds good," I say. "Thanks, and good luck today. We'll probably be talking again later." Then I make a quick call to the USCP Command Center, to see how things are shaping up on the Hill.

Situation normal, nothing unusual to report.

7:33 a.m. I check in with Assistant Chief Jeff Carroll at the MPD. Carroll was one of my captains at the SOD, and I was happy to see him take the helm there when I retired at the end of 2015. We discuss the day's events, and I tell him I've just checked in with Glover. As I'm about to pull into my secure parking lot at USCP headquarters, I ask him to reach out if he needs anything.

I swipe my entry badge to lower the security barrier to our parking lot, wishing him luck as we conclude the call. I back into my parking space, grab my computer backpack and overnight bag, and head up to my office on the seventh floor.

I drop my bag off in my office, log on to my desktop computer, and do a quick check of my emails. A few months earlier, I had a stand-up computer assembly installed in my office. I often tell people it is my healthy way to be sedentary. I always hate being stuck at a desk. Even as the lead

MPD planner, when I was typing up hundreds of pages of DC event manuals, I still got out as often as I could. I'd check perimeters and staging locations, inspect fencing and Jersey barriers, and survey the locations for road closures. As chief of Capitol Police, I still go out into the field any chance I get, often taking one or both of my assistant chiefs with me.

Only yesterday, the three of us drove the perimeter of the Capitol. I still was not comfortable with the size of the perimeter and the number of personnel I had available to staff it. But to be clear, we weren't expecting anything we can't handle.

7:49 a.m. I see that I've missed a call from Stenger. This is unusual. I rarely hear from him this early, so I call him right back. We talk about the day's events, about what I heard from MPD on my way in and what it looks like around the campus. Stenger has heard about the incident last night with Senator Romney being harassed in the Salt Lake City airport and on the flight to Washington National. Stenger is concerned that other members of Congress flying into town for the joint session may be subjected to similar harassment or acts of violence.

I tell Stenger I will reach out to Pittman to have Protective Services Bureau and some USCP uniforms deployed over to National Airport for visibility and to escort members to their cars if needed. I also tell him I will reach out to the Metropolitan Washington Airports Authority Police and make them aware of our increased concern over the members' safety.

I call Pittman and discuss the coverage at the airports. This is something both she and Thomas have handled before, and I am confident she'll be able to implement it fairly quickly. I tell Pittman I'll be back at the Command Center shortly. After handling a few more emails, I grab another cup of coffee and head to the back of the chief's complex, toward the Command Center. The chief's complex houses my office and those of my two assistant chiefs, as well as administrative offices and staff to support their operations, and the office of the public information officer (PIO). I check in with my administrative lieutenants and then stop in to speak with my PIO. I then visit Pittman to talk about Stenger's request regarding the airports.

8:17 a.m. Trump tweets: [1]

Donald J. Trump ✔
@realDonaldTrump

States want to correct their vote, which they now know
were based on irregularities and fraud, plus corrupt
processes never received legislative approval. All Mike
Pence has to do is to send them back to the states, AND
WE WIN. Do it Mike, this is a time for extreme courage!

JAN 6, 2021

9:32 a.m. I return to my office and call Deputy Chief Timothy Tyler at the Metropolitan Washington Airports Authority. I've known Tyler for many years, and we've coordinated quite a few details together, especially after the 2017 congressional baseball-field shooting in Alexandria. Tyler is already aware of the Romney incident and will assist with some added visibility. I tell him that USCP will be sending some officers and then thank him for his support.

I then put a call in to Irving, to provide him with an update on what we are seeing downtown and around the Capitol. I also inform him of the added visibility we've coordinated at National Airport. Irving appreciates both the update and the coverage at the airport. In his classic Irving way, he says, "Phenomenal. Thank you, Chief."

I check my inbox for any new correspondence and then walk down the hall, past the two assistant chiefs' offices, and into the Command Center. This particular door leads from the chief's office to the Command

1. Jenni Fink, "Jan. 6 Capitol Riot Timeline: From Trump's First Tweet, Speech to Biden's Certification," *Newsweek*, January 6, 2022, www.newsweek.com/jan-6-capitol-riot -timeline-trumps-first-tweet-speech-bidens-certification-1665436; Shelly Tan, Youjin Shin, and Danielle Rindler, "How One of America's Ugliest Days Unraveled Inside and Outside the Capitol," *Washington Post*, January 9, 2021, www.washingtonpost.com/nation /interactive/2021/capitol-insurrection-visual-timeline/?itid=hp-top-table-main-0106.

Center and makes a loud *snap* as the lock disengages when I swipe my security badge, followed by a *whoosh* as I push the heavy door open. I've always wondered if the sound was intended as a warning to anyone in the center that someone was coming from the chief's office.

Lieutenant John Wisham, the watch commander, says his customary "Good morning, Chief." Wisham is fairly new as a supervisor in the Command Center. He was previously a sergeant with our bomb squad and is a well-seasoned veteran of the department. He knows his way around a suspicious package but is still in the learning phase as a lieutenant in the Command Center.

This morning, some people in the Command Center, including the watch commander, are preoccupied with the threat to fly a plane into the Capitol. The FBI and the FAA received this threat just days before January 6. As a result, several of my officers in the Command Center are busy facilitating calls with the FAA and the National Capital Region Coordination Center (NCRCC) regarding air traffic in the area of the Capitol. The NCRCC is made up of various representatives of security organizations and military agencies, including the FAA, collocated to ensure coordinated and rapid decision making in the event of an aviation threat in the National Capital Region.

I step up onto the dais, where my seat is located, and wish him a good morning back. The Command Center, the nerve center of all USCP operations, is a futuristic-looking room about forty feet long and thirty deep, with workstations scattered throughout and multiple video monitors on three of the four walls. It houses not just our agency but also staff from numerous other agencies. It's always a little dim so you can see the screens better, and it's usually kept fairly cold for the electronics. Many people in the Command Center wear a jacket or zip-up for the cool temperature.

In the center of the room is a raised dais with a U-shaped desk and seating for about ten workstations facing the front wall. The dais is reserved for my command staff, the public information officer (PIO), and the watch commander during major incidents. To the right of the dais is a long table with seating and phones for our partner agencies' liaisons, including the US Supreme Court Police, Federal Protective

Service (FPS), US Park Police, FBI, and MPD. On this day, only the liaisons from the US Supreme Court Police and the FPS are present in the Command Center. We also have an official assigned to the MPD's command center to facilitate information sharing.

Behind where I sit on the dais is a desk with workstations for the liaisons from the House and Senate sergeants at arms and the Architect of the Capitol. They're placed here so that they can relay my communications and directions back to the CPB.

Yet another, smaller U-shaped workstation to the left of the dais houses the nerve center, which monitors all the camera systems, radios, alarms, and a computer-aided dispatch terminal to monitor USCP and MPD calls for service. This area is always humming with activity and is affectionately called the "pit." I regularly spend a good bit of time with the staff in the pit, often having them pull up various camera views and reviewing video footage.

On a small ledge between the dais and the pit sits the "red phone," an old-fashioned telephone with no number pad or rotary ring—just one red light that flashes to signal an incoming call. The red phone is the emergency "ring down" phone that immediately connects the watch commander to all our partner command centers.

In the far back corner of the room sits the communications hub, which handles all calls into the center from the congressional community, our special agents with the Dignitary Protection Division who are on travel, and our partner law enforcement agencies. This is also where all after-hours calls to the department or chief's office are handled.

The purpose of the USCP Command Center is to maintain an overall situational awareness of activity occurring on the Hill or anywhere else that could affect members of the congressional community. The Command Center also plays an important role in managing critical incidents and special events, housing liaisons from our partner agencies for seamless communications, and coordinating support during a major event or emergency. Ever since the tragic events of 9/11, US law enforcement has learned a lot about incident management and the National Incident Management System (NIMS). Most major law enforcement agencies, including the USCP, have subsequently adopted the use of NIMS, making it a key part of their policies and procedures. NIMS dictates that during an incident, the lead agency shall identify an incident commander (IC), who will establish an incident command system to manage the event and coordinate the response. Everyone has a designated role to help support the incident commander. I've said many times during training that in a chaotic situation, NIMS allows us the ability to "work smarter, not harder," while ensuring that the IC is not overwhelmed. And today, the responsibility for running area command operations resides with my two assistant chiefs at the dais and me.

On this day, January 6, the USCP has two events taking place on the Hill. We are, of course, hosting a joint session of Congress with the vice president in attendance inside the Capitol, and at the same time we are watching a number of demonstrations outside the Capitol Building. Each of these events has its own management structure and incident commander. Deputy Chief Eric Waldow has been designated the incident commander for the CDU response to the demonstrations outside. Waldow was the IC for the previous two MAGA rallies and managed those events successfully.

Inspector Thomas Loyd, as the commander of the Capitol Division, is in charge of all events inside the Capitol. The Capitol Division is the largest and most prestigious division within the USCP, having responsibility for protecting the crown jewel of the complex: the US Capitol Building itself. Loyd is a seasoned USCP veteran, with a thin build and a genuine smile. Loyd cares deeply about his officers and his service to the congressional community. In return, he's well liked by all his officers, by the labor union, and especially by his stakeholders in the congressional community.

After I settle into my seat on the dais, I am joined by Assistant Chief Pittman and my general counsel, Thomas "Tad" DiBiase, who are seated to my left. Everyone is gearing up for a long shift. I ask for the latest information on events downtown.

"We're seeing large crowds in the area of the White House," Wisham responds.

I turn to address the liaisons from the Supreme Court Police and the Federal Protective Service: "Are you two seeing anything related to today's events?"

They both relay that they do not have any concerns or issues at any of their facilities.

I turn again to greet the three liaisons from the Capitol Police Board. Ira is the liaison for the Senate sergeant at arms and a by-the-book retired Maryland State Police official. Melissa represents the House sergeant at arms. She's detail-oriented, always diligently typing and reporting back to her boss. Doug and Kisha are the liaisons sent from the Architect's Office.

Then finally, I turn back to the watch commander: "Hey, John, can you see if you can find the event on the Ellipse and put it on three?" I'm referring to the number-three video screen in the center of the front wall, above the news feed. (We usually maintain a constant feed from CNN and Fox.) John finds the video feed and puts it on the center screen. I ask him to turn up the volume so we can hear if there's any concerning rhetoric regarding the Capitol.

I call Waldow for a quick check-in to make sure he has everything he needs and that he has Glover's contact information. Checking and double-checking—that has been my usual course of action throughout my career. I believe there's always time to do one last follow-up to make sure everyone is ready—something that would drive my old MPD guys crazy.

10:00 a.m. Small crowds are beginning to form on the East Front of the Capitol. Some people are congregating around the permitted areas near the grassy area on the Senate side. At one point, we observe someone with a pull wagon containing a box and several gallon-size jugs. I ask the video operators in the pit of the Command Center to bring the video of the individual onto the front screen. We zoom in on him and see that he is heating a kettle of water over an open flame against one of the short walls on the East Front. I ask Pittman to reach out to Waldow and have him send an officer to tell the man to extinguish his stove. We watch on the video monitors as the USCP officer approaches the individual. The officer's interaction with the individual draws the attention of a few other people around him, but without any arguments the individual extinguishes the flame, packs up his wagon, and is last seen walking eastbound toward the Supreme Court.

Open flames are not allowed on Capitol grounds and can subject the individual to arrest. This was one of the first lessons I learned when I came on board with the USCP. I once recommended bringing a grill to the west lot of USCP headquarters and having a barbecue for the officers, but the attorneys quickly informed me that the Capitol traffic regulations would not allow it. That regulation doesn't seem to apply to members of Congress, though, who have regularly sought waivers from the Capitol Police Board to barbecue on the balconies and exterior areas near their offices. Texas Representative Louis Gohmert is one of the regular waiver-seekers. He often sends some of his barbecued ribs to us at the USCP headquarters. I have to say, he makes some pretty good ribs.

As the day progresses, events and incidents begin occurring in rapid succession, sometimes simultaneously. For me, the day will begin to swing wildly—I'll feel as if I am moving at hyperspeed one moment, then trying to run in deep mud the next. To better understand everything that is about to happen, it's important to have a general picture of the layout of the Capitol grounds.

The Capitol Building is built on a significant incline, its West Front gradually sloping down toward the National Mall. The architectural design of the West Front had to address this considerable slope of the hill up to the Capitol Building and did so in a terracing design process, like the layers of a wedding cake. A beautiful grassy area with trees and walkways, known as the West Front lawn, leads up to the Capitol. Where this grassy area meets the first white limestone terrace is known as the lower West Terrace. There, two large marble staircases lead up to the base of the Capitol. Halfway up these marble stairs, another, smaller terrace connects the two staircases. In the center of this small terrace is an ornate tunnel formed of limestone blocks, leading to the lower West Terrace door. This is the door that the president-elect is always pictured walking through on Inauguration Day, en route to the inaugural platform to be sworn in.

On January 6, the presidential inaugural platform is in the finishing stages, so parts of the two staircases are covered with sections of the platform and scaffolding. At the top of the stairs is the upper West Terrace. The upper West Terrace surrounds the west side of the Capitol and leads all the way up to the doors and windows of the first floor, or what I would call the "skin" of the building. Four doors on the upper West Terrace lead into the Capitol. Directly above the lower West Terrace door is the upper West Terrace door. In the two hallways connecting the House and Senate wings of the Capitol to the central rotunda section are two emergency doors, and there is one final door onto the upper West Terrace from the House wing.

Over on the East Front, the ground is level and leads directly to the first floor of the Capitol Building. There is no terracing on the East Front. The flat hardscape area that extends from the building out to the House and Senate grassy areas and the Capitol Visitor Center entrance is called the East Plaza. Three large flights of stairs on the East Front lead to the third level of the Capitol. The center flight of stairs leads up to the rotunda entrance, the stairs to the right lead to the Senate Chamber, and the stairs on the left lead to the House Chamber. There are also several other entrances on the east side of the Capitol, as well as doors on the north and south sides of the building.

Beyond the East Plaza are a number of grassy areas that lie outside our established metal barricade perimeter for this day. Six groups have been issued permits to hold First Amendment assemblies there today. Across First Street, on the east side, are the Supreme Court and the Library of Congress. Constitution Avenue runs along the north side of the Capitol near the Senate wing, and Independence Avenue runs along the south side by the House wing.

10:51 a.m. I call United States Park Police Major Mark Adamchik for an update on how things are going on the Mall and at the Ellipse. Mark says they have large crowds in and around the Ellipse and the Washington Monument grounds. I tell him what we are seeing around the Capitol and that I have been in touch with Glover and Carroll.

It's a fairly short call, and Mark concludes by saying, "They are going to be coming your way soon, brother." I don't fully grasp the importance of this, because I don't realize that even while we're talking, Rudy

Giuliani is on the stage, firing up the crowd and calling for them to go to the Capitol and have "trial by combat." I don't think anyone else in the Command Center picks up on the magnitude of this statement either.

10:56 a.m. I call my wife to let her know that I'm in the Command Center and that I've reached out to several of our partner agencies and that everyone seems prepared for the day. The call lasts only a few minutes. She's been a police official's wife long enough to know that a quick check-in is better than no check-in.

"I love you, sweetheart," I say.

"I love you too," she says. "God bless, and stay safe."

10:59 a.m. I am seeing that the crowds at the Ellipse are substantial. Although I have not heard of any issues with any groups down at that end of the National Mall, I continue to be concerned for the perimeter and the number of officers I can deploy to support it. Having been involved in the planning of major events with the Metropolitan Police Department for well over half of my law enforcement career, I know that a big part of the planning involves staging CDU resources close to where you may need them.

I call Jeff Carroll. "Jeff, would it be possible for you to stage some CDU platoons near the Capitol, maybe on Louisiana Avenue or Constitution Avenue on the north side of the Capitol?"

"I can put some bike platoons on Constitution Avenue," he replies. "Would that work?"

"That'll work," I say. "Thanks." I now have MPD next to the Capitol, which makes me feel a little better. I have some good, experienced, immediate backup if needed.

11:00 a.m. We receive reports of about two hundred members of the Proud Boys marching on the Capitol grounds. The group was first seen marching through Garfield Circle from Maryland Avenue and then up to the East Front. They spent a little while at the permitted grassy areas (8 and 9) on the Senate side of the East Front. Within twenty minutes, the group marches west, off Capitol grounds. It appears they are headed back toward the Washington Monument and the Ellipse.

11:05 a.m. MPD officers patrolling in the area about four blocks west of the Capitol grounds, in the 700 block of L'Enfant Plaza SW, locate a vehicle with a scope-mounted Savage .22-caliber rifle lying in plain view.

11:17 a.m. We receive a report of a suspicious package behind the Supreme Court. Even though the Supreme Court has its own police force, it relies on the USCP for certain technical services, such as explosives ordnance response. I call Thomas to advise him of the suspicious package and ask him to come into the Command Center.

Our Hazardous Device Unit (bomb squad) is activated, and the immediate area is evacuated while we conduct an investigation. When I hear the description of the package—a red wagon—I suspect that it's the same wagon that belongs to the individual who was earlier told to leave the East Front. I call Waldow since the bomb squad is under his command and say, "This suspicious package sounds a lot like the wagon from earlier. We're looking at the previous video footage of the individual with the stove to see if we can locate him and have him claim his property, but we're not seeing him anywhere."

The bomb squad clears the suspicious package at 12:16 p.m. and declares the area safe. The USCP returns to normal operations.

11:26 a.m. I receive an email about a posting on Twitter indicating that someone is distributing a flyer around the Capitol calling for the formation of a militia. The flyer reads, "Notice of Levee En-Masse." *Levée en masse* is a French term used for mass conscription in the face of a military threat. The flyer indicates that militia members should self-identify as lawful combatants by affixing a silver armband, and concludes by saying, "The tree of liberty must be refreshed from time to time with the blood of patriots and tyrants. —Thomas Jefferson."

I review the email and immediately send a copy to Pittman and Gallagher so they can have IICD evaluate it. It appears that the IICD has already seen this information, and they push out an intelligence bulletin and photo to the appropriate people immediately after I forward it to Pittman and Gallagher.

11:32 a.m. Tom Sullivan, the chief of the United States Secret Service Uniformed Division, calls me on my cell phone to give me a quick update on the event at the Ellipse. "POTUS is at the Ellipse and should be starting his speech soon. We've got big crowds at the Ellipse and the Mall, and they may be coming your way soon."

Noon. On the news feed, I see that President Trump has taken the stage at the Ellipse. I ask the watch commander, "John, can you turn it up a little?" But even with the increased volume, it's hard to pay attention over all the phone calls and activity in the Command Center.

Right around the time Trump takes the stage, the MPD receives information about a possible suspect with a rifle near Fifteenth Street and Constitution Avenue NW. MPD and USPP officers begin looking for the suspect and locate an individual in some trees near Seventeenth Street and Constitution Avenue NW, near the World War II memorial. He is in possession of a firearm and is arrested without incident.

12:20 p.m. I hear someone, possibly the watch commander, call out that there are reports of a group of about a hundred, possibly members of the Proud Boys, on the National Mall. They appear to be marching toward the Capitol. We try to locate this group on our video cameras but can't.

We are also beginning to see large numbers of people starting to fill Constitution Avenue in the area east of the Ellipse. They look as though they could be staging in anticipation of a march to the Capitol. I am sitting at the dais with Thomas, Pittman, Gallagher, and DiBiase as President Trump is on the video screen in front of us. The president's image is on the center screen, surrounded by CCTV images of crowds starting to form around the Capitol. I turn toward DiBiase and Pittman and ask, "Did the president just say he was coming up to the Capitol? That would not be good for us."

"I thought I heard him say something like that," DiBiase answers.

"Secret Service isn't going to let that happen," Gallagher adds.

I turn to Sean and say, "Put a call in to Secret Service to make sure POTUS didn't have any plans to come up to the Capitol."

Shortly thereafter, Gallagher advises that USSS reports there are no plans for POTUS to come to the Capitol.

12:36 p.m. I am monitoring the approach and arrival of Vice President Pence's motorcade. The fleet of black government Suburbans is escorted onto the East Plaza by twelve police motorcycles with their red-and-blue lights flashing: three MPD, three USPP, three USSS Uniformed Division, and three USCP. Due to the size of the crowd, the motorcade arrives via the south barricade. The vice president's armored limousine pulls in for a secure drop-off at the Senate carriage entrance. Pence gets out of his limo and is greeted by Senate Sergeant at Arms Stenger, who escorts him inside with the Secret Service and Capitol Police. The vice president is safely inside.

12:42 p.m. The Command Center receives a call about another suspicious package. An employee of the Capitol Hill Club has located a device that looks like a pipe bomb in the rear of the Republican National Committee Building, in the 300 block of First Street SE. USCP officers respond and quickly cordon off the area and call the bomb squad. We've turned the president's speech down so I can monitor the radio communications about the pipe bomb.

The bomb squad arrives quickly and assesses the device. Captain Kathleen Pickett, the commander of the Hazardous Incident Response Division, takes over as incident commander for the suspicious package. Wisham is monitoring the actions of the bomb squad, and one of the technicians sends a picture of the device to his phone for our situational awareness. I watch John open the image, and I can see his eyes widen. He quickly comes over and hands me his phone.

Having overseen the bomb squad at the MPD for five years, I have some basic knowledge of what to look for, and this picture raises a number of concerns. I can clearly see a large metal pipe with the end caps screwed on. One of the metal end caps is drilled with wires protruding from it and leading to what appears to be a kitchen timer. At first glance, it looks like a device whose timer would have to be manually set, but looks can be deceiving, and the one thing every explosive-ordnance disposal technician knows is that when dealing with bombs or explosives, you never take things at face value. You have to consider every possibility, or as some techs like to say, you have to "think like the Jackal"—a reference to a film about a paid assassin. And in this case, the manual timer could just be a cover for an electronic timer or a remote detonator. It is determined to be a legit, workable device.

I immediately pick up my phone and notify Irving and Stenger about the device. USCP officers are sent to canvass the area and look for any other suspicious packages. I advise my two assistant chiefs and the Command Center that we need to be careful because this could be a diversionary tactic.

Officers are also sent to canvass the area around the Democratic National Committee Building as a precaution. There are two protective details at the DNC—one for Vice President-elect Harris and the other for a member of the House leadership—and we can't take any chances.

While the bomb squad is responding to the pipe bomb and officers are canvassing the area, we begin monitoring a large group near the Reflecting Pool on the west side of the Capitol, near Third Street. In preparation for the upcoming inauguration, a large portable cell tower has been installed near the corner of Third Street and Constitution Avenue NW. The tower has been enclosed with temporary fencing that also encircles a portable toilet. As we're looking at the crowd using our virtual video patrols, we observe a group trying to pry open the fencing to get access to the toilet. I ask Thomas to send someone down there to resecure the fence and let the group know they aren't allowed to open it. We watch two USCP motor officers arrive on the scene and begin talking to the group. The group appears to accept the officers' direction and leaves the area. The motor officers then begin to resecure the fencing around the cell tower.

The video feed of President Trump giving his speech from the Ellipse is still on the monitor, with the volume turned down as we continue listening to the radio communications at the bomb scene. Suddenly, someone in the pit yells out, "There is a large group approaching the perimeter on the West Front!"

I look up from my seat and see the group walking quickly across Garfield Circle toward the officers who are manning the metal barricades at the Maryland Avenue walkway. I see that these officers on the line are dressed in soft gear. No CDU officers in hard gear are in sight. This troubles me, especially after the lessons learned from MAGA I and II. We've already activated several hard platoons, and I was expecting them all to be suited up, at their posts, and ready to go well before a march like this could happen.

12:53 p.m. The large group of protesters arrives at the barricade and immediately begins yelling at the officers on the line. They're trying to tear down the metal barriers. The officers are doing their best to hold the barriers in place. There are only a handful of officers manning this barricade, and the CDU platoon assigned to the West Front of the Capitol is nowhere to be found.

The confrontation grows more violent as the protesters become increasingly agitated. The size of the crowd grows quickly. The officers are clinging to the barricade, visibly terrified of what might happen if they no longer have its protection. The enraged group begins shoving the barricades harder, pinning one officer to the ground and punching the others with their fists. I'm shocked. I have never seen a group turn so violent so quickly.

I turn to Chad and yell, "Where the hell is our CDU? Get them down there now!"

As Thomas gets on his cell phone and calls Waldow, I can now see hundreds of protesters approaching the barricade where the small contingent of officers is still fighting desperately to keep it in place.

The situation is going south fast.

12:55 p.m. I call Carroll: "Jeff, we have a situation, and we are getting our asses handed to us. I need assistance on the West Front now! Can you send CDU?"

Carroll immediately directs the CDU assets that we had coordinated earlier in the day to the West Front. Minutes later, I see swarms of MPD CDU bike officers, wearing their distinctive yellow-and-black "bumblebee" jackets flooding into camera view. I have never been so happy to see MPD officers!

These are experienced, street-hardened officers, well-accustomed to violent confrontation. I deployed them in the past when I was at the MPD, and I know their capabilities. I'm hopeful we can end this confrontation here and now. But the rioters have forced the barricade out of the way, and dozens are now running up the three steps to the walkways on the West Front. I see my officers quickly backing up to the lower West Terrace, where the next series of barricades has been set up, staffed with another group of officers. More and more protesters are flooding onto the West Front and making their way up the Maryland Avenue and Pennsylvania Avenue walkways to an area near the inaugural viewing stand and the lower West Terrace. What I'm witnessing sends a jolt of electricity through me, vestiges of which I will feel long after this day.

The USCP radio blares: "West side, all units respond now!"

I'm watching the rioters battling with the USCP and MPD officers. The officers are trying to hold the metal barricades in place around the base of the inaugural platform, which is still in the building process. The attackers keep trying to drag the barricades away from the officers, striking the officers' hands with metal pipes, flagpoles, and other objects. USCP officers start hastily evacuating the construction workers off the inaugural platform to safety. But in the rush, many tools are left behind and quickly become weapons in the hands of the rioters.

12:58 p.m. After I get off the phone with Carroll, I hit the speed dial for Irving. When he picks up, I say, "We are getting overrun by protesters on the West Front! I need approval to request the National Guard immediately!" I already asked for the National Guard to assist on the perimeter three days ago, but the two sergeants at arms made it abundantly clear that this wasn't an option for me. Now I am hoping for a much different response.

"Let me run it up the chain," Irving replies, referring to the House leadership. I know he can hear the stress in my voice, and I trust he understands the gravity of the situation. "I'll call you back."

1:01 p.m. I receive a text from Sullivan at the USSS Uniformed Division: "If you need help I can send platoon to you." I text back, "I will take whatever you can send."

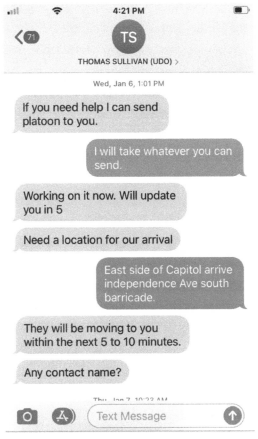

Figure 2.3. Texts with Chief Sullivan at USSS

Minutes later, Vice President Pence puts out a statement indicating that he will not attempt to claim unilateral authority to overturn the votes.

I am urgently trying to reach Stenger, chairman of the Capitol Police Board, to expedite approval for the National Guard. I try to call his cell phone, but the call goes straight to voice mail. I don't realize that he is presently walking the VP and Senate members and leadership across the interior of the Capitol Building to the House Chamber. As they are approaching the House Chamber, Speaker Pelosi pounds the gavel on the rostrum, calling the House to order. Just minutes after I have urgently requested the National Guard, Irving escorts the Senate entourage into the House Chamber and loudly proclaims, "Madam Speaker, the vice president and the United States Senate."

I try to call Jennifer Hemingway, Stenger's deputy sergeant at arms, but my calls to her also go directly to voice mail.

Around this same time, USCP officers canvassing for other suspicious devices in the area of the RNC locate a truck parked on the street in front of the building. As they look inside, they make a disturbing discovery: a cache of eleven Molotov cocktails, many knives, and several firearms.

1:06 p.m. Stenger calls me back. I describe the rapidly deteriorating situation outside and tell him that I need the National Guard immediately.

"Have you asked Paul?" he says.

"Yes, Paul said he was running it up the chain."

"Okay," Stenger says. "Let me know when Paul gets back to you."

The House and Senate are in joint session, and both Irving and Stenger are inside the House Chamber. But right now I need both their approvals to request the support of the National Guard across the Hill.

As soon as I get off the call with Stenger, I see a text from Hemingway, which reads, "Need me to call?"

I text back, "No, just briefed Stenger we had a breach of the fence line on the West Front by several thousand protesters."

1:06 p.m. USCP and MPD officers begin to form a police line several officers deep. They are trying to prevent the mob, now thousands strong, from progressing past the lower West Terrace and up toward the Capitol

Building. The fight on the lower West Terrace is raging and turning into an outright brawl. Waldow, supported by a hard USCP CDU platoon, begins to issue warnings to the rioters. The crowd is given one last opportunity to disperse.

The warnings have no effect. The rioters have torn down a barrier of plastic construction fencing that was midway up on the west lawn and are trying to get onto the inaugural platform. The officers are now involved in vicious hand-to-hand combat with thousands of rioters who are clearly focused on doing whatever it takes to get into the Capitol. The rioters are systematically trying to pull the metal barricades away from the officers. When they're successful, they use the barriers as weapons, striking officers with the metal ends, jabbing at them with the sharp metal feet, or hurling them as projectiles.

Both Waldow and Loyd have responded to the West Front. They make their way to the front lines, where the officers continue their battle. Protesters are targeting officers' faces, eyes, and hands. It is brutality without mercy, as if these fellow citizens had become foreign invaders. Such a sick irony to be stabbed with a Blue Lives Matter flag or to be knocked unconscious by someone who, back home, is a fellow first responder.

Both Waldow and Loyd can see how serious this has become. Everyone, every officer and every commander, knows at this moment that we have to do everything we can to prevent a breach of the Capitol Building. But we are becoming more and more outnumbered with each passing minute. We desperately need more bodies on the line.

1:08 p.m. I call Matt Miller, director of the Washington Field Office for the USSS. I give him an update on the situation and tell him we can use all the support we can get.

1:10 p.m. I make a one-minute call to my wife to tell her I'm safe and we're doing the best we can to repel the mob. I know my wife is watching this on television, seeing many familiar faces getting hurt, and waiting for an update. She would never call or text me, for fear of interrupting something or distracting me, but I can tell she's very worried about my officers and me.

1:12 p.m. The joint session goes into its first recess over the objection of Republican members to the certification of Arizona's Electoral College vote. The members of the Senate then traverse the interior of the Capitol, heading back to the Senate Chamber to debate the objection.

At the same time, Gallagher sends an ongoing situational awareness email to the staff of the House and Senate sergeants at arms, which reads: *"Update #4 Priority Update- There has been a breach by thousands on the West Front. Performing CPR, and 10-100s, with photos."* (The term *10-100* is the USCP code for a suspicious package.)

1:12 p.m. As Trump is concluding his speech, I am watching the violent struggle on the screen in front of the dais. It's a view from directly above a group of officers and rioters on the north side of the inaugural platform on the lower West Terrace.

Someone in the Command Center says, "There is a protester down." I see a heavyset male demonstrator unconscious on the sidewalk, directly between the police officers and demonstrators.

A responding officer advises the dispatcher: "We have an unconscious person down and not breathing. Notify the board." (A reference to the DC Fire and Emergency Services.)

There is a temporary, very localized pause in the fighting as everyone clears an area around the fallen man. A USCP officer starts CPR. An ambulance makes its way down crowded Northwest Drive to get as close as it can to the group, and a path is cleared for the incoming stretcher. The victim is loaded onto the stretcher and pushed through the crowd and into the ambulance with the assistance of both cops and rioters. After the ambulance leaves, the temporary truce quickly dissolves, and the officers and rioters go right back to fighting each other. It's one of the strangest things I've ever seen.

(At the hospital, the fallen man, later identified as Kevin Greeson, will be pronounced dead from cardiac arrest.)

The rioters continue to push forward, hitting and spitting at the officers on the line, including Waldow and Loyd. Waldow calls for the less lethal teams over the radio and authorizes the deployment of less lethal projectiles. The less lethal teams take position on the upper West Terrace and on the inaugural platform, which gives them the tactical high ground. They begin firing PepperBalls and FN 303 chemical projectiles in an effort to push the crowd back.

Both Waldow and Loyd are wearing their soft duty gear, but they're at the front of the fighting as they try to hold the line at the base of the inaugural platform. They are punched and sprayed, but they continue to fight back. At one point, Loyd is seen turning from the line and throwing his hat like a Frisbee toward the back of the melee. Anytime you see Loyd around the Capitol, he's always wearing this hat as a sign of respect for the people he works for, but right now, it was just getting in the way and had to be discarded.

I continue to watch the fight on the monitors. It is brutal, relentless, and only getting worse. I can see people in the crowd deploying chemical spray at the officers, many of whom do not have respirators to protect them. I hear someone in the Command Center say that there are reports of bear spray being used. Bear spray is a very potent form of pepper spray—stronger than anything police use for crowd control or self-defense.

The mob continues to push the officers back. Glover, who arrived shortly after my call to Carroll, has been coordinating the MPD's response on the West Terrace but is now being flanked by the rioters. Glover calls out the USCP, via MPD radio, for a fallback position. There is no response from those in the Command Center responsible for monitoring the MPD radio channel.

As the fighting wears on, the overall command structure is beginning to fall apart. Too many things are being thrown at us from too many directions. While I am coordinating resources and communicating with the two sergeants at arms, my two assistant chiefs, both in charge of operations, fail to detect the breakdown in communications with officers and do not establish an effective area command. The on-site officials who normally direct officers in the field are involved in physical altercations with the violent crowd instead of focusing on tactics and strategy.

Officers begin to try to make arrests. It takes two officers to make a single arrest under normal circumstances. They quickly find they cannot transport the arrestees out of the area. Doing so would leave their fellow officers even more shorthanded. In several incidents, arresting officers are encircled and forced to release their arrestees when they are boxed in and threatened by an aggressive crowd.

Both Waldow and Loyd are hit with the spray from the crowd, Waldow taking a number of direct shots to the face. He falls back from the front lines to pour water on his face, then quickly returns to the fray using his hands and his PR-24 baton. When he's hit with another direct shot of chemical spray, he has to move back and seek treatment at a decontamination station.

MPD and USCP officers will hold the lower West Terrace for over an hour until the mob can finally force its way past the barriers and up the steps to the upper West Terrace. Rioters are now under the inaugural platform, trying to push up the stairs. Some in the crowd are now climbing up onto the platform, throwing various projectiles, construction tools, and debris at the officers. At one point, a rioter throws a fire extinguisher down from the platform at the officers below.

MPD units have been backed into the tunnel leading to the lower West Terrace door. Here they can get additional reinforcements from inside the Capitol to try to hold this critical entrance. The violent battle in the tunnel to the lower West Terrace door will rage on for hours, resulting in many serious injuries to officers. I can see the battle from a camera mounted near the lower West Terrace door. The rioters are hitting the officers with everything they've got. I see two-by-fours from the construction of the inaugural platform being thrown at the officers. A chair, even a large ladder, is hurled into the tunnel at the officers. During the battle for the door, a rioter pulls the gas mask away from an MPD sergeant while he is sprayed with bear spray. Then the gas mask is released, trapping the concentrated chemical irritant in the sergeant's mask and burning his eyes and face. The sergeant falls to the ground, inhaling the chemical and burning his lungs. USCP and MPD officers will describe this scene as some of the most brutal fighting they have ever seen. MPD Officer Daniel Hodges is trapped and crushed in the lower West Terrace door. Officers defending the door suffer broken bones, torn ligaments, and dislocated joints, but they hold the door.

1:16 p.m. Inspector Glover, the designated MPD incident commander, using the radio call sign "Cruiser 50," is on the West Front with his officers. Glover advises dispatch of multiple USCP injuries. Glover is frantically calling for hard MPD platoons to assist. It is clear that the MPD is sending everything they have available to the Capitol.

"Give me DSO up here now," Glover calls over the radio, referring to the MPD's Domestic Security Operations Unit. It's the unit I once commanded at MPD, and it is responsible for training all the department's CDU officers and providing special support and munitions capabilities. Officer Steven Hebron, from MPD's Special Operations Division, is manning the equipment truck that carries all the CDU chemical munitions. After responding "Code One" to the Capitol, Hebron opens the back of the truck to start deploying the munitions.

A winded DSO officer runs up to the truck, and Hebron asks him what he needs.

"Give me everything you've got!" the officer says. "Everything! Bring it all!"

1:19 p.m. Deputy Senate Sergeant at Arms Jennifer Hemingway calls as a follow-up to my previous text. I inform her that things are bad on the West Front and that we need to activate the National Guard. She tells me she will reach out to Stenger.

1:21 p.m. Stenger calls me back for an update on the situation outside. I advise him that it has gotten worse and that we have thousands of protesters fighting with the police. I explain that MPD has hundreds of cops on the West Front assisting but that we are still having trouble holding

the line and need the National Guard. He tells me he'll get back to me
and hangs up.

Officers in the field are reporting that some rioters are throwing
homemade explosives and large firecrackers like M-80s at the officers
on the line. Others report hearing what sounds like flash-bang devices
being set off on the West Front. Rioters are trying to jump the metal
barricades and climb the walls to gain access to the upper West Terrace.

1:22 p.m. Trump tweets:

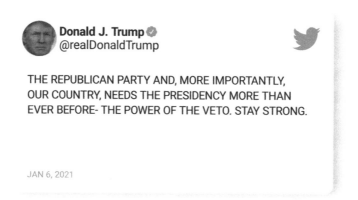

Donald J. Trump
@realDonaldTrump

THE REPUBLICAN PARTY AND, MORE IMPORTANTLY,
OUR COUNTRY, NEEDS THE PRESIDENCY MORE THAN
EVER BEFORE- THE POWER OF THE VETO. STAY STRONG.

JAN 6, 2021

Demonstrators on the West Front have pushed forward a very large
blue Trump flag, about eight feet by twelve feet in size and held taut by
a frame of white PVC tubing. I can clearly see the banner moving over
the heads of the rioters, being passed from protester to protester, all the
way to the front of the battle.

A banner of this size creates a lot of concern for anyone in law enforcement. I've seen such props used to conceal criminal behavior during
a violent confrontation. Even this summer, during the violent protests
in DC and around the country, we've seen rioters using umbrellas as
cover, hiding behind them to conceal the lighting of fireworks or explosives before throwing them at the police or to throw rocks, bricks,
or urine-filled bottles. So this large banner worries me. As it reaches the
front of the line, an aggressive tug-of-war begins between the police and
the rioters. I watch as the rioters appear to gain control of the banner and

pull it over to their side, but in the next moment, several MPD officers manage to regain control. The frame is twisted and broken down as the banner is passed to the rear of the police line, not to be seen again. The police have won this small battle.

1:22 p.m. USCP begins to evacuate the Cannon House Office Building due to its proximity to the pipe bomb located at the RNC.

1:23 p.m. USCP reports the arrest of two people on the upper West Terrace. A third is arrested two minutes later. During the battle for the upper West Terrace, it's reported that a rioter has pried a two-by-four plank from the presidential inaugural platform, has approached the line of USCP officers who are trying to hold the metal barricades in place, and has struck an officer in the head with the plank. Another officer on the line sees the struck officer looking dazed and disoriented and grabs him by the back of the collar to pull him behind the police line. Because the officer's face is so red, those providing first aid first think it is a chemical irritant dye on his face, but when they clean his face, they see blood streaming from his hairline. The two-by-four plank that hit him had several nails protruding from it. The officer is rushed into a room with another officer to keep an eye on him while they wait for medical support that never arrives. Medics just cannot get through the crowd. (They will ultimately walk him to the other side of the building for medical assistance.)

Officers are trying to hold the cold metal barricades in place with their bare hands, doing everything they can to repel the attack. At the same time, the rioters are striking at their hands and fingers with bats, pipes, hockey sticks, hammers, and pieces of wood they have taken from the construction site. They are grabbing at officers' gas masks, trying to rip them off their faces, and tearing at their uniforms.

1:28 p.m. I am growing increasingly impatient. I again call Irving to tell him how bad things are on the West Front and that we are doing everything we can to hold the line. I ask if there is an update on the Guard.

"Still waiting," he answers.

I get off the phone wondering what the hell everyone is waiting for. Not for the first time, I see that this whole crazy town is all about following protocol and procedure, with no common sense or acknowledgment of reality. Why can't they just tell me I can call the Guard myself to get more people on the line? No more waiting. We need to end this NOW!

1:30 p.m. I receive a call from Chief Ron Pavlik with the Metro Transit Police Department. He has transit officers with civil disturbance training and is offering to send them my way. I quickly accept his offer and ask him to direct them to the north side of the Capitol on Constitution Avenue.

1:30 p.m. The DHS National Operations Center, which is located two miles from the Capitol, sends an email to the Pentagon Operations Center. It reads, in part: "There are no major incidents of illegal activity at this time in Washington, DC."

At the time of the attack, Acting DHS Secretary Chad Wolf was out of the country and of little benefit to his agency as it fumbled with its response to the attack.

1:34 p.m. I make yet another call to Irving, trying to get an update on the request for the National Guard. Again his response: "Still waiting."

The sense of desperate urgency is mounting. Everyone in the Command Center can see me making these calls, and those around me can sense my growing frustration. As I hang up the phone, I tell them, "We are still waiting on Irving to make a decision."

At this point, the radios broadcasting the two USCP channels, along with the MPD radio zone, are blaring loudly and often competing. Calls are coming in and ringing throughout the center. More people keep coming into the room from other USCP units, including from the IICD, the Public Information Office, the Dignitary Protection Division, and others. A dozen different discussions are going on throughout the room.

Because of the growing din in the Command Center, I have to step out into the hall to make and receive some of my calls. At those times, I hand over incoming resources to Thomas on my right, while Pittman and Gallagher continue meeting with their unit commanders on my left. My chief of staff, Salley, is constantly checking to see if I need anything and is dutifully updating me on the ever-increasing number of inquiries coming in over the phones.

Having heard of the attack on the West Front, the head of the USCP Dignitary Protection Division (DPD), Inspector Kimberly Schneider, comes up to the Command Center. She is standing behind me, near the Capitol Police Board liaisons, and watching the wall of rioters viciously fighting with the police. The situation is both shocking and surreal, and she is rightly growing very concerned for the safety of the congressional leadership under her protection. She talks briefly with Gallagher and Pittman, then steps to the back of the room with another DPD official to discuss how best to start taking proactive measures.

At 1:35 p.m., Schneider has DPD start preparing to evacuate leadership, relocating vehicles and the officers assigned to the DPD teams should evacuation become necessary.

1:36 p.m. I call Chief Sullivan at the USSS to check on the status of the CDU he promised to send over.

1:39 p.m. I receive a follow-up call from Stenger, asking for an update. I explain that things have only gotten worse even as we keep doing everything we can to prevent the rioters from accessing the upper West Terrace. I again advise him that I am still waiting on approval from Irving regarding the National Guard.

As soon as I end my call with Stenger, I'm immediately back on the phone to coordinate assistance, this time with Ashan Benedict, the special agent in charge of ATF's Washington Field Office. Ashan is sending resources to the location of the explosive device and also pulling together several squads of ATF agents to help me at the Capitol.

1:40 p.m. The Pentagon Operations Center sends an update to military leadership, including Lieutenant General Charles Flynn: "There are no major incidents of illegal activity at this time."[2] It would be an understatement to say that this is a gross mischaracterization of the fierce battle I am witnessing as officers try to defend the Capitol and prevent an assault on the lawmakers.

1:42 p.m. I receive a call from Sullivan at the Secret Service: "Steve, I'm sending a platoon of CDU officers. Where do you want me to have them respond?"

I confer with Thomas and tell Sullivan to have them come to the north side of the campus on Constitution Avenue, near the north barricade. Thomas then advises Waldow that they are on the way.

I realize we're going to have many other law enforcement resources coming, and I want to make sure we have a structure in place to account for all of them and to deploy them as quickly and effectively as possible. In the past, I've dealt with incoming resource issues—for example, while I was the incident commander at the Navy Yard shooting in 2013. I know it's imperative that we not lose track of anyone.

I tell Thomas that we need someone good with logistics to start tracking the incoming resources and designate a staging location for them to respond to. Thomas recommends a lieutenant and lot 16, a large, mostly empty parking lot across the street from USCP headquarters. I ask Thomas to send the lieutenant to the lot and to have another official come up to the Command Center to deploy the incoming resources to Waldow and Loyd and to track their locations on a map.

1:44 p.m. I receive a call from Assistant Chief Carroll at MPD to coordinate resources and try to get more support for Glover on the West Front. I explain to Carroll that I have resources coming in from other agencies

---

2. Betsy Woodruff Swan and Lara Seligman, "'No Major Incidents of Illegal Activity': DHS Told Pentagon as Pro-Trump Mob Breached Capitol," *Politico*, September 28, 2021, www.politico.com/news/2021/09/28/dhs-pentagon-jan-6-capitol-riot-514527.

and that we will be deploying them as soon as they get on-site. I also advise Carroll that I have requested the support of the National Guard but that the Capitol Police Board has not yet approved my request.

1:45 p.m. I again put in a call to Irving to check on the status of the request for the Guard. I give him a detailed description of the actions of the rioters and how they are advancing on the Capitol from the West Front. Additionally, large numbers of protesters are now forming on the East Front. I advise him of the resources we have coming, but that we clearly need more support, and again I ask about my request for the National Guard. Irving tells me he's still waiting on approval for the Guard.

As I sit in my Command Center watching the video screens, my frustration at the repeated delays from the sergeants at arms, along with my concern for my officers' safety, is redlining. To be more precise, I am *fucking livid*.

1:49 p.m. I pick up the phone and call General Walker. I advise him that my perimeter has been breached by thousands of rioters and that I need the National Guard's help immediately. "I need as many as you can muster. I do not have the Capitol Police Board's approval to request the National Guard," I tell him, "but I should have it any minute now. Could you please get the ball rolling?"

Walker says he will notify the secretary of the army and start moving on my request.

1:49 p.m. A report comes in over the USCP radio about a second hazardous device. Wisham yells over to me, "This one's at the DNC and is identical to the first one."

The situation is getting more serious by the minute. We are being violently attacked by thousands of demonstrators who have breached our perimeter, they're advancing on the Capitol Building, and now we have a second explosive device. With one bomb at the RNC, right next to the Capitol grounds, and now another at the DNC, just a few blocks south of our primary jurisdiction, I'm thinking, *What else are we going to be looking at?*

My bomb squad is still working on the first package at the RNC. And I don't want to divert resources to the second bomb, in case we encounter more. "Make sure you roll the MPD Explosive Ordnance Unit to the DNC," I tell Wisham, "since that's in their jurisdiction."

The FBI and ATF will also respond to both locations to assist.

1:50 p.m. DC Fire and EMS dispatch an ambulance for an individual just three blocks from the West Front to the intersection of Third Street and Maryland Avenue SW. They are responding to the report of an individual who has had several fingers blown off by some type of explosive. This location is just off the Capitol grounds, next to where the demonstrators are marching toward the West Front.

At this point, I have been waiting for the National Guard approval for damned near an hour. I have made repeated calls to the two sergeants at arms, but to no avail. The situation is becoming absolutely absurd. We are all well aware of the House's reluctance to use the military on the Hill, but Irving and Stenger clearly know the situation outside. I have briefed them repeatedly, and Gallagher has been sending updates to their staff, telling them just how bad the situation is. In addition, the Capitol Police Board liaisons are doing exactly what they are supposed to: staying near me, watching, and reporting everything back to their bosses in real time. Yet Irving will not make a decision, and Stenger will not proceed without Irving.

Irving is obviously terrified of the potential blowback he could get from leadership, so he has called a 1:50 p.m. meeting of leadership staff in Stenger's office to discuss the question of bringing in the National Guard. Stenger is just returning to his office after escorting the Senate and the vice president to the Senate Chamber and is surprised to see the large group in his office. House leadership staff, along with some from McConnell's office, are in attendance.

When they are all informed that the Guard has not yet been called, they are reportedly furious. I can only imagine the environment in Stenger's office, with its large windows looking out over the West Front and the thousands of attackers viciously fighting with police, trying to get into the Capitol. I have no doubt they can hear explosions and possibly even smell the munitions being deployed, and now Irving wants to discuss whether he can get approval to call in the National Guard?

As my officers are battling on the West Front, more rioters begin forming up on my East Front perimeter. This group, however, is acting more like the rioters we were expecting: energized and loud, but compliant. So far, they have stayed behind the metal barriers, neatly gathering there. Just as you would expect at a normal demonstration, they are waving flags and banners, chanting, shouting, but all while staying behind the barriers.

As I watch on the video monitors, this crowd on the East Front continues to grow and is becoming more and more agitated. At a precise moment, right around 1:50 p.m., the whole demeanor of the East Front crowd changes. They are now screaming at the officers and pushing and pulling at the barriers in an attempt to break through. The USCP officers hold the line as the crowd grows more and more enraged. When they see their fellow rioters from the West Front flooding around the base of the Capitol and making their way to the upper West Terrace, the levee breaks. In one giant wave, they break through the East Front perimeter, rushing toward the Capitol's center rotunda steps. Glover screams over the radio that this is "effectively a riot" and calls on officers repeatedly to "HOLD THE LINE! HOLD THE LINE!" Forty-pound bike racks are ripped out of officers' hands. It looks so effortless, like a gate being swung open. Overwhelmed officers at this last exterior perimeter are quickly overrun and, in an effort at self-preservation, must retreat to the safety of the Capitol.

I watch it all happen on the video screen. "Someone, get me the number to the Metropolitan Washington Council of Governments!" I yell to the pit. "I need to activate mutual aid from Maryland and Virginia!"

Even though I'm talking to the operations people in the front of the room, it's Tad DiBiase who goes to his computer first and asks, "Which department?"

"Public Safety," I say.

A few seconds later, I'm on the call as hundreds of people are pouring onto the East Plaza. We now have violent rioters rushing toward the base of the Capitol Building from all sides. On the exterior, officers in soft gear become surrounded. The CDU officers who have been on the line have now fallen back, and many are taking up positions inside the building. Officers try to get their colleagues to fall back, but radio communication is useless. It's too loud, it's too congested, or they're on other radio channels. Officers begin frantically waving at law enforcement from various jurisdictions to fall back to the interior. But even the inside of the Capitol seems less safe as the rioters bang on the doors and windows.

1:51 p.m. I call Scott Boggs, director of the Metropolitan Washington Council of Governments (MWCOG) Department of Homeland Security and Public Safety. Scott must already know what's going on at the Capitol because his first words are, "What can we get you, Chief?"

I advise Scott that I need to activate MWCOG's mutual-aid agreement. "We need any and all available crowd-management resources every agency can send us, as soon as possible."

"I'm on it," he answers. "I'll call you right back."

1:52 p.m. As I finish up the call with MWCOG, I hear another call incoming. It's Congresswoman Maxine Waters's chief of staff. When I switch over and answer, I hear the voice of Representative Waters herself: "Chief Sund, I told you this was going to happen. What are you doing about it?"

I explain to her that the Metropolitan Police Department and other agencies have arrived to assist us and that I am still calling in more agencies.

"I told you this was going to happen," she says again, cutting me off.

"Ma'am," I say, "I am doing the best I can."

"I told you this was going to happen," she says yet again. "I told you!"

I'm still at the dais, now watching rioters on the east side flooding up to the base of the building and up the rotunda stairs, running over the chain on the stairs that designates the restricted area and up to the rotunda door. The situation is getting worse by the second, and this call is going nowhere but in circles.

I take the phone away from my ear, look at it for a second, still hearing the congresswoman on the other end, and hit the End Call button. I'm not trying to be disrespectful to the congresswoman. It's just that time is critical right now.

I turn to my general counsel and say, "Tad, I just hung up on Waters. I wanted to make sure you were aware because I'm sure I will be hearing about it."

I get right back on the phone with MWCOG. They are pushing out the mutual-aid request and want to know the location of the staging area where responding units should report. "Lot sixteen," I say, "located on First Street Northeast, between D Street and Massachusetts Avenue." I tell him we'll have personnel on the scene to check them in and give them an assignment. Scott tells me he's waiting for the agencies to start calling in and will get them to me as soon as possible.

1:59 p.m. I call Ashan Benedict with the ATF to provide a response location and a point of contact for the ATF squads he is sending to the Capitol.

2:01 p.m. I again call Irving, and he tells me to give him just a couple more minutes.

I am watching the battle rage, the rioters approaching the upper West Terrace, with USCP and MPD trying to hold the line. I can see chemical munitions being sprayed from both sides, and rioters using all sorts of improvised weapons, striking my officers on the line. Pittman orders a lockdown of the building. (She will later extend the lockdown to include the entire congressional campus.) I have all the resources coming that I can get, but I still haven't received a response from the sergeants at arms regarding the National Guard.

Word that the protesters are taking out some of our camera systems quickly reaches my Security Services Bureau. SSB is the unit within the USCP responsible for installing and maintaining our physical and technical security equipment, including the closed-circuit television camera system. Sergeant Scott Nagiel, one of the supervisors within SSB, decides to head over to the Capitol to assess the situation. Sergeant Nagiel, wearing a dark suit, gray wool overcoat, white dress shirt, pink tie, and face mask, walks the two blocks from his office to the West Front, where he is astonished by what he is witnessing. He can see the chemical munitions being deployed and, even at a distance, can feel the effects. His

lungs burn when he inhales. His eyes are stinging. He notes the many
rioters wearing heavy body armor and tactical equipment and calls back
to his office to alert them that some in the crowd may be armed.

Rioters are now climbing all over the construction scaffolding and
onto the presidential inaugural platform. They have also climbed onto
the media riser that has been built farther out on the West Front. The
security cameras on the media riser, and those mounted near the platform, have been torn down and smashed. Nagiel, walking alone and
bearing an uncanny resemblance to Senator Josh Hawley, quickly finds
himself surrounded by rioters.

Nagiel, who also happens to wear a lapel pin like those worn by
members of Congress, is accused by many in the crowd of being a congressman. He denies this and tries to move away, but now the crowd
around him has grown larger, and they demand to see his identification.
He is starting to grow concerned about his own safety. Finally, he pulls
out his wallet and shows them his badge. "I'm a Capitol Police officer."

Some members of the crowd are appeased by this. Others don't like
the fact that he is a police officer any more than if he were a member of
Congress, but in the moment of indecision, he slips away from them.
He walks around to the East Front to continue investigating the security cameras, along with the windows and doors that have now been
breached. He is confronted two more times by rioters on the East Front.
He pulls out his badge both times, but at this point, he decides it's better
for his own safety to leave the area completely.

Nagiel will report later that it seems our camera systems have been
specifically targeted, observing that some of the rioters brought rope
and climbing equipment to tear down cameras and defeat some of our
physical security systems.

2:08 p.m. Seventy minutes have passed since I first called Irving to approve
the use of the National Guard. Seventy agonizing minutes of watching
my officers and MPD being brutally assaulted, literally fighting for their
lives, and still not receiving permission to bring in the next largest level
of personnel to help stop the attack.

I again call Irving for an update. This time, he tells me that the use of the National Guard has been approved. *Finally!* I think. I immediately call Stenger, unaware that he is with Irving, and tell him that Paul has finally approved the National Guard. With Pittman sitting to my left and DiBiase beside her, I look at the digital clock on the wall and shout across the room to the watch commander, "John, mark the official time that the National Guard was approved as two ten."

Between 12:58 and when I finally receive approval for the National Guard at 2:09, I have made thirty-two calls to coordinate response support for my officers, including at least eleven calls to the sergeants at arms regarding my request for the National Guard.

While I am on the call with the SAAs, the rioters, now numbering well into the thousands, have broken through four rows of metal barricades and countless police lines, injuring many officers and making their way onto the upper West Terrace. Rioters flood onto the terrace. I see them on the video feed running toward the skin of the building. Initially, many only peer into the windows, but then they begin pounding on the door to a hallway that connects the Senate wing to the center of the Capitol. The officers are trying to find some way to keep them out, but their options are narrowing.

2:11 p.m. Dominic Pezzola, a rioter who stole a Capitol Police riot shield on the West Front, begins to use the end of the shield to break through a window to a hallway on the Senate side of the Capitol Building. This hallway is not far from Stenger's office. The single-pane window appears to break with relative ease. The watch commander yells across the room, "Chief, they breached the Capitol!"

Rioters begin to climb in through the window and into the hallway, quickly opening a nearby emergency exit door to allow more rioters in. Multiple entrances are now infiltrated, and police have to spread out to try to maintain control of the hallways, stairs, and walkways leading to the center of the building. *How bad is this going to get?*

Inspector Schneider has been watching the advancing rioters and is now preparing to evacuate leadership. She has been discussing the evacuation plans with Pittman and Gallagher since the attack began and coordinating actions from the back of the Command Center on a separate DPD radio channel. Although there may have been some dis- agreement between Pittman, Gallagher, and the DPD commander on where to evacuate leadership, Schneider knows that a scenario this se- rious requires that leadership be evacuated off campus.

2:13 p.m. DPD agents advise congressional leadership and the Secret Ser- vice of the increasing threat posed by the mob. Vice President Pence is escorted from the Senate Chamber by USSS and USCP.

To the Dignitary Protection Division, this is rapidly becoming a worst-case scenario. Protesters are flooding into the building. Evacua- tion of House and Senate leadership has begun. Senator Grassley gavels the Senate into recess. Grassley's DPD security team enters the Senate Chamber and rushes onto the rostrum where the senator is standing. As they are trained to do, one agent quickly moves behind Grassley, placing a hand on his upper back and one on his shoulder as another agent stands in front and guides the senator to safety. This allows the team to better control the senator if they encounter crowds as they are evacuating. The three agents evacuate Senator Grassley off the floor and exit from the north door of the chamber. Other leaders are escorted out the same way.

2:14 p.m. It is reported that rioters have breached the second floor of the Capitol. Capitol Division officers are directed to respond to the Senate Chamber, where they begin to barricade the doors. For the first time I can recall in my four years with the USCP, the Command Center issues an alert through the mass notification system, warning of an "inside threat." Hundreds of rioters flood into the Capitol, ransacking offices and destroying furniture.

The center steps on the East Front leading up to the rotunda doors are filled with angry rioters. Dozens of people at the top of the stairs are fighting with a group of officers who are trapped between the mob and the rotunda doors. MPD deploys gas at the top of the stairs to try to push back the crowd. USCP Officers and federal agents manage to pull the officers to safety, but now the mob is trying to break in through the doors. Officers inside the rotunda are doing everything they can to prevent the doors from being breached, but the mob finally overpowers them and gets the doors open. The officers then try to form a blockade to prevent the mob from accessing the rotunda, but there are just too many of them.

2:19 p.m. Some two hundred rioters breach the line of officers and surge into the rotunda. A minute later, rioters breach the Senate door and the north door on the upper West Terrace. Hundreds of rioters are now flowing into the Capitol Building and rampaging through the halls. USCP Officer Eugene Goodman encounters the mob on the stairs leading to the second floor. He realizes they are approaching the area where members are located and tries to engage the mob. He begins posturing and challenging them, swinging his baton even though he is badly outnumbered. They take the bait and follow him away from the members located in the Senate Chamber.

Elsewhere in the Capitol, in an area known as the Crypt located right below the rotunda, USCP officers make a valiant stand against a huge mob to prevent them from penetrating deeper into the Capitol. Trying to form a line against the mob, with batons swinging, they hold it as long as they can. But the mob's numbers are too great, and they overrun the officers, forcing them to another location to regroup. The large circular room with its forty massive columns is completely filled with protesters. The sudden rush of banner- and flag-bearing rioters is reminiscent of a castle under siege.

2:20 p.m. Deputy Chief Jeffrey "J. J." Pickett arrives in the Command Center. Pickett has come in from the USCP training center in Cheltenham, Maryland, with his training staff. Thomas gives him a job handling the logistics of deploying the incoming resources inside and outside the Capitol. I promoted Pickett to a two-star deputy, and I know him to be very detail-oriented, so he's the right pick for such a dynamic and critical task. The cavalry is coming, and we must have a clear process of accounting for the officers and deploying them as quickly as possible to where they can do the most good.

I ask Pickett and Thomas to step into a back room with me so I can explain the process I want implemented. We have three goals: secure the building, clear the building, and reestablish our security perimeter. Thomas has already sent a captain from one of his divisions over to lot 16 to help Lieutenant Willis check in the responding agencies. Captain Verderese will swear the officers in as special police officers. Pickett will send his training staff over to lot 16 to escort outside agencies to their reporting locations, then coordinate with Loyd and Waldow to send them where they are needed most. Pickett's staff will then quickly walk the officers from lot 16 to the northwest door of the Dirksen Senate Office Building and then escort them through the subway tunnel to the Capitol and the location of their assignment.

The Capitol Building has a very confusing floor plan, and it's easy to get lost. After four years at the USCP, I still have some difficulty finding certain locations inside the building. In fact, it is this confusing layout of the building that will raise suspicions when some in the crowd quickly and unerringly make their way through the vast corridors of the Capitol in what appears to be a direct path to Majority Whip James Clyburn's office in room H-329. This gives the strong impression that they had advance knowledge of the location.

2:24 p.m. Trump tweets:

Donald J. Trump ✔
@realDonaldTrump

Mike Pence didn't have the courage to do what should have been done to protect our country and our constitution, giving states a chance to certify a corrected set of facts, not the fraudulent and inaccurate ones which they were asked to previously certify. USA demands the truth!

JAN 6, 2021

2:25 p.m. The House Chamber Officers, a unit within the USCP Capitol Division, initiates the evacuation of the remaining representatives from the House Chamber.

2:25 p.m. I receive word that the Department of Defense is trying to get me on a conference call to discuss my request for the National Guard. I receive a text message from Dr. Christopher Rodriguez, director of the DC Homeland Security and Emergency Management Agency. The text provides a telephone number and an access code for the conference call. A second text follows: "This is Chris Rodriguez."

I immediately call the number from my desk phone, enter the access code, and am placed on hold with elevator music. While on hold, I continue calling my partner agencies on my cell phone to coordinate support.

I wait maybe another minute and think something must be wrong, even though I've received a second text with exactly the same call information from General Walker. I hang up and call back several times, getting the same result. Between 2:25 and 2:34 p.m., I make several more attempts to get onto the DoD conference call, with no luck. It's bizarre—I make these types of calls several times a week without any problem.

2:26 p.m. I make a follow-up call to Assistant Chief Michael Anzallo with the Metro Transit Police to coordinate assistance coming to Capitol Hill.

2:28 p.m. I call Deputy Chief Tim Tyler with the Metropolitan Washington Airports Authority to coordinate the assistance they are sending us.

As I wait to be patched into the call with the Pentagon, Glover, who is fiercely fighting on the West Front and is now surrounded by the violent mob, screams over the radio: "Ten-thirty-three! Ten-thirty-three!" This is the distress call for "officer in trouble, send all available units." The MPD police dispatcher comes over the air: "Ask all military and sworn officers to come to the Capitol."

2:34 p.m. I text Rodriguez: "I am on the call. Only person."

Rodriguez calls me right back on my cell and patches me into the

Pentagon conference call, which is already in progress. Several people are on the line, including General Walker, Lieutenant General Piatt, Lieutenant General Charles Flynn (brother of General Michael Flynn), and other members of the DC National Guard and Pentagon military staff. Also on the call are various DC government officials, including Mayor Bowser, MPD Chief Contee, and Chris Rodriguez.

After waiting over seventy minutes to get the Capitol Police Board's approval to deploy the National Guard, I now have to sell my urgent request to the Pentagon command. It should be noted that the military operations center in Washington, DC, has police radios from the MPD and the USCP. I have little doubt they've already heard the fighting and the frantic pleas for assistance. With every big-screen TV in every office at the Pentagon tuned to the special reports from Washington, surely they already know what I am requesting.

"I have Chief Sund of the Capitol Police on the line," Rodriguez says. "Chief, are you requesting the assistance of the National Guard?"

At this point, I have been watching the battle rage on all sides of the Capitol for almost two hours. The rioters have now breached the building and are inside, along with members of Congress and the vice president. It is a true worst-case scenario. "Yes," I reply, "this is an URGENT, URGENT request for the National Guard," I say. "We are being overrun. I need assistance to reestablish the perimeter around the Capitol."

Lieutenant General Walter Piatt responds, "I don't like the optics of the National Guard standing a line with the Capitol in the background. I would much prefer to relieve USCP officers from other posts so they can handle the protesters."

It's safe to say he doesn't quite comprehend the gravity of the situation. "That is not an option," I say, my voice shaking with frustration. "I don't have officers on posts that I can swap out."

But Piatt doesn't like this answer and again states that he'd prefer to relieve my officers on traffic posts so they can respond to the riot. Once again, I try to explain to him that I don't have officers on traffic posts to swap out. They are ALL engaged in the fight!

As I am imploring—some would even say begging—the National

Guard for assistance, real-time images of my officers being beaten and bloodied are playing on the screens all around me. The brutal attack is being broadcast not just in my Command Center, but all around the world. One would think my request would be an easy decision for our military leaders. I am asking them to help us defend our Congress, the vice president, and our democratic process from this attack. But it just isn't sinking in for these people.

Piatt announces that he is getting ready to brief the secretary of the army and that his recommendation will be "not to support the request." It's a response I will never forget for the rest of my life. I am thunderstruck, dumbfounded, to hear these words from a military commander while the Capitol is under active siege. I feel nauseated.

Chief Contee, who can be a little forward sometimes, speaks up: "Whoa. Hold up a second. So you are denying the request from the chief of the Capitol Police?" Then he asks me to restate my question: "Steve, you are requesting National Guard assistance?"

"Yes," I say, going over the same ground yet again. "This is an urgent, urgent request. I need immediate assistance with National Guard at the Capitol. I do not have the option to swap out officers!"

But once again Lieutenant General Piatt repeats that he doesn't like the visual of the National Guard standing a line at the Capitol and repeats his useless suggestion to swap out my officers. He closes the subject by saying that he will run the request up the chain of command at the Pentagon.

John Falcicchio, the chief of staff for DC Mayor Bowser, will later say, "Literally, this guy is on the phone, I mean, crying out for help. It's burned in my memories."[3] Mayor Bowser will also be quoted: "Sund had made it perfectly clear that they needed extraordinary help, including the National Guard. There was some concern from the Army of what

3. Carol D. Leonnig, Aaron C. Davis, Peter Hermann, and Karoun Dimirjian, "Outgoing Capitol Police Chief: House, Senate Security Officials Hamstrung Efforts to Call in National Guard," *Washington Post*, January 10, 2021, www.washingtonpost .com/politics/sund-riot-national-guard/2021/01/10/fc2ce7d4-5384-11eb-a817-e5e7f 8a406d6_story.html.

it would look like to have armed military personnel on the grounds of the Capitol."

2:38 p.m. President Trump tweets:

> **Donald J. Trump** ✔
> @realDonaldTrump
>
> "Please support our Capitol Police and Law Enforcement. They are truly on the side of our Country. Stay peaceful!
>
> JAN 6, 2021

2:43 p.m. Even as I'm still on this absurd conference call with the Pentagon, I hear the frantic voice of an officer on the Command Center radio: "Shots fired in the Capitol, shots fired in the Capitol." The watch commander confirms the report and tells me that one person has possibly been shot.

My frustration has reached a boiling point. I am mad as hell at the repeated delays and stupid excuses I'm hearing as I try to get the military's assistance. Infuriated, I shout into the phone: "There are shots fired in the Capitol! Is that urgent enough for you now?"

The shooting means I need to get off the call and notify the two sergeants at arms so they can pass along the information to the congressional leadership. Once I make that call, I reach out to the commander of my Office of Professional Responsibility, Inspector Michael Shaffer. I ask Shaffer to connect with MPD to coordinate the use-of-force (and subsequent homicide) investigation.

(According to some reports, immediately after my conference call with the Pentagon, General Milley requested to get the attorney general on the phone so he could "get every cop in D.C. down there to the Capitol this minute, all seven to eight thousand of them."[4] But I find

---

4. Carol Leonnig and Philip Rucker, *I Alone Can Fix It: Donald J. Trump's Catastrophic Final Year* (New York: Penguin, 2021), 469.

this story patently ridiculous. Since when does the military order civilian police departments from multiple jurisdictions to deploy? Besides, I had already started calling police reinforcements myself within minutes of the attack and had already activated the MWCOG mutual-aid program before my conference call with the Pentagon. Instead of focusing on *my* job as the lead law enforcement officer, the general should have been focusing on *his* job and getting us the military assistance we so desperately needed.)

We heard an earlier report of shots being fired inside the Capitol, but luckily, these turned out to be false. But this time, we start to receive additional information about a victim and the request for medical assistance, all but confirming the shooting. I'm unsure whether it's a police officer or a rioter who has been shot.

For almost two hours now, the rioters have been viciously fighting with the police, breaking through barrier after barrier, getting closer and closer to where the members of Congress are located. We are repeatedly overrun. Police reinforcements are streaming in, but just when we think we can outmaneuver them, more rioters show up. Thousands of them will punch, kick, and club their way through the police lines onto the West Front and into the Capitol Building. As many as twenty-five thousand more protesters are still outside the building, chanting, pushing, shoving, and encouraging their more aggressive comrades.

The chamber officers are protecting the evacuating members. They can hear their fellow officers calling for help over the radio and the reports of multiple injuries to police as the mob continues to push forward and breach the building itself. Panicked voices from seasoned police officers shouting over the radio as they confront the riotous mob in hallways, passages, and staircases are not something the chamber officers ever imagined they would hear.

And now they know the mob is headed their way.

It's a terrifying reality that they are the next target, for a large group has finally arrived at the glass doors of the entrance to the Speaker's Lobby. The Speaker's Lobby is the area behind the House Chamber, where members of Congress, staff, and invited VIP guests can meet to hold discussions or wait to access the chamber. This is the very last physical barrier separating the remaining members of Congress from the mob, who are harassing the officers standing outside the glass door. One rioter raises his fist toward the officer's face but decides to smash the glass instead. One can only imagine the fear these officers are feeling as the blows keep flying past their heads. The attackers continue their assault on the door until they break the final pane of glass that separates them from the members of Congress. A member of the mob begins to climb through the window. Fearing for the lives of the members of Congress still in the chamber, a House Chamber officer on the other side of the glass pulls his service weapon and orders the individual to stop. When she does not comply and continues to climb through the window, the chamber officer fires at her, striking her once in the upper body.

Members of our CERT are just coming up the stairs to the entrance of the Speaker's Lobby when the shooting occurs. The officers immediately go to work, rendering first aid to the rioter who was shot. She is put on a stretcher and transported to the hospital as quickly as possible. The female, identified as Ashli Babbitt, will succumb to her wound and be pronounced dead at the hospital.

Almost simultaneous with this breach of the Speaker's Lobby is the breach of the Senate Chamber. Thankfully, the Senate Chamber has been completely evacuated before the mob can enter the chamber and defile the inner sanctum.

3:08 p.m. More resources are responding to my mutual-aid activation. I speak to the head of the Virginia State Police, Colonel Gary Settle, who says, "Steve, I have a platoon stationed here across the river just on the other side of the bridge. I'll probably take some flak for this but, brother, I can tell by your voice you need help, and I'm sending them your way."

3:10 p.m. Fairfax County Police Chief Ed Roessler receives approval from Fairfax County Deputy Executive Dave Rohrer to send police

officers to assist me. They both know me and realize that if I'm calling for help, it must be bad. Fairfax County Police sends a first wave
of civil disturbance unit officers, who will arrive at the Capitol around
4:00 p.m.

3:13 p.m. President Trump tweets:

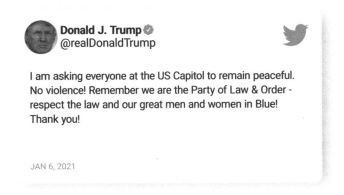

Donald J. Trump ✔
@realDonaldTrump

I am asking everyone at the US Capitol to remain peaceful.
No violence! Remember we are the Party of Law & Order -
respect the law and our great men and women in Blue!
Thank you!

JAN 6, 2021

In addition to the calls I'm handling with other law enforcement
agencies, I quickly learn that the press is very effective in finding my cell
phone number. Even in the middle of the attack, I have media outlets
reaching out to me. Needless to say, I don't have time for them.

3:15 p.m. MPD Officer Michael Fanone responds to provide relief for the
MPD officers. Once inside the Capitol, he hears a call for a 10-33 (officer
in distress) at the lower West Terrace door. When he and his partner
respond to the 10-33, he observes dozens of MPD officers positioned in
the tunnel leading to the lower West Terrace door, where they have been
fighting hundreds of rioters for over two hours. Fanone moves to the front
of the line to relieve the officers closest to the rioters. The rioters quickly
grab him and pull him into the crowd, separating him from his other MPD
officers. Once separated, he is beaten, stunned with a Taser, and threatened
with death from his own gun. Fanone is knocked unconscious and suffers
a heart attack before someone in the crowd assists in getting him back to
the officers near the door. He is taken to safety to seek medical assistance.

3:19 p.m. The highest levels of congressional leadership begin calling the Pentagon, demanding help from the military.[5] Both Pelosi and Schumer are told that the use of the National Guard has been approved but that the Guard still will not arrive on the Hill for another two hours. Schumer and Pelosi are unaware that I have just gotten off my Pentagon conference call, and hence know nothing of my repeated pleas for help from the military, who are clearly doing everything they can to keep the troops out of the fight on the Hill. It's ironic that I've been denied and delayed in getting the National Guard because of concerns about how it would go over with the Speaker, and yet now she can't get them here fast enough.

The military will report that they spend the next ninety minutes developing a plan to deploy to the Capitol, but none of that planning is being conducted in my Command Center, where it would make the most sense. We have maps of the campus, video feeds inside and outside the buildings, and the latest situational awareness. All I asked for on the call with the Pentagon was support to reestablish the perimeter of the Capitol. I don't need them inside clearing the Capitol! I need them to help maintain a perimeter line outside. How much effing planning does that take? Just days before, Miller and Milley had reportedly been so damned concerned about large-scale violence that they were considering locking down the city and revoking demonstration permits at the Capitol. If that was indeed the case, why the hell didn't they develop contingency plans in advance?

In between calls with the SAAs, I receive several calls from the FBI. The first is from Steve D'Antuono, director of the Washington Field Office. I met him virtually yesterday during my video call with the heads of the military and law enforcement agencies in the District of Columbia and, luckily, gave him my cell number. D'Antuono tells me that the number two at the FBI, David Bowdich, wants to talk to me about resources.

5. Lisa Mascaro, Ben Fox, and Lolita C. Baldor, "'Clear the Capitol,' Pence Pleaded, Timeline of Riot Shows," AP News, April 10, 2021, https://apnews.com/article/capitol -siege-army-racial-injustice-riots-only-on-ap-480e95d9d075a0a946e837c3156cdcb9.

I've met Dave before on a couple of occasions, including once when he came to the Hill for a Fourth of July celebration. Bowdich tells me that numerous members of Congress are calling him directly, requesting that he send support. He wants to send me tactical resources, specifically his SWAT teams, directly to the members' location. I tell him I'll take any support he can send but that I'll need to coordinate the resources with him or his designated official so we can use them in an efficient and coordinated fashion.

I feel that this is important, especially when dealing with heavily armed tactical units. The last thing I want is a lot of law enforcement agencies self-dispatching to the Capitol and trying to enter the building without any coordination. A lot of people coming into the Capitol in unusual olive-drab uniforms could create a very dangerous situation during such a chaotic event. I would always want a couple of clearly recognizable USCP uniforms with them to reduce the chances of a catastrophic *blue-on-blue* incident. Also, the FBI SWAT teams will need someone to guide them through the confusing Capitol layout. I end the call with a promise that Gallagher will reach out to Bowdich to coordinate.

About 3:30 p.m., I am advised that I have an important call in the office and need to step out and handle it. I walk out of the Command Center and down the hallway to my office and take the call from a desk in the outer office. A male voice comes on the line, and I immediately recognize it as the VPOTUS.

"This is Mike Pence. Is this Chief Sund?"

"Yes, sir."

"Chief, how are you doing?"

I'm a little surprised by the question, but I give him my best answer: "Sir, I have had better days."

"How are things going outside and in the Capitol?"

"Sir, it's bad." I tell the vice president that the Capitol has been breached by thousands of rioters and that the officers are fighting hard and that I am very proud of them. I describe the violent attack that began on the West Front, telling him, "It was some of the worst violence against law enforcement I have ever seen." I explain that the building and perimeter are still unsecured but that more law enforcement resources are arriving and that we are working diligently to take back control of the Capitol.

The vice president then asks me to come to his location and brief him on when we can get him back into chambers to certify the vote. "Sir, we are doing everything we can to regain control of the Capitol, but I'm not in a position to leave the Command Center." I tell him that I need to stay here and that it will be at least an hour before I'm available.

He accepts that and makes it clear that he doesn't want to distract me any longer. In a calm voice, he tells me he is adamant that he's going to stay at the Capitol and wants to make sure I understand "the importance of Congress getting back into session as soon as possible to certify the election."

"Sir, I completely understand your desire to get back into session, and I share that same interest," I reply. "I am doing everything I can to make that happen."

He asks for a good contact number and says he'll call me back in an hour. He then thanks me for everything the USCP and other law enforcement officers have been doing. With all the challenges of the moment, the VP is taking the time to inquire how the men and women in blue are doing, and it's greatly appreciated.

When I complete the call, I swipe my access card to reenter the Command Center. I tell the two assistant chiefs about the call, and then we're all back to work coordinating incoming resources. We've been receiving reports of members being stuck in their offices and hideaways inside the Capitol, afraid to come out. They're calling the USCP, the sergeants at arms, the FBI—anyone who can possibly help them. USCP and some of our federal partners head to locations on both the House and Senate sides of the complex to extract members and staff from offices and meeting rooms.

3:35 p.m. Pence tweets from his secure location on the Hill, "The violence and destruction taking place at the US Capitol Must Stop and it Must

Stop Now. Anyone involved must respect Law Enforcement officers and immediately leave the building.'"

3:37 p.m. Even though the military isn't sending resources to the Capitol in response to my urgent pleas for help, the Pentagon is sending resources to protect the homes of military leaders.[6] Their own security forces are guarding homes, even though no rioters or criminal attacks are occurring at those locations. This demonstrates to me that the Pentagon fully understands the urgency and danger of the situation even as it does nothing to support us on the Hill.

3:42 p.m. We are trying to gain control, but we are spread too thin. We've had breaches at multiple entrances and a shooting inside the Capitol. Hundreds of people are roaming around inside. At one of the exit doors to the West Front, dozens of protesters are filing past a limited number of officers who feel vulnerable. These officers, like others across the expansive building, are surrounded. They have seen the violent battles with the rioters and have heard the repeated calls for injured officers over the radio. To their credit, they are still manning their position and have not abandoned their post at the door. They know that things don't look good, and their training tells them to try to de-escalate the situation, especially if they don't have the resources to engage the group physically. In an apparent attempt at de-escalation in an unimaginably stressful scene, one Capitol officer obliges a protester with a selfie. This is clearly an act of self-preservation and nothing more. The very idea that he is somehow showing support for the insurrection is nothing short of ridiculous, as any officer who was there will tell you. None of these officers had ever imagined a breach of the Capitol by a mob of thousands, and now they were living it.

Elsewhere on campus, an African American official dons a MAGA hat, again in an effort to de-escalate and establish some kind of communication with the group. It will later be reported that he was successful in getting a group of protesters to move to another location, which allowed a group of trapped officers to escape and regroup with others.

(That said, while over 99 percent of my officers acted courageously and fought valiantly, there may have been a small handful of cases involving officers and officials of various demographics who performed less than admirably in the field that day.)

3:45 p.m. Three dozen Virginia State Police vehicles carrying almost seventy state troopers come rolling across the Fourteenth Street Bridge with their lights flashing and sirens blaring. Marked and unmarked sedans, vans, pickup trucks, and an armored personnel carrier—Colonel Settle is sending the cavalry from Arlington, Virginia. The caravan of emergency vehicles comes screaming out of the Third Street tunnel onto Massachusetts Avenue toward Union Station, turning south toward the Capitol. (Only two days ago, MPD arrested Proud Boys Leader Enrique Tarrio in this very tunnel after stopping his vehicle.) The caravan is obliged to take this route to the Capitol to avoid the thousands of protesters in the streets. The caravan stops on Constitution Avenue near the Capitol, and dozens of fully equipped troopers quickly create a platoon formation and double-time to the Capitol. These guys are huge, and the platoon formation looks like a moving seven-foot wall. They help us begin to clear the area of the lower west door to bring some relief to the MPD officers in the doorway. For the first time today, it feels as though the tide is finally beginning to turn in our favor. My officers will later tell me how happy they were to see the Virginia State Police, saying, "It was like the Three Hundred had arrived"—a reference to the Spartans at the Battle of Thermopylae.

3:47 p.m. USCP, supported by MPD, deploys gas inside the Capitol rotunda to try to clear the crowd. This is the first time in history that riot-control munitions are deployed inside the building. When the rotunda is cleared, the teams move to secure the broken doors.

3:48 p.m. SECARMY McCarthy leaves the Pentagon, heading to DC Police Headquarters on Indiana Avenue to go to the Joint Operations Command Center on the seventh floor to continue planning with the mayor and the chief of MPD.

Former DHS Secretary Chad Wolf will later say that the USCP initially turned down assistance from the DHS during the attack.[7] That could not be further from the truth. One of my first calls for support, within minutes of the attack, was to the DHS. In fact, I called and received support from a number of DHS agencies. The USSS (part of DHS) immediately sent me officers after the initial attack. In addition, at 3:32 p.m., DHS Police reported to lot 16 with a forty-member hard platoon.

Stenger offers to ask Senator Mitch McConnell to call the Pentagon and help move along our request for assistance from the National Guard. I answer him that any assistance would be appreciated. I call him back twenty minutes later to inquire about the request to McConnell, but it sounds as if this request has not yet been made. (I still don't know that the request was ever made.)

Meanwhile, more of the law enforcement resources I have been requesting are arriving on the scene.

3:58 p.m. Jim Dawson from the FBI calls me to coordinate additional support. Dawson is with Bowdich, and they are going to provide resources to secure the members of the Senate who are sequestered on the Hill. Dawson advises that they are still getting multiple calls from members of Congress asking for the FBI's help. Once they arrive, they are paired with USCP officers and deployed throughout the Hill.

FBI and ATF teams, combined with USCP officers, begin clearing parts of the building and responding to areas where officers need assistance. Captain Neysha Mendoza, who was the field force commander

7. Grace Segers, "Former DHS Chief Chad Wolf Says Capitol Police Initially Rejected Help on January 6," CBS News, March 4, 2021, www.cbsnews.com/news /capitol-riots-police-declined-help-january-6/.

during the MAGA I and MAGA II events, responds to provide assistance in the Capitol. MPD's CDU and DSO members have also joined forces with USCP officers.

Many of the officers from the USCP, MPD, and partner agencies report being involved in some fierce fighting inside the Capitol and genuinely fearing for their lives. A young USCP officer who recently joined the department after serving in the military has found one of the rioters' military-style tactical radios, and the transmissions he hears over the radio sound like something right out of a military playbook, using cryptic call signs and reconnaissance-style semantics.

4:06 p.m. The Senate sergeant at arms puts out a mass message via email and text advising members needing assistance to call the USCP. Some members are too afraid that the people at the doors could be members of the mob and not police officers. USCP Captain Sean Patton is working with Stenger's office to develop a process to help the members trapped in their offices validate the identity of the law enforcement officers who are responding to assist them.

4:07 p.m. I send an email to General Walker with the first of two formal letters requesting the National Guard. Even though we are in the middle of an attack, I still have to submit a formal written request. It may seem like a mere formality, but it's a key requirement for the National Guard.

4:08 p.m. Pence calls Acting SECDEF Miller, asking for the same information he was requesting from me. Pence wants to know when the Capitol will be secured. The military, however, is still trying to coordinate its response and develop a plan for sending the National Guard. No troops are coming—not even the quick reaction force that is fully prepared, equipped, and sitting at Andrews Air Force Base, right outside Washington. Pence's call to Miller lasts only a minute, and it doesn't appear that Miller can give the vice president the information he wants to hear.

Within minutes of this call, SECARMY McCarthy arrives at MPD headquarters to discuss the National Guard support with Mayor Bowser and Chief Contee. Months later, he will tell the DoD Inspector General that he went there "for situational awareness." But how can he get situational awareness regarding the Capitol from anywhere outside the Capitol and without involving the Capitol Police? Why didn't McCarthy come to Capitol Police headquarters for mission planning? (It has been suggested that McCarthy went to MPD headquarters because that is where Mayor Bowser was. The gossip around the office had him being considered for a job in the incoming Biden administration, and he needed Bowser on his side to help him solidify his future political position.)

The mission I am tasking the National Guard with involves my specific federal jurisdiction on the Capitol grounds. I am already in the process of deploying hundreds of law enforcement officers to defend the Capitol, and I can very easily integrate the National Guard into the forces being deployed to the perimeter. Again, we have the maps, video feeds, and latest situational awareness to handle this coordination most effectively, yet McCarthy has gone to the MPD command center instead, blocks away from the Capitol.

4:13 p.m. USCP has made enough progress that we can begin making limited arrests inside the Capitol.

4:17 p.m. Trump tweets a video from the Rose Garden telling the rioters,

Donald J. Trump ✓
@realDonaldTrump

We love you, go home and go in peace.

JAN 6, 2021

4:19 p.m. We have cleared and secured the Senate Chamber.

4:28 p.m. We have secured the basement of the Capitol and the subways. The first floor of the Capitol, including the Crypt, is secured. Officers begin securing all access points and the breached and broken doors and windows. The second floor of the Capitol is cleared, including the House Chamber.

4:30 p.m. According to the military leaders, officials at the Pentagon have now completed their planning, and General Walker has received word he can send his troops to the Capitol.

4:40 p.m. Pelosi and Schumer conduct a follow-up call with SECDEF Miller and General Milley. Pelosi and Schumer again call for the military to secure the perimeter. This is two hours after my call with the Pentagon in which I repeatedly pleaded for the military's assistance in securing our perimeter. Congressional leadership is now making the same plea and appears to be getting the same response. The call is reported to last thirty minutes and includes a discussion of the "obvious intelligence failures that led to the insurrection."[8] Even the governors of Maryland and Virginia are having trouble activating their National Guard forces and sending them to the Capitol as a result of Miller's January 4 memo directing the Guard not to "interact physically with protestors." (See Figure 4.4.)

For the past several hours, we have been battling a mob at the Capitol, and the fight has been televised around the world. We have multiple fatalities, including a fatal shooting inside the Capitol. We have had to secure members of Congress, the vice president and his family, and the next three levels of succession to the presidency of the United States. And the military has made no effort whatsoever to help end this.

(Knowing now that Miller and Milley had expressed such grave concern for mass violence at the Capitol in the days leading up to the attack, why did they then take such unprecedented steps to keep the National

8. Mascaro, Fox, and Baldor, "'Clear the Capitol,' Pence Pleaded."

Guard away from the Capitol? Some in the congressional leadership have even accused the military of knowing that the protesters planned to storm the Capitol.[9])

By now any "emergency response" from the military no longer matters. The USCP and our law enforcement partners have been left to defend the Capitol, the democratic process, and the Constitution, which we all swore to defend, on our own. Thank God I have not relied solely on the military today. My calls to my fellow law enforcement leaders paid off. We now have significant resources on-site and are in the process of methodically clearing the building and the grounds. Pickett and Thomas continue deploying the resources to Loyd and Waldow, and the tables are turning in our favor.

4:43 p.m. My cell phone rings, and the screen shows an odd sequence of numbers with no identifier. I've received similar calls in the past and know that it is probably going to be a call from somewhere or, more importantly, *someone* very important. I'm still in the Command Center, where it's hard to hear, so I leave the room for a secure hallway.

"Chief Sund. May I help you?"

A female voice on the other end of the call responds: "This is the White House. We are trying to reach Chief Sund of the US Capitol Police."

I thought this might be the POTUS calling to see what support or assistance we needed, so I reply, "Yes, ma'am, this is Chief Sund," and prepare myself to speak with President Trump.

"Stand by for the vice president of the United States," she says.

Okay, I was not expecting that, but Pence did say he would call me back. He is still in a secure location on the Hill under my watch, with his Secret Service detail and a team of USCP officers.

I update Pence on the current situation at the Capitol and tell him, "We are close to regaining control of the building and our perimeter." He again expresses concern for the officers and asks me to come to his

9. Mascaro, Fox, and Baldor, "'Clear the Capitol,' Pence Pleaded."

location to discuss when I think we can get Congress back into session to certify the vote. But I know we are at a critical point in our operations, and it is still not a good time for me to step away. I again advise Mr. Pence that I need more time, and he agrees to call me again in thirty minutes. I feel bad making the vice president wait, but I don't have another option.

4:45 p.m. USCP deploys munitions at a group trying to rebreach the rotunda doors. We are successful in pushing them back and away from the entrance.

4:46 p.m. USCP and partner agencies push the mob off the upper West Terrace, forcing some down toward the lower West Terrace and the West Front and forcing others around the Senate wing of the Capitol toward the East Front.

4:48 p.m. Partner agencies deploy chemical munitions at the lower West Terrace and at the door where some of the fiercest battles occurred earlier. The police are now pushing the mob off the stairs and away from the lower West Terrace door. The police line begins to push rioters away from the lower West Terrace down to the West Front lawn and toward First Street.

4:52 p.m. It is reported to the Command Center that USCP are making more arrests inside the Capitol.

5:00 p.m. For the first time, I feel confident that we are in a position to regain full control of the Capitol and Capitol Square. We have USCP, MPD, USSS, ATF, FBI, and other agencies inside the building, methodically clearing the various levels of the interior and doing final checks of offices, hallways, and hideaways. We are also conducting a final sweep of the Capitol to ensure that no explosives, weapons, or other hazardous devices have been left behind.

I can see on the video feeds that the East and West Fronts are beginning to be cleared of rioters. Many of the agencies I've contacted are now on the exterior with the MPD and USCP, reestablishing the perimeter and pushing the riotous mob away from the foundation of the building.

I step away from the dais and motion Pittman to join me in the hallway. She follows, and we meet Thomas in the hallway. I tell both of them the vice president has again requested that I come and brief him on the situation. I feel we are at a point where I can step away and head over to the Capitol, not only to meet briefly with the VP but also to do a personal assessment of the situation.

Pittman returns to the Command Center, and Thomas steps into his office. I head toward my office to make some calls. I speak to the lead for the vice president's Secret Service detail, Special Agent Tim Giebels. I advise Giebels that I can be over to brief the VP in about twenty minutes. Before leaving, I tell Chad I'll be available on my cell if needed and that he has command until I return. I then head toward the bank of elevators to go to the ground floor of headquarters.

5:08 p.m. Army Chief of Staff General James McConville finally informs General Walker that the Secretary of Defense has authorized the DC National Guard to deploy to the Capitol in support of the USCP.

As I walk out of police headquarters, it's starting to get dark. I can see the aura of the bright white floodlights reflecting off the Capitol dome into the dark sky. I think back on all the appalling things I've witnessed today. Then I look across D Street to lot 16, at all the activity going on under portable lights brought in by the Architect of the Capitol. This is where all the outside agencies I contacted are still checking in and getting their assignments. It's a comforting sight.

On my way to meet the VP, I walk through the congressional subway system, from the Dirksen Building to the Capitol. I see a haze of dust in the air and smell the chemical riot-control irritant. It's a smell I know well, having used it as a police officer in defensive situations at violent mass demonstrations, as well as being on the receiving end a couple of times during my career. I can't believe I'm now smelling this inside the US Capitol.

The marble floors of the hallways are wet with a mixture of chemical and pepper spray, powder from fire extinguishers, vomit, and other bodily fluids. There is dust on the floors and walls. The once pristine hallways are littered with debris, broken furniture, flags, water bottles, and trash.

I have never seen, nor could I have ever imagined, parts of the Capitol looking this way. All I can think is, *How did this happen? How did we go from a demonstration to an attack on our government by angry Americans?*

I run into officers on my way. Many are standing in groups, stunned and silent. They look dazed as if they've been to hell and back. Their uniforms are covered with dirt and dust. Many look at me with a vacant expression, the thousand-yard stare, barely blinking. They have just been through a situation that we never imagined—an attack on the Capitol by thousands of violent, rioting fellow Americans. I stop to check on all of them that I can as I walk through the halls. Many of the officers I recognize from my regular walks through the Capitol, others from recent graduating recruit officer classes. Many are covered in stains from various fluids, their eyes red and swollen, tears and snot still running down their faces. They keep pouring water on their faces to wash off the stinging chemical cocktail, with little relief. Uniforms are torn and missing badges and insignia, lost in the attack. Uniforms that started the day midnight blue are wet, crusty, more gray than blue, and the crisp, bright-white shirts are stained shades of yellow, orange, red, and brown, each hue telling a story of a separate attack, a distinct incident involving another assailant and another substance. I can see that these officers are hurting physically, mentally, and emotionally. They're in shock and disbelief, trying to make sense of everything that has happened, yet they're concerned enough to ask me how I'm doing.

The knot in my stomach that has been there ever since I first saw the officers on the outer perimeter getting hit has grown even bigger and more painful. The electric buzz flowing through my body has not stopped, and it feels as though it never will. I fight back tears, seeing my officers and my Capitol look this way.

We were violently attacked, and parts of the building were taken over. And now we're all hurting together, but we have no idea what nasty digs and diatribes are already coming from the media, the public, and even some of our members of Congress. We don't know yet about the condemnations that will come from all sides—from the Left because they think we're the stereotypical racist, hateful police who only beat and shoot unarmed Black people; and from the Right for fatally shooting an unarmed female "patriot." Even Biden will chime in, angrily accusing us of a double standard—the same man who, just five years earlier, was shaking my hand and telling me not to retire from the MPD because the world needs good cops.

None of us know any of this yet because we're all still too busy doing our jobs in the best way we can.

5:36 p.m. I arrive where we've relocated the vice president and his family. As I round the corner, I immediately recognize Pence's distinctive white hair and stature. He's standing near a couple of black USSS Suburbans, talking to his lead agent and another gentleman in a suit. I briefly speak with a couple of my USCP Special Ops guys and some of my SWAT officers who are protecting the vice president. Several USSS Counter Assault Team (CAT) officers are also there. The USCP CERT and the USSS CAT are SWAT team officers, equipped with special weapons and highly trained. I step down a couple of stairs and walk a short distance to where the vice president is standing. He turns to me and in his characteristic soft voice says, "Chief, thank you for coming to see me. How are you and your officers doing?"

I tell him that it's been a pretty tough day and that the officers put up a hell of a fight. "Everyone's doing about as well as could be expected."

He asks me if I know his brother, motioning to the gentleman with him. He introduces me to Greg Pence, a member of the House of Representatives. Greg shakes my hand and says, "I appreciate everything the Capitol Police do for us on the Hill."

The vice president tells me he would really like to get back to certifying the votes and that no one has been able to give him a clear idea when this could happen. He again reiterates that he doesn't want to leave the Capitol and is willing to wait as long as necessary.

I tell him that it's been awful outside but that we've secured the perimeter and are in the process of clearing the Capitol. I want to get the latest update, so I ask Pence to give me a minute so I can make a call to confirm. I step away and call Thomas, ask him a series of specific questions, and then tell him I'm with the VP and need to confirm the details as soon as possible.

Thomas tells me he'll call right back. I go back to my conversation with Pence, and then a few minutes later I get the call with the update I need. Based on the latest updates from the commanders on the ground, Loyd and Waldow, we can get both houses of Congress back into their chambers around 7:00 p.m. But the Architect of the Capitol needs another thirty minutes to clean up the chambers before they can be reoccupied.

When I tell Pence we can have him back in the chambers by 7:30 p.m., he responds, "Chief, based on what you're telling me, I think we should call the Speaker and have you relay this to her with me on the call."

I know my information has to be as accurate as possible, so I ask the VP for another minute to make one more call. I want to call Irving to let him know that Pence is getting ready to call Pelosi and to make sure Irving doesn't have any issues with the proposed timeline to get the House back in session. Pence is waiting politely, but now he's starting to pace, and I feel terrible making the vice president of the United States wait. But I want to make sure every detail is in place before the call to the Speaker.

When everything is finally confirmed, I tell Pence that I'm ready to make the call with him. He dials Pelosi on his cell phone and places it on a ledge so we can both hear the call.

I hear the distinctive voice of Speaker Pelosi: "Mr. Vice President."

"Madam Speaker," Pence says, "I have the chief of the Capitol Police, Steven Sund, with me, and he is advising me that we will be able to reconvene to certify the election tonight." Then he looks at me and says, "Chief, can you tell the Speaker the same information you told me?"

I tell the Speaker that we're in the final stages of clearing the building of rioters and checking for any hazardous devices. I advise that we have reestablished the perimeter and are in the process of pushing the rioters off Capitol grounds, that I have talked to the Capitol Division and we will be ready to get both the House and the Senate back into their chambers by 7:30 p.m. I also tell her we've reached out to the Architect of the Capitol, and they'll be able to do a cleaning of the House Chamber by that time as well.

Pelosi responds in a very concerned voice: "Are you confident about this timeline?"

"Yes, ma'am," I answer. "I am certain."

Pence tells the Speaker that based on my information, he would like to get back into session as soon as possible. Pelosi says she will discuss this with the other congressional leaders, and the call concludes.

As Pence puts his phone away, he says to me, "Thank you, Chief. I appreciate you confirming that and speaking to her with me."

Throughout this meeting, a White House photographer has been present in the room with us. When I first arrived, the photographer was about to take a shot of Pence and me, but Pence waved him off. But now, at the conclusion of our meeting, perhaps feeling that the timing might be more appropriate, Pence allows the photographer to take a photo of the two of us before I depart. Within minutes, my picture with him will appear on Pence's official Twitter feed.

Little did I know that as I was meeting with the vice president, the first contingent of the National Guard had finally arrived on the Hill.

5:40 p.m. Over four and a half hours after the violent attack on the West Front began, Captain Brian Verderese swears in the first 155 troops as special police officers, and they begin to be deployed to assignments to help support the perimeter. By now, all the fighting is over, and by the time the National Guard troops reach their assigned posts, the rioters have been pushed out of Capitol Square and the perimeter is already secured. General Walker arrives on the Hill with the troops and will later confide in me, saying, "Steve, I felt so bad. I wanted to help you immediately, but I couldn't. I could hear the desperation in your voice, but they wouldn't let me come. When we arrived, I saw the New Jersey State Police. Imagine how I felt. *New Jersey got here before we did!*"

He says all this even though the DC National Guard headquarters and armory are less than two miles east of the Capitol.

5:50 p.m. All rioters are cleared off the West Front to First Street.

5:52 p.m. All rioters are pushed off East Front Plaza.

5:59 p.m. At the conclusion of my meeting with the vice president, as I leave the secure location with the officers protecting the second-in-command,

I give a nod to my officers and head down a long hallway. I then call Irving to update him about my call with Pence and Pelosi.

"Thank you, Chief," he says. "How are you holding up?"

"Like shit," I say.

He says he feels the same way, and ends the call.

6:00 p.m. The rioters have been pushed away from the Capitol and off Capitol Square, and the security perimeter has been successfully reestablished.

While I've been away from the Command Center, the room has become flooded with more personnel from the USCP and the various agencies that responded to assist us. It is reported that Thomas, Gallagher, and Pittman have all left the dais. Although Thomas and Pittman are officially part of the Critical Incident Management Team—a group of key officials designated to implement command and control of extreme situations—they both have left the dais and are not providing any command presence. With the command positions vacant, Jeff Carroll and Morgan Kane, with whom I worked closely at MPD, step in to fill the void and the seats at the dais.[10]

At one point, Carroll approaches Pittman, who is on her phone, and interrupts her to recommend that the USCP consider obtaining eight-foot antiscale fencing to reinforce the perimeter in case the mob tries to return once we succeed in pushing them out of the area.

But there is reportedly some concern on Pittman's part about who is going to authorize and pay for the fencing. After informing Pittman that he will authorize the fence, Carroll calls Contee on his cell phone. Contee is sitting in the MPD Joint Operations Command Center with Mayor Bowser and Secretary of the Army McCarthy. When McCarthy hears that there is a concern about who's going to pay for the fence, he steps in and agrees to have the DoD pay for it.

As the head of the Dignitary Protection Division, Schneider has evacuated off the Hill with the congressional leadership to the secure

10. United States Capitol Police, *USCP Directive 1052.003: Incident Command System* (internal restricted document).

location. House leadership is in one room, and Senate leadership in another, a short distance away. Senator Grassley keeps moving between the two rooms, getting information from Pelosi and then returning to the Senate side. Pelosi is reportedly growing increasingly impatient and angry, looking for someone to brief her. Schneider does her best to brief Pelosi regarding the condition of the Capitol, but based on the information she has at this time, Schneider advises Pelosi that neither chamber will be in any condition to be occupied until tomorrow morning at the earliest. Pelosi is reportedly not happy with this, having just received conflicting information from me during the call with her and Pence. She asks her director of operations, Emily Berret, to get the USCP chief on the phone.

6:01 p.m.: Trump tweets a post suggesting that the Capitol riot was the result of a fraudulent election.

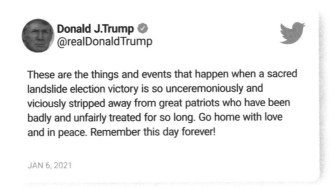

Donald J. Trump ✓
@realDonaldTrump

These are the things and events that happen when a sacred landslide election victory is so unceremoniously and viciously stripped away from great patriots who have been badly and unfairly treated for so long. Go home with love and in peace. Remember this day forever!

JAN 6, 2021

He says before deleting the tweet.

6:05 p.m. As I'm walking back to the Capitol, I run into Stenger. He looks tired and weary. He's walking with some of the staff from his office, and I join in with the group. Unlike Irving, who always seems to speed-walk, Stenger takes it at a much slower pace. As I'm telling him about the meeting I've just had with Pence and the progress we've made clearing the Capitol Building and securing the grounds, someone in the group passes a phone up to me and says, "Chief, Speaker Pelosi is on the phone, and she wants to talk to you."

I step a couple of feet away to take the call. "Why did you tell the VP that we could be back in chambers tonight?" Pelosi asks me. "I just received a briefing and am being told that the chambers would not be in a condition to be reoccupied until tomorrow morning at the earliest."

I can tell by the tone of her voice that she's very upset. "Ma'am, the information I provided you and the VP is correct," I say. "I am not sure who is advising you otherwise."

Just then I hear another female voice speak up. Pelosi's phone is on speaker. "Chief Sund, this is Inspector Schneider. I have been in touch with Inspector Loyd and he advised that the chambers would not be ready until tomorrow."

I've always been afraid of conflicting and divergent information being briefed by different people, especially during critical incidents. I've seen it happen before, and I have no doubt it will happen again. It is just the nature of everyone needing immediate information and looking for it from any available source. "Kim, that is no longer the case," I tell her. "I just spoke to Assistant Chief Thomas, who confirmed this timeline with both Inspector Loyd and the Architect of the Capitol. The chambers are secured but will need thirty minutes for the AOC to clean them. So the chambers will be ready to be occupied by seven thirty p.m."

"Ma'am, I trust this information," Inspector Schneider says to Pelosi. "It appears that the chambers will be ready by seven thirty."

At this point, the call abruptly ends. I pause, take a breath, and return the phone to its owner. This is my second time to speak with Pelosi since the attack.

As I continue to walk with Stenger, he informs me he's on his way to where they've sequestered the Senate. He may have to provide them with an update on the current status of the Capitol and asks if I would be available to attend with him.

"No problem," I say. As we continue through the Capitol complex, I see more signs of destruction and more injured officers. Finally, we arrive at the location where the Senate is gathered, and we are met by the

FBI's Hostage Rescue Team—a large group of heavily equipped agents, here from the Quantico Marine Base in Virginia. I'm told that when they arrived, they fast-roped off their Black Hawk helicopters into lot 16. As I walk through the big team of heavily armed SWAT operators, I know the Senate is well protected, but I can't help wondering what might have transpired if the rioters had made it this far.

We arrive in a narrow, brightly lit hallway. Unlike most of the other hallways around the Capitol, it has no pictures on the walls, and it's lined with hidden access doors into adjacent rooms. We enter an office that looks more like a waiting room in a funeral home than a workspace. My eyes have to adjust from the brightly lit hallway to this dim room. Two ornate couches are positioned against opposite walls, next to end tables with colonial-style brass lamps, and there are four armchairs with a damask print that matches the couches.

Several people are seated around the room. Many of them I recognize as leadership staff: Kelly Fado, Democratic liaison to the Senate sergeant at arms under Senator Schumer, Secretary of the Senate Julie Adams, and Robert Karem, the national security and defense advisor for Senator McConnell.

Stenger sits down on the couch along the far wall. I take a moment to look at him and think to myself that he doesn't look good. He's spent four decades in law enforcement, and I know that seeing all the injured officers today has to be taking a toll on him.

I don't feel like sitting down, so I remain standing. Fado asks me how it looks outside and how the officers are doing. I tell her how bad it was and that the officers fought hard against a mob of thousands for well over an hour before the group managed to break into the Capitol. I add that we were able to get a lot of support from our partner law enforcement agencies and that we are in the process of clearing Capitol Square of protesters.

Stenger says, "Chief, tell them about your plan to get the House and Senate back into chambers."

I give them the same information I gave to Pence and Pelosi: "We are in the final stages of sweeping the Capitol Building for rioters and hazardous devices, and the chambers will be cleaned and ready to be reoccupied by seven thirty p.m."

Everyone in the room appears satisfied with this information, and there are no additional questions. But Karem tells me that leadership is also waiting for a briefing. "I'll see if I can get them all on a call," he says as he pulls out his phone and starts dialing.

About 6:25 p.m. Robert Karem places the call to the congressional leadership from his cell phone. He speaks briefly before putting his phone on speaker and placing it on a table in the middle of the room. On the call are Speaker Pelosi, Senator Schumer, Senator McConnell, Representative Clyburn, and possibly others. The leaders of the most powerful institution in the United States and, arguably, the world are all on this one phone on this little table. They all were whisked off campus to shield them from a rapidly advancing violent mob. Waiting at the secure location, they all watched the news reports of the attack and received text updates and inquiries about their safety. They are furious about the attack and having to flee the seat of democracy, a place they had always felt was safe and secure, a place that many of them have called home for decades.

"I am here with the chief of the United States Capitol Police, Chief Steven Sund," Stenger says. "I'm going to have the chief provide an update."

I don't have notes to brief from, but addressing a group and thinking on my feet is one of my better skills. First, I want them to know just how hard the USCP, MPD, and many other agencies fought to protect them and defend the institution. I explain that I contacted a number of my federal, state, and local law enforcement partners for immediate assistance and that they all came without delay or hesitation. I explain that officers battled for hours: "Because of the support the USCP has received from other law enforcement agencies, we have been able to regain control of the building and the Capitol grounds." I inform them that we are in the process of doing a final sweep of the building for suspects and hazardous devices and that we found firearms on the grounds and inside the Capitol during the sweeps. The last thing I want is to return Congress to its chambers and have someone injured by a hazardous device or a discarded firearm.

I advise them of my current timeline for getting the House and Senate back into joint session and discuss the condition of the Capitol. Finally, I inform them that there has been significant damage and that the building will require a major cleaning, but the chambers will be ready by 7:30 p.m.

As I brief, everyone is silent. Once I finish, there are some discussions on the other end of the line between the congressional leaders, about when each side feels that it will be ready to get back into session. I think some are surprised that I'm telling them they can be back in as little as an hour.

At the conclusion of the call, both the House and the Senate decide to go back into session at 8:00 p.m. But then shortly after the call, the House pushes its start time to 9:00 p.m.

This briefing of congressional leadership is the third and final time I've spoken to Pelosi since the attack began five and a half hours ago. This fact will matter tomorrow.

Everyone leaves the office to go and brief the remaining members of the Senate. As Stenger walks past me, I tell him I need to use the restroom. When I walk in and turn on the light, I see my face in the mirror. I look like crap and feel worse. When I finish, I wash my hands and splash cold water on my face. I dry my face off and look back in the mirror one more time. *Yup, still look like shit.*

It's the first moment I've had to myself since the attack began at 12:52 p.m. When I step out of the office to rejoin Stenger in the hallway, he says, "If you need to leave and return to headquarters, I understand. I can brief the senators on my own."

I tell Stenger I really need to get back to the Command Center and I would rather pass on participating in the next briefing. I get the impression that he'd like to pass on it too, but he agrees I'm needed back at the Command Center and lets me go.

As I'm walking back to headquarters, Schumer returns to the location where the Senate is safely sequestered. Senator Schumer, Stenger, and USCP Captain Sean Patton go to the front of the room to brief the senators and their staff. The briefing doesn't go well for Stenger. He usually talks in a fairly low, quiet voice, and the senators get frustrated when they can't hear him. They're already mad about the whole situation, and the poor performance at the briefing doesn't make things any better. The senators are brutal with him. He's a goldfish swimming into a school of piranhas. Some at the briefing report hearing Stenger mumble to himself, "I wish I had just retired last week."[11]

Shortly after 7:00 p.m., uniformed USCP officers and the FBI tactical team escort the Senate back to the Capitol.

7:00 p.m. Pelosi returns to Capitol Hill from the secure off-site location with Representative Steny Hoyer. They stop by the Longworth House Office Building to brief members of the House before continuing to the Capitol.

Sometime after 7:00 p.m., as I walk by the Dirksen Senate Office Building back toward USCP headquarters, I see that activity in lot 16 has picked up quite a bit. At least one large command vehicle is now set up in the lot, along with a lot of military personnel and other vehicles in the area. More portable lights illuminate the area, and I see groups of soldiers in formation. I'm glad they've finally arrived. It's about time.

I walk to the west door, swipe my security card, and enter the building. As I walk down the first-floor hallway, I look at the pictures of various Capitol Police officers on the wall. Officers from the Ceremonial Unit, K9 officers, officers on mountain bikes. Sadly, I know that the history of this department moving forward will forever reflect January 6. I pass the plaque memorializing the Capitol Police officers lost in the line of duty: Eney, Crenshaw, Gibson, and Chestnut. I tap on the glass partition separating the security screening area from the lobby to get the attention of the officers posted there. I do this every time I enter or leave the building, just to check on the officers and acknowledge them. I hit the elevator button and head up to the seventh floor.

As soon as the elevator doors open, I am met by a number of military personnel and some police officers from partner agencies in my outer

11. Rosalind S. Helderman, Beth Reinhard, Karoun Demirjian, and Carol D. Leonnig, "House Security Chief Said Lawmaker Wariness of Military at Capitol Drove His Resistance to Early Request for National Guard," *Washington Post*, January 18, 2021, www.washingtonpost.com/politics/paul-irving-capitol-attack/2021/01/18/59fb4aae -567d-11eb-a931-5b162d0d033d_story.html.

lobby. I don't go back to my office but head down an exterior hallway that leads directly to the Command Center. I swipe my security badge on the sensor and hear the loud clunk of the door lock disengaging, and I push open the door. The Command Center is packed.

I make my way up to the dais, where MPD's Assistant Chief Jeff Carroll and Commander Morgan Kane are sitting. Jeff, who has bright-red hair and is about six feet six, stands up and says, "Let me get out of your chair."

I take my seat and say to both Carroll and Kane, "Thank you for coming and saving our ass. I know MPD has been through hell. Please let them know how appreciative we are."

When Kane asks me how I'm doing, I say, "About as well as can be expected." I recognize Dean and Ebert, friends from DC National Guard, and give a quick hello. Then I go back to work.

I ask for an update on where we are, what's been done, and what still needs to be done. Carroll says they have reestablished the perimeter and are pushing people all the way back to Third Street. He adds that the Department of Defense is procuring fencing to better secure the Capitol and that it should be arriving in the morning.

I ask Carroll what his intel is seeing as far as the protesters leaving the area. He tells me many have already left, some returning to buses that brought them to DC, others returning to their hotels. Carroll tells me that a lot of people are still milling around outside the police lines, and he wants to make sure we're not vulnerable to a repeat attack.

Pittman gives me an update on the leadership, and I relay the information from my meetings with the VP and briefing of congressional leaders. Thomas is working with Pickett regarding the immediate deployment of the National Guard and advises me that they'll be developing a plan for the deployment to cover the next several days. He adds that Pickett will be acting as the National Guard liaison and is in the process of developing the staffing requirements needed for the Guard to help secure the Capitol and the congressional office buildings. Thomas also gives a brief update on the law enforcement agencies that have responded to assist. Pickett, Verderese, and Willis have done a good job of accounting for and deploying the resources as quickly as possible.

Carroll mentions that the mayor has implemented a 6:00 p.m. curfew that is now in effect. My general counsel then chimes in: "Chief, in order for us to be able to enforce the curfew, we would need to get an approved Capitol Police Board order." *Again, more bureaucracy.*

"Please prepare one for my review to send over to the Board," I tell him. Then I ask Wisham for an update on our assessment of the damage to the Capitol Building. The damage is significant. Several exterior windows and doors have been smashed. The inaugural platform has some damage, but it appears that it could be repaired before inauguration day. The inside of the Capitol is a mess. Offices have been ransacked. Debris is strewn throughout the hallways, and the residue of chemical munitions and fire extinguishers covers the floor, furniture, walls, and statues. Members of Congress must be told to be careful touching anything, over concerns about cross contamination or disturbing dust containing chemical irritants.

While clearing Capitol Square and enforcing the curfew, police give chase to an individual who was involved in the riots and is now violating the curfew. The individual is apprehended in the 100 block of First Street NE, between the Capitol and the Supreme Court. He is found to be in possession of a loaded 9mm handgun and is charged with a number of violations, including possession of a firearm on Capitol grounds and a curfew violation.

Things are finally beginning to calm down. The DoD is now on the scene, and I have representatives from many of my partner agencies in the Command Center: MPD, US Park Police, Metro Transit Police, Federal Protective Service, Supreme Court Police, and the National Guard. A more organized command structure is beginning to settle in. But several critical issues remain to be dealt with. One of the most important is developing our security plan moving forward and also a plan to relieve the law enforcement agencies that have provided assistance, so we can get their officers back home.

7:20 p.m. The remaining floors and offices of the Capitol are declared to be clear of rioters and any hazardous devices.

8:00 p.m. I do another quick check-in with my wife to let her know I'm okay. She tells me our teenage son is having a rough time with all the negative coverage.

"They're making you guys out to be the Keystone Cops, who gave up the ship at the first sign of trouble. The stuff they're spewing is just awful. They are saying cops were waving people in and that they opened gates for them."

"Gates? We don't *have* any gates!"

"I know that, but that's what they're all reporting. All this BS is affecting the kids. Maybe you can call and talk to him for a bit?"

I put in a quick call to our son.

"Dad," he says, "some people are saying some pretty bad things about you and the police."

I tell him people say all sorts of things and he should try not to spend too much time on the internet. I don't want him subjected to that kind of negativity. I want him to know that I couldn't be prouder of my officers and all the police officers who came to assist. "I'm okay," I say, "and everything will be all right. I love you."

"I love you too, Dad."

I tell him I'll call him in the morning and to try to get some sleep tonight.

I continue on the phone with a series of calls to Irving, Stenger, Thomas, and Pittman, coordinating security as the House and Senate prepare to come back into session.

8:06 p.m. The Senate is gaveled back into session.

9:01 p.m. The House is gaveled back into session.

Although I have already ordered Pittman and Gallagher to request that the House and Senate recording studios preserve their records and footage from the chambers, Representative Ryan sends us an email directing us to preserve videos of the event. He is calling for an investigation, which I support unequivocally. But instead of investigating the overall security failings, the politicians are focused more on the allegations of officer misconduct.

9:26 p.m. Less than ten hours after the attack, Tim Ryan is featured prominently in a Politico article titled, "Capitol Police Firings Imminent after 'Attempted Coup,' Top Appropriator Warns." In the article, Ryan addresses the allegations that officers were opening the barricades and letting rioters through, stating, "I have no idea why that would be permissible. That's unacceptable." Ryan also says, "If Black people were storming the Capitol, they would have been treated so much differently than they were today. I don't think there's any question that communities of color would have been handled much, much differently. I think it's pretty clear that there's going to be a number of people who are going to be without employment very, very soon."

The following day, Jamie Fleet, from one of my oversight committees, will request a comparison of our arrest numbers from January 6 compared to other protests on Capitol grounds, specifically the Black Lives Matter protests. After everything law enforcement has been through today, I am perplexed by the interest in comparing January 6, a major climactic day for my agency, to the anticlimactic Black Lives Matter protests we experienced on the Hill. We had very limited Black Lives Matter protests on the Hill during 2020, and I provided briefings on these demonstrations to my oversight committees. We had only six arrests at Black Lives Matter protests and no reported use of force. In fact, we had restricted the deployment of certain less lethal weapons as a direct result of some of the reported injuries at Black Lives Matter protests across the country. There is NO comparison, and the only people drawing one are just trying to score cheap political points at our expense.

Later that evening, I run into Waldow in our headquarters. His face is still swollen and red from the burning of the chemical munitions, and his uniform is dirty and disheveled from battle. I can see he has been through hell, and this large and powerful man has been reduced to tears over what he faced today. It's gut-wrenching to see such a respected and admired police officer so emotionally and physically scarred. His is just one of many untold stories of the heroism and bravery that happened today.

10:02 p.m. The secretary of the CPB distributes the final version of the board order to the three voting members, officially implementing the emergency declaration necessary for me to legally call in the assistance of the National Guard and other federal resources.

As usual, Salley Wood is anticipating my future needs. She is my Radar O'Reilly without the grape Nehi soda. To the extent that I've done well during the pandemic and in my time as chief, it is in large part because Salley is such a brilliant chief of staff. Salley knows that members of Congress and my oversight committees will be calling for briefings. House and Senate Appropriations have already reached out and scheduled a call for eleven o'clock tonight. Salley had the foresight to begin developing a briefing sheet with the initial information we had about the attack and details on the impact on the agency.

Although the National Guard sends ranking representatives over to the Command Center this evening to help coordinate their resources, I don't hear anything about the secretary of the army coming to the Capitol until General Walker texts me at 10:20 p.m. The text reads, "The Secretary of the Army would like to come to your office to meet you and discuss the way ahead for additional support at 2330 hours. Please let me know if we can meet with you tonight. Thanks so much. VR MG Walker."

I immediately respond to Walker, letting him know I will be available.

10:40 p.m. I am notified that Officer Brian Sicknick has collapsed and is unresponsive. Officer Sicknick, who was involved in the battle, collapsed while walking with a group of officers to get something to eat. One of the officers in the group with him was Chris Grzelak, a Virginia state trooper and a tactical medic. Grzelak immediately went to work on Brian, providing CPR and trying to resuscitate him until DC Fire and Emergency Services arrived on the scene. Brian never regained consciousness and was transported by DC Fire to George Washington University Hospital.

11:00 p.m. Accompanied by my two assistant chiefs and Tad and Salley, I join the call with my appropriations committee to discuss the attack. On the call is the chairman of the Appropriations Committee, Representative Tim Ryan. Also on the call are Senator Chris Murphy, Senator Cindy Hyde-Smith, and Representative Jaime Herrera Beutler. I already received a notification earlier in the day that Ryan would be calling for an investigation, but right out of the gate, he is extremely upset. Actually, *livid* would be a better description.

"How can something like this happen!" he shouts. "How could you allow something like this to happen? Why were you not prepared for this to happen?"

Try as I might to explain our preparations, he doesn't want to hear it. It's his call, and he has plenty he wants to say, starting with blaming the police for everything that went wrong. It's apparent he has no faith and no trust in his police department, and although we end up discussing a number of topics including arrests and the allegations of misconduct against some of the officers, a big part of the call revolves around our use-of-force policy. Ryan is upset that officers didn't resort to shooting the protesters. "How come the officers didn't open fire? You just let them in!" As if not shooting them dead were equivalent to an open invitation.

When I explain our standard law enforcement policy and training regarding the use of lethal force, he shouts, "Then why didn't you change the policy!"

"You cannot just change the policy in the middle of an incident," I say. "Officers are trained when and when not to shoot." I go on to explain that there were thousands of rioters and that even though some police officers faced a number of situations where lethal force may have been justified, tactically it was not the right decision.

"So if, on an ordinary day, someone ran past one of your officers at an entrance and into the building, you wouldn't shoot them?" he asks.

"The officer would have to assess the situation," I say. "Simply running past an officer at one of our entry points is not a lethal-force situation. There could be other reasons someone runs into a building besides nefarious ones. You could be dealing with a distraught person or an emotionally disturbed person, or possibly a staffer who is late to an important meeting."

I conclude by saying, "Unless that individual posed an immediate threat of death or serious bodily injury, no, we would not shoot them."

"So you wouldn't shoot," Ryan says. "Then why do we have you here?"

He continues his loud diatribe while everyone else on the call remains silent. It's kind of ironic: Ryan has written a book on "mindfulness," and here he is, definitely in the moment, digging into my ass.

Putting people down or shouting has never been my style, though I do understand, given the emotions of today, how some people may need to vent. So I stay calm and explain to him, "Sir, there is a reason why seventeen law enforcement agencies responded and *all* of them utilized the same level of force. It is how law enforcement is trained. There were thousands of people in the crowd, and officers were fighting for their lives and highly stressed. Officers are accountable for every bullet that they shoot. Under those circumstances, even in a justifiable situation, the chance of missing your intended target and hitting another law enforcement officer or an unintended individual is high. Turning to less lethal weapons and chemical munitions were the better options."

Ryan still isn't having it. He's actually hoarse now from all the yelling. "We will continue this conversation in the morning!" he says, and sure enough, a follow-up meeting is placed on my calendar for nine the next morning.

When the call ends, I look around at my staff. They're silent and look stunned. Tad will later describe the call as "brutal."

I leave the room and go to my conference room with my executive team to wait for McCarthy. The secretary of the army is coming to the Command Center to meet with some of the National Guard representatives. I'm tired now, sick to my stomach, and I have a million things going through my mind.

McCarthy walks in wearing khaki pants, desert-sand-colored boots, and a zip-up jacket. The rest of his military entourage are dressed in fatigues. I immediately think about telling him how much I really needed his help earlier, but instead decide to keep it to myself. I know the National Guard will be our long-term security strategy, so I'm not about to make any snide comments on their emergency response capability.

When I shake his hand, he transfers a challenge coin to my palm. The coin reads, "Ryan D. McCarthy Secretary of the Army." I really don't think this is the time or place to exchange coins, but I thank him anyway, and everyone takes a seat around the table. He is accompanied by General William Walker of the DC National Guard, among others. I have my two assistant chiefs, Deputy Chief Pickett, Salley, and Tad with me. We discuss the plan for deployment of the National Guard around the campus moving forward. They anticipate having almost three hundred Guard personnel on-site overnight, and some eight hundred tomorrow. I designate Pickett as our liaison with the Guard. He will work closely with them to develop our staffing requirements.

We discuss the layout of the Hill and how we'll be needing National Guard support to guard the entire campus, with further resources deployed around the House and Senate office buildings. Pickett volunteers to develop a staffing plan to provide twenty-four-hour coverage for all the office buildings and the Capitol. "This is likely to require several thousand troops to provide the necessary coverage," Pickett says.

I ask Tad if we have all our official requests submitted. I already signed off on two formal letters for the Guard earlier, in the middle of the attack. Tad says that our official request has been submitted to General Walker. We wrap up our meeting, and McCarthy decides he wants to go out and visit the troops in the field. Part of his team stays behind in my conference room to begin working on logistics with Pickett.

January 7, 12:45 a.m. I return to my office. Salley and I begin discussing the development of an official timeline and a press statement regarding the events of January 6. My public information officer, Eva Malecki, comes into the office, and the three of us start working on a draft statement. Over the next several hours, I will talk to Stenger and Irving about our security posture going forward, about the press statement, and about answers to various questions coming in from members.

I also check in on the USCP officers who have gone to the hospital, such as Officer Caroline Edwards. Edwards was knocked unconscious during the battle on the West Front.

2:17 a.m. I send an email to General Walker with the third formal letter requesting the National Guard. Additional edit requests will keep coming in from lawyers.

It's been a long day, but it's not over yet. Throughout the morning, I will check in on Thomas and Pickett regarding the development of the National Guard staffing plan. At the time, no one anticipates the fencing or the Guard to stay as long as they will. The official media statement goes through numerous revisions between 3:30 a.m. and 10:50 a.m. when it is finally sent to my oversight committees and released to the media. It is critical to me that regardless of the criticism we are facing externally, the officers are acknowledged for responding heroically and that they know I am very proud of them.

3:44 a.m. I am in the Command Center watching the final proceedings of the certification of the Electoral College results. Senator Amy Klobuchar reads off the final determination from the House and Senate on the official counting of the Electoral College: "Joe Biden and Kamala Harris will be the president and vice president according to the ballots that have been given to us."

Vice President Pence then reads off the final vote count, indicating that Joseph R. Biden Jr. of the state of Delaware has received 306 votes and that Donald J. Trump of the state of Florida has received 232 votes. For the vice president of the United States, Kamala D. Harris of the state of California has received 306 votes, and Michael R. Pence of the state of Indiana has received 232 votes. Vice President Pence, as president of the Senate, then certifies the vote. Chaplain Barry Black then gives a moving prayer to close—appropriate following the events of the past sixteen hours. Vice President Pence then bangs the gavel on the rostrum and dissolves the joint session of Congress.

After this conclusion of the joint session, I thank everyone in the Command Center as I wait for the vice president's motorcade to depart the Capitol grounds.

4:00 a.m. Mike Stenger is escorting Vice President Pence from the House Chamber back to his armored limo at the Senate carriage entrance. They walk side by side through halls that are still being cleaned and cleared of debris and broken glass. As they walk, Stenger observes yellowish powder residue on the floor, discharged from a fire extinguisher. He says to Pence, "Watch your step, sir, it could be slippery."

"If I slip, you catch me," Pence says. "And if you slip, I'll catch you."

As the vice president gets into his limo, Stenger says, "Sorry about the situation, but it has been a privilege having you here tonight."

To which Pence responds, "It has been an honor."

The vice president's motorcade then departs the East Plaza of the Capitol, escorted by police motorcycles with their red-and-blue lights flashing. I watch on the video screens in the Command Center as the motorcade fades from view and then return to my office.

Overnight and into the early morning hours of January 7, I hear from a lot of officers, many sharing their stories. Although I try to lie down to get some sleep on my couch for a few minutes, my legs keep cramping up, and I continue to receive too many calls to even try to get one minute of shut-eye.

9:00 a.m. I have another call with Tim Ryan, this one a little more subdued. Afterward, I have a string of calls with the director of the FBI's Washington Field Office, Steve D'Antuono. We want to develop a joint investigative task force to start going through the evidence and begin to identify suspects in this attack. I offer to provide a joint workspace on our first floor. I also put in a request for the FBI's Critical Incident Response Group to assist in developing an after-action report (AAR). Steve concurs with my recommendations, and we are moving forward on the joint investigation.

My chief of staff is busy working with Tim Blodgett, deputy sergeant at arms for the House of Representatives. Although I already started briefing my oversight at eleven last night, the two of them have been developing a schedule for me to provide briefings for my oversight committees and congressional leadership. We reach out to Blodgett several times to schedule a briefing with Speaker Pelosi, but we still don't have a confirmed time from her office.

10:50 a.m. We publish my official statement regarding the events of January 6.

UNITED STATES CAPITOL POLICE

FOR IMMEDIATE RELEASE: January 7, 2021

AUTHORIZED BY: Steven A. Sund, Chief of Police

CONTACT: Eva Malecki, Communications Director ████████████████

Statement of Steven A. Sund, Chief of Police
Regarding the Events of January 6, 2021

WASHINGTON, DC - United States Capitol Police (USCP) officers and our law enforcement partners responded valiantly when faced with thousands of individuals involved in violent riotous actions as they stormed the United States Capitol Building. These individuals actively attacked United States Capitol Police Officers and other uniformed law enforcement officers with metal pipes, discharged chemical irritants, and took up other weapons against our officers. They were determined to enter into the Capitol Building by causing great damage.

As protesters were forcing their way toward the House Chamber where Members of Congress were sheltering in place, a sworn USCP employee discharged their service weapon, striking an adult female. Medical assistance was rendered immediately, and the female was transported to the hospital where she later succumbed to her injuries. She has been identified as Ashli Babbitt

As per the USCP's policy, the USCP employee has been placed on administrative leave and their police powers have been suspended pending the outcome of a joint Metropolitan Police Department (MPD) and USCP investigation.

As these other violent events were unfolding across the Capitol Complex, the USCP officers were simultaneously responding to a report of a pipe bomb in the 300 block of First Street, SE, and a second pipe bomb in the 400 block of Canal Street, SE. A suspicious vehicle was also identified in the 300 block of First Street, SE, at this time.

The USCP Hazardous Materials Response Team determined that both devices were, in fact, hazardous and could cause great harm to public safety. The devices were disabled and turned over to the FBI for further investigation and analysis.

The suspicious vehicle was thoroughly investigated by the USCP, FBI, and ATF. It has been cleared of any hazards. The USCP arrested the vehicle's owner along with 13 additional suspects for unlawful entry of the U.S. Capitol. The USCP is continuing to review surveillance video and open source material to identify others who may be subject to criminal charges.

(MORE)

UNITED STATES CAPITOL POLICE

The Department is grateful for the assistance provided today by more than 18 local, state, and Federal law enforcement agencies and the National Guard. More than 50 USCP and MPD sustained injuries during today's attack on the Capitol. Several USCP officers have been hospitalized with serious injuries.

The violent attack on the U.S. Capitol was unlike any I have ever experienced in my 30 years in law enforcement here in Washington, D.C. Maintaining public safety in an open environment – specifically for First Amendment activities – has long been a challenge. The USCP had a robust plan established to address anticipated First Amendment activities. But make no mistake – these mass riots were not First Amendment activities; they were criminal riotous behavior. The actions of the USCP officers were heroic given the situation they faced, and I continue to have tremendous respect in the professionalism and dedication of the women and men of the United States Capitol Police.

The USCP is conducting a thorough review of this incident, security planning and policies and procedures.

# # #

Figure 2.11. Chief Sund's official statement

12:10 p.m. I begin preparing for a 2:00 p.m. briefing with Senator Roy Blunt and the Senate Rules Committee. I'm sitting at the small conference table in my office with Salley when Eva Malecki comes into my office. Eva says she's been called by a reporter who told her they heard I was planning to resign. The reporter wants to know if it's true, and if so, when?

Both Eva and Salley give me a look of concern, apparently hoping there is no truth to the rumor. I'm a little taken aback by the question. "Hell no," I say. "I don't plan to resign. We just went through all that, and I intend to see this thing through."

I tell Eva to relay my response to the reporter: "I have no intentions of resigning. I plan to ensure that a complete AAR is performed regarding the security breach, and once we see what it reveals, we can discuss any resignations then."

In the end, the women and men of the United States Capitol Police did not fail in their mission. Not a single member of Congress was injured during this unprecedented attack. We were faced with a violent attack by thousands, Americans attacking Americans. USCP officers and the numerous responding law enforcement agencies showed tremendous dedication, professionalism, and restraint in their response. They were true heroes that day. I could not be prouder of how they defended the Capitol and our democracy.

Seventeen law enforcement agencies came to our assistance, providing over 1,700 officers. These agencies included the following:

- Metropolitan Police Department of Washington, DC
- Maryland State Police
- United States Park Police
- United States Secret Service
- FBI
- Virginia State Police

- Montgomery County Police Department, Maryland
- United States Marshals Service
- Metropolitan Washington Airports Authority Police
- Department of Homeland Security Police
- Fairfax County Police Department, Virginia
- Prince William County Police Department, Virginia
- Metro Transit Police Department, Washington Metropolitan Area Transit Authority
- Pentagon Force Protection Agency
- Arlington County Police Department, Virginia
- Prince George's County Police Department, Maryland
- New Jersey State Police

Any public perception that we did not make arrests that day is simply uninformed and untrue. The insinuations and accusations by politicians, pundits, and media that arrests were not made due to supposed police sympathies for MAGA supporters are ludicrous and illustrate the level of bias and downright hate toward the law enforcement profession in this country. Before anything else, we are cops. We uphold the law. Lawbreakers get arrested. Arrests are often done at the site of the crime, but that isn't always the case. Most arrests can be made at any time after the commission of a crime. On January 6 and in the early morning hours of January 7, the USCP made a total of fourteen on-site arrests related to the attack on the Capitol. It doesn't seem like a very big number, but what people need to understand is that in a mob situation, it takes a few officers to conduct *each* arrest. With an entire police department exhausted from hand-to-hand combat, many officers covered in chemical irritants, many injured, and many unable to move from their critical posts and assignments supporting the joint session of Congress, you can see how arresting, handcuffing, and transporting an individual becomes less of a priority—especially when we know we will locate additional lawbreakers by using forensics, footage, and assistance from the FBI. My priority on January 6 was to protect the members of Congress, clear the Capitol, reestablish a secure perimeter, and reconvene the joint session of Congress. I did not have the available personnel to make more arrests.

Although we stopped and detained more than fourteen individuals, a number of those had to be released due to the size of the crowd, the inability to safely transport the individual, and the crowd's aggressive demeanor toward the arresting officers. Maintaining the arrests was not worth the risk, either to the officers or to the detained individual.

Of the fourteen arrests made by the USCP, twelve were for unlawful entry into the US Capitol and two for gun-related charges. The USCP confiscated seven firearms related to the events of January 6:

- One handgun was located by a Senate Division CDU sergeant in the Capitol Building.
- Two handguns were found on a suspect during a response to a suspicious package.
- Three long guns were found in a suspect's vehicle at 400 First Street SE.
- One handgun was taken from a suspect arrested at 200 Maryland Avenue NW.

MPD made a total of seventy-three arrests citywide, including forty-six at the Capitol. Also, MPD confiscated six guns, two of them on Capitol grounds.

The USPP made one arrest and confiscated one rifle.

The investigation into the death of Ashli Babbitt was conducted by the Metropolitan Police Department, the United States Capitol Police, the FBI, and the US Attorney's Office. Nevertheless, there has been a great deal of speculation surrounding why the shooting was classified as a homicide. The MPD investigates all deaths and homicides in the city, regardless of where or in whose jurisdiction they occur. It was the MPD Homicide Branch that investigated Babbitt's death, and it was classified as a homicide. That is how all fatal shootings, with the exception of suicides, are classified in the District of Columbia. The listed manner of death would be homicide, and the listed cause would be gunshot wound.

The US Attorney then made a determination whether there was a basis to bring criminal charges in reference to the shooting. In this case, the US Attorney's Office declined to pursue criminal charges. There has been significant public scrutiny and also ridicule, including from the former president, of the official's use of lethal force in the case. Any loss of life is tragic. But any law enforcement officer with a mission to protect the president, vice president, or members of Congress, when faced with similar circumstances, would likely have done the same to prevent serious bodily injury or loss of life.

Regarding President Trump, I and many others in law enforcement appreciated that he had always publicly supported the police, even when doing so was unpopular. But his response and actions on January 6 troubled me deeply. He riled up a crowd, sent them to the Capitol, and then retreated to the safety of the White House, where he reportedly watched coverage of the events all afternoon as police were bloodied and abused. Not only were USCP and MPD officers being injured, but his own beloved Secret Service had a detail on the Hill with Pence and with CDU squads assisting me with the riots. Yet the law-and-order president sat and allowed the attack to go on. His half-hearted attempts at de-escalation via tweeting to the crowd were not what I would have expected from a leader who, only six months earlier, was "taking swift and decisive action to protect our great capital . . . to stop the rioting, looting, and wanton destruction of property." Where was the support for my men and women and all the other law enforcement officers who were trying to protect the Capitol, Congress, and his vice president?

He watched as a mob laid siege to the Capitol, but unlike in the summer, he was not publicly outraged at *this* violence and destruction, perpetrated by *this* group of people, to whom he made a point of saying, "We love you," as he finally, reluctantly asked them to stop. In June, he had spoken of never giving in to anger, hatred, and malice, but on January 6, he did not immediately and publicly condemn those who, *in his name*, were spitting on and striking officers and roaming the halls of the Capitol, looking to hang Nancy Pelosi and Mike Pence. He was the president, the commander in chief sworn to preserve, protect, and defend the Constitution. He had the ability to assist us and protect the men and women in blue, whom he had so staunchly supported a few short months ago. Where was his leadership in directing the military to respond to my repeated requests for life-and-death assistance? Thank God the president didn't come up to the Capitol during the riot. I can't even imagine what my officers and law enforcement would have been faced with if that occurred. In the end, law enforcement was left to fight and restore order alone, unsupported by its law-and-order president, hamstrung by the security apparatus on the Hill, and abandoned by the military.

CHAPTER 3:
AFTERMATH

As the sun came up on January 7, I knew that I had just witnessed an event as tragic as it was historic. The Capitol had been breached only once before—by British troops over two centuries ago. The assault on the Capitol by American citizens was unprecedented, and it happened on my watch. I knew when I saw the mob overrun my officers that it was a potential career ender, and I fully expected to find myself in front of Congress regarding this incident.

It had been just a little under eighteen months since the Senate sergeant at arms and chairman of the Capitol Police Board, Michael Stenger, swore me in as the tenth chief of police for the United States Capitol. That was one of the proudest days of my career.

That day, I had been excited about the possibilities this could bring, and I was looking forward to leading this agency for many years. Stenger, who talked very quietly with a bit of a New Jersey accent, chuckled as he told me on the day I was sworn in, "Just remember, your role as chief is to be the fall guy if things ever go bad."

Stenger had a cop's sense of humor, and I laughed it off at the time. But I guess that behind every joke is a little truth.

Like many law enforcement officials who operate in the high-stakes security environment of Washington, DC, I knew I was always one critical incident away from the possibility of a congressional inquiry. I had been involved in many DC special events and had responded to several active-shooter incidents in my career. Any high-profile matter in DC has the potential to pique congressional interest. I had been called before Congress when I was with the DC Metropolitan Police Department most recently in 2015, regarding a suspected explosive device near the White House. And as chief of the Capitol Police, appearing before Congress was part of my job description. As chief, I had to speak at budget hearings, congressional briefings, and events. But even as I tried to process everything I had just seen on January 6, I knew this time it would be much different.

THE SPEAKER SPEAKS

It was 2:00 p.m. on Thursday, January 7, 2021. I had not slept in over thirty-two hours. Adrenaline and a painful knot in my stomach were all that kept me going from one phone call, briefing, or meeting to the next. I had been briefing members of Congress since eleven the night before and was at it again at 9:00 a.m. I was sitting in the chief's conference room at a wooden conference table with seating for twelve, surrounded by many video screens, with the US and US Capitol Police flags behind me and a speakerphone in front. I was on a conference call with Senator Roy Blunt and staff from the Senate Rules Committee, briefing them on the attack and the current security posture of the Capitol. Other staff members from the Rules Committee were on the call, including Fitzhugh Elder and Rachelle Schroeder, but Senator Blunt was the only one talking to me. Unlike some other members on recent calls, he was calm and respectful.

I described the horrific attack and how officers had fought for hours to defend the Capitol and the members of Congress. A total of seventeen law enforcement agencies had brought in over 1,700 officers to help us secure the Capitol. I described the various chemical sprays that had been used against my officers and the various weapons some of the rioters had on them. Many of the responding agencies, including the MPD, expended all their chemical munitions during the fight, but the rioters had come with masks, respirators, and goggles to withstand the effects of police munitions. The mob threw projectiles and used our barriers as weapons against us. They slammed them into the officers, knocking them down and pummeling them. One of our female officers at such a barrier sustained a head injury and was knocked unconscious.

We discussed the pipe bombs and the fact that I believed it was a co-ordinated attack. I briefed the senator on the arrests that we had made, as well as on the ongoing investigation we were conducting with the FBI. Senator Blunt listened intently as I described what we had been through.

In the room with me at the time were Chad Thomas, Tad DiBiase, and my chief of staff, Salley Wood. Salley was always high energy, un-stoppable, and a force to be reckoned with—in other words, the perfect chief of staff. Only two days earlier in this same conference room, I had hosted a video conference with a dozen of the top law enforcement and military officials in Washington, DC, to discuss the joint session of Congress and the upcoming presidential inauguration.

As I was briefing Senator Blunt on one of the most horrific days in my career, I was unaware of the train wreck still to come.

At 2:04 p.m., while still in the briefing, I looked at my cell phone and saw that I had an incoming call from Jamie Fleet, the staff director for the House of Representatives. Jamie worked directly for Chairper-son Zoe Lofgren but also for Speaker Pelosi and her office. Since I was in the middle of briefing a senator, I elected to let the call go to voice mail, knowing I could call Jamie back in a few minutes. As I continued to brief the senator, I saw Salley grab her phone and walk out of the conference room. A minute later, she returned and tapped Tad on the shoulder, and they both stepped out. As I continued to brief the senator, Salley walked back into the room and motioned for me to check my phone. I looked at the screen and saw a text from her asking me to step out because she had something very important to discuss. I could see by the look on her face that it was serious.

I apologized to Senator Blunt and explained that I needed to step out to address an urgent matter and would be turning the call over to

Assistant Chief Thomas. I had always had a good relationship with Senator Blunt, and he had always been a strong supporter of law enforcement and the USCP. He answered in his Missouri accent, "No problem, Chief."

I stepped out of the conference room into the chief's reception area, where Salley and Tad were waiting. Salley took a deep breath and said, "I just received a call from Jamie Fleet and he wanted to give you a heads-up that the Speaker is about to go on television and call for your resignation."

Salley and Tad watched my reaction. They could see that I was taking a moment to process this news. No other information had been given about the press conference. All I knew was that Speaker Pelosi was about to publicly end my thirty-year career.

I knew the role of a police chief and how things work on the Hill, so I wasn't completely blindsided by this decision, but I was perplexed at why it was so sudden. I looked toward my conference room and said, "I'm going back to finish briefing the senator."

"You aren't going to watch the press conference?" Salley asked.

I shook my head. "Why? I already know how this movie ends."

I was about to walk away, but both Salley and Tad stopped me and convinced me to stay and watch the press conference. I went into my office and picked up the phone. "I need to call my wife and tell her what's about to happen," I said. In the next instant, I heard her voice on the line.

"Tell me what?"

"Honey, I have some news to tell you. I just got word that the Speaker is about to go on TV and call for my resignation."

There was a long pause. "Are you okay?" she asked.

"I'm fine. I've got Salley and Tad here."

She immediately went into protection mode. "Don't worry about us, we'll be fine," she said. "It's okay. If this is what's meant to be, so be it."

Then she switched to wife mode. "I guess you can come home now. When do you think you'll be home?"

I told her I still had a lot to do and wouldn't be home until much later.

She sighed. "All right, do what you have to." Then she added, with emphasis, "Screw 'em. They don't deserve you anyway!"

"Thanks for always being there," I said. "I love you."

Salley, Tad, and I sat down in my office to watch the press conference on the wall-mounted TV. What followed was a twenty-three-minute televised press conference by the Speaker of the House. During the press conference, Speaker Pelosi blamed the incitement of the riot on the sitting president of the United States. She finished her statement and began taking questions. At first, we thought maybe she had changed her mind. But when a reporter asked her about Schumer threatening to fire Stenger and whether she would be taking similar actions in the House, she replied, "That is a very important question. Let me hold for a moment because it is not . . . We have to do the after-action review."

At this moment, I thought she was planning to wait until after the AAR was completed, which I thought would be a fair way to proceed. Instead, she continued. "I have, uh . . . uh . . ." And then after a long, awkward pause, she said, "I am calling for the resignation of the Capitol chief, the chief of the Capitol Police, Mr. Sund."

There they were, the words I never thought I would hear, let alone on national television. And I knew that once she said those words, there was no walking them back. She went on to cite a failure at the top of the Capitol Police for the security breach, which basically illustrated to everyone that she had already concluded the results of the AAR before it was even started.

But there was more. I listened in disbelief as the Speaker went on to give the press corps and the American television audience blatantly false information. "Mr. Sund . . . he hasn't even called us since this happened. So I have made him aware that I would be saying that we're calling for his resignation." She said I hadn't even called her since the incident occurred, implying I might have something to hide or I was ashamed of my actions or those of my officers. It painted me as a callous, disrespectful person. But did she already forget about the three times I had personally spoken to her since the attack started? Did she forget that one of those times was in the presence of Vice President Pence, using his cell phone? Was she unaware that I'd been conducting briefings for members since eleven the night before and that we had been trying to schedule her briefing through Irving's office all morning?

(An aide to Pelosi later clarified that the Speaker was referring to "the hours since the last conversation with Sund, which occurred early in the evening Jan. 6." I find these comments by her staffer to be a patently disingenuous attempt to backtrack and provide cover to the Speaker's blatantly untruthful public statement.)

During the press conference, Richard Braddock, my chief administrative officer and part of my executive team, came into my office. As soon as Speaker Pelosi said those words, my whole team fell silent. Their faces turned pale. But my concern at that moment turned immediately to them and the future of the department. I don't know what came over me. Perhaps it was a defense mechanism after seeing them so upset. But I shrugged my shoulders and said, "Well, that sucks."

Then, as I looked at everyone in the room, I said, "We are witnessing a significant moment in history—might as well record it." I took a couple of selfies with members of my team, with Pelosi still on the television behind us. Even though I felt my heart breaking, I encouraged everyone to try to muster a smile for the picture.

After we took the pictures, I turned to Tad and Richard, two people with decades of experience working on the Hill, and said, "You just saw Pelosi go on television and call for my resignation. What are the chances of me surviving this?"

They looked at each other for a quick second, and then Braddock said, "Your chances are pretty slim."

I knew he was right. There is a reason why the Speaker is the highest-compensated congressional employee. She wields a lot of power. She's like the godfather of the Hill. Once you are in her crosshairs, you are pretty much done. Even if I tried to push back, I knew I'd be fired by the CPB by the end of the day.

I called Paul Irving. Apparently, he, too, had watched the press conference, because the first thing out of his mouth was, "Wow, that was tough," followed by, "How are you doing?"

I told him I had discussed the press conference with my wife and close colleagues and he would have my resignation by the end of the day.

I then called the chairman of the Capitol Police Board, Michael

Stenger, and told him the same. Unlike Paul, who took it as business as usual, I could tell by Mike's voice that he was deeply upset at my fate. He and his predecessor, Frank Larkin, had recruited me four years earlier, and he felt a sense of responsibility for my coming to work on the Hill.

Even though I was at the bottom of the law enforcement structure as it exists on Capitol Hill, I was the first and only one singled out by the most powerful person in Congress. I don't know if either of the sergeants at arms stepped in on my behalf, but at that point they probably couldn't do anything since their resignations would be demanded shortly after mine. I finally called Jamie Fleet and thanked him for the heads-up. Jamie and I had a good working relationship, and he knew how much I cared about the department. I told him I would submit my resignation by the end of the day, with a separation date of January 16. He said that would be acceptable.

At 4:45 p.m., a little over two hours after Pelosi's press conference, I submitted my resignation to the Capitol Police Board via email with an effective date of January 16. It was the usual course of business to separate from service at the end of a pay period because separating earlier could create accounting issues. This would also allow me enough time to make the transition out of the office and tell everyone goodbye. My email to the CPB stated, "Attached please find my letter of resignation, effective January 16, 2021. It has been an honor to serve. Please let me know if you have any questions." It was done.

Writing that email and hitting the send button was one of the toughest things I've ever had to do. Just eighteen months before, I had been heralded as a new type of chief, a "breath of fresh air." Back then, both Republicans and Democrats appreciated my reputation, valued my law enforcement experience, and admired my relationship with the rank and file. I had made significant changes to move the USCP, an agency I loved, forward and to increase employee morale. Now, with a click of a button, it was all over.

I had been torn away from a department I had worked so hard to develop, at a time when they would need me the most. I had dozens of officers and officials come through my office almost immediately. They were in shock and disbelief. Some were upset at me, thinking I was abandoning them in their hour of need. I explained it wasn't my decision. Some were angry and visibly agitated. A few cried openly, while the rest tried to remain professional, even as they wiped their eyes while speaking to me.

Less than an hour later, at 5:23 p.m., Paul Irving responded by email, stating, "Chief, we have received your notice of resignation effective January 16, 2021. The Capitol Police Board accepts your resignation. We appreciate your service to the congressional community."

Not long after that, Assistant Chief Thomas hurried into my office. He kicked my door stopper out of the way, and the door shut behind him. It was just the two of us, and I could tell he was upset. "Why didn't you tell them you had requested the National Guard?"

He clearly wanted me to fight for my job. "I am so sorry I let you down," he said. No matter how I reassured him, he kept repeating that he had let me down.

When I was finally by myself again, I went back to work on some things in the office. I had received many calls from staff on my oversight committees, expressing their sadness at my resignation and concern for the USCP moving forward without me at such a critical time. They knew the relationship I had with my officers and were concerned that my departure would only compound the impact of the trauma they were experiencing. Several staffers were considering ways to postpone my departure, and one even said, "If we can get the temperature to come down, would you consider staying?"

As I worked at my stand-up desk, I found myself often glancing tearfully around my office, realizing that all this was coming to an end. I scanned the pictures on the wall and those standing on my desk. I looked at the pictures of me with various presidents, on an MPD Harley-Davidson motorcycle at the White House, and on the streets of DC. I looked at the photos of my wife and kids and thought about how difficult this must be for them. As I looked at all this, I asked myself, *Am I done carrying a badge? Is it time to end a career I've loved for almost thirty years?*

When I went over to the Command Center, the door made its usual *click* and *swoosh* sound. As I walked inside, everyone's head turned. They all had heard the news. "Why should you be the one to resign when it was the Pentagon who refused to respond?" one officer asked me.

"Chief, this isn't right," Deputy Chief Pickett said. "You brought in the resources to retake the Capitol. Sir, I had MPD tell me if it weren't for you being in the chair, we wouldn't have gotten the building back as quick as we did. I'm sorry, boss, but this is just fucked up."

I didn't respond, but inside I had to agree with him. I went around the Command Center as I usually did to check on the staff and see how they were doing. But today it was so much harder.

I walked back to my office and worked on things for the next couple of hours. I called my wife again. She told me the kids were doing okay and that she found a note and a bottle of wine on our doorstep from our next-door neighbors. The note read, "Yesterday was leadership on display." *What a stark contrast to the narrative out there*, I thought. Even though we had managed to resecure the Capitol effectively and expeditiously, Hill leadership made it perfectly clear they were focusing only on the breach. My department and I were to be criticized for that breach, but not commended for anything that happened after—including possibly saving many lives.

Maria told me how two of her friends had stopped by and brought her an orchid. Vera and Ingrid would go on to be wonderfully helpful and steadfast in their support. Vera would often shout, "Team Sund!" to the reporters outside our house. That night, two more neighbors stopped by our house with a meal of pasta, pizza, garlic bread, salad, and ice cream for dessert. They delivered it to our door and handed the bags and baskets to my wife with tears in their eyes. They didn't say anything because what could they say? Seeing Tammy and Dannielle holding back tears prompted my wife to break down crying, which in turn led the two of them to start crying. It was a strange new experience for all the ladies because how often do you see your neighbors cry?

Meanwhile, at work, I asked that an official be present at the hospital to speak to Sicknick's family while he was on life support. Captain Mendoza was the senior Special Operations Division official on duty and went to the hospital. I greatly regret not going myself, but I felt I was in an odd predicament. I was technically still the chief, even though everyone knew I had resigned. I stayed in contact with Mendoza as she arrived at the hospital and relayed updates on Brian. Things were not looking good. I had been keeping Irving and Stenger informed of his condition, and at 9:45 p.m., I received the tragic news.

I was deeply saddened by Brian's passing. So many things seemed to be happening at once. I immediately began working on a statement to the force and an email to my oversight committees. I reached out to MPD and Mendoza about coordinating an escort for Officer Sicknick from George Washington University Hospital to the medical examiner's office. MPD was already on it, and Sergeant Ford with our motor unit was coordinating with them. Mendoza, along with other officers at the hospital, escorted Officer Sicknick's body out to a waiting van. A short time later, a long procession of police motorcycles and cars with their red-and-blue lights flashing escorted the van carrying his body as it slowly passed the United States Capitol on its way to the DC medical examiner's office. It was a terrible ending to a terrible day.

When I finally arrived home late Thursday evening, I found a security detail in place at my house, established by the USCP and the Fairfax County Police Department. The detail had been established because of statements made on social media following Pelosi's press conference. I went over to talk to the detail, thanking them for being there.

When I walked into the house, I was greeted by my wife. We had a long hug. There was no need for words. There was prepared food in the kitchen, but no one was in the mood to eat. I helped my wife put everything away, and we went to bed.

———

I had heard the concern regarding "optics" many times during my career with the USCP. But during the week of January 3, I would experience the impact of this obsession with optics on several devastating occasions. The first was Irving's apprehension on January 3 regarding the optics of having the National Guard on the Hill. The second came from the Pentagon regarding sending troops to the Capitol.

And now I would soon be hearing it one more time. It was Friday, January 8, and I had gotten up before 6:00 a.m. I began doing more follow-up work. I was developing a record of departmental actions, handling member briefings, and preparing responses to department media inquiries.

Everyone on the Hill knew Stenger was retiring in January. Nonetheless, Schumer went on TV demanding Mike's resignation. Again, it was all about *optics*. Initially, it looked as though Paul was safe, but he too was forced to resign later that day.

I kept going through my emails and my briefing notes for the various conference calls I had on my schedule. I also knew that an after-action report would be needed after such an incident. I thought back to the many AARs I had been involved with while at the MPD. I began composing an email to Steve D'Antuono of the FBI, requesting the support of the FBI's Critical Incident Response Group (CIRG) to assist with the USCP's development of the after-action report.

About 10:00 a.m., I got a call from Jennifer Hemingway, now the acting Senate sergeant at arms and chairperson of the Capitol Police Board. I was working on my laptop at my kitchen counter and had just gotten up to make another cup of coffee when her call came in. Jennifer told me she was trying to get in touch with Pittman and that she had been unable to reach her. She wanted to know where she was. I told her Pittman was at a personal appointment and would be available after 11:30 a.m. At that point, Jennifer hit me with the third concern for *optics*. "We are concerned about the optics of the chief leaving three days before the inauguration," she said.

Well, I thought to myself, *maybe they have reconsidered my resignation, or maybe they are going to postpone it and have me stay through the inauguration.* Then Jennifer let the hammer drop. Without any hesitation or even emotion in her voice, she continued, "So we are going to make your resignation effective today."

I didn't think I had another level to drop, but those words floored me. She went on to ask me who I would recommend to the board to be the acting chief of police.

I was annoyed at the question. She had called me looking for Pittman, so I had a pretty good idea who she was considering for the position. "I don't know, Jennifer," I said. "Who would *you* like to pick?"

Traditionally, the acting chief is someone next in line in the rank structure. That would be either Assistant Chief Thomas or Assistant Chief Pittman. "Pittman has a good relationship with the committees and the sergeants at arms, so I think she would make the best choice," she said. "We are planning to swear in Pittman around 12:30, and I want to tell her as soon as possible so she can notify her family."

"I will notify her to contact you when I hear from her," I said. "I will just take leave for next week so I'm not in the way and Pittman can have a clean transition."

Hemingway agreed this would be fine and ended the call.

I'll be damned, I said to myself. *The hits just keep coming.*

Interestingly, only minutes later at 10:21 a.m., Jamie Fleet texted Paul Irving: "Heads up that Sund is going to take leave next week, so Jennifer is planning on swearing Yogi in today," referring to Yogananda Pittman.

So instead of explaining that I was taking leave because Hemingway was making Pittman acting chief, he made it appear that Hemingway had to make Pittman the acting chief of police because I had chosen to go on leave. To this day, I have no idea why it was portrayed this way.

Irving replied, "Can you flag it for Terri?" referring to Speaker Pelosi's chief of staff, Terri McCullough.

And then Fleet answered, "Yes, I'll send an email."

Despite everything going on, I remembered I was in the middle of coordinating support to assist with the after-action report. I knew Pittman didn't have the connections or the experience with AARs, so I decided to proceed with contacting the FBI to request the support of the Critical Incident Response Group. CIRG had previously assisted me with the AAR for the Navy Yard active-shooter incident in 2013, and I knew they would be an effective resource. I sent D'Antuono the email and included Pittman, making her the point of contact since she would be the acting chief of police within a matter of hours.

Shortly thereafter, I called into a previously scheduled conference call with my executive team. I had to explain to everyone on the call that today was now going to be my last day as chief and that Pittman would be sworn in within a few hours. The news was met with stunned silence.

I told them I would miss them very much, but that Pittman would do a good job and that they needed to have her back. I got choked up as I spoke, and I could tell I was not the only one. My wife stood in the kitchen doorway and heard the entire conversation. When I got off the call, we tearfully hugged to the sound of my two cell phones ringing and dinging from all the texts and calls coming in.

"It's unfair," my chief of staff, Salley, told me. "We had so much going for us under your leadership. All those initiatives in your five-year plan—what's going to happen to them now?"

I hadn't thought that far ahead yet, but she was right. The field offices, the restructuring, the training programs—everything in the plan could be derailed now. "It is what it is," I said, and I consoled myself by thinking, *It's all someone else's headache now.*

Just as I finished my call with Salley, a worried official texted me: "We need you. The inauguration is in two weeks; you're the most experienced on the Hill. What are they thinking?"

The next day was a Saturday. I went to the police headquarters early in the morning. I had to return all my gear and my uniform, and I needed to pack up my office. Most of the department was working because days off had been canceled following January 6. It felt strange coming to work out of uniform. I was wearing blue jeans and a long-sleeve Marine Corps Marathon shirt. I thought the packing would take only a few hours, but a flood of officers came by the office throughout the day to check on me and say goodbye. A group of motor officers stopped by and gave me a barrel stave with my last name on it. They explained the stave represents one of the integral parts of the unit (the barrel) and that I would always be one of them. The day was getting more difficult for me emotionally.

But it was about to get far worse.

At 10:45 p.m., Captain Mendoza came into my office and sat down on the couch. She had already been physically exhausted and emotionally spent like the rest of us, but now she looked even more stricken. We talked about January 6 and her trip to the hospital, how hard it had been for her to coordinate the escort of Officer Sicknick's remains from the hospital. She told me she was upset about my departure and wasn't sure she wanted to stay with the Capitol Police.

I told her that many people looked up to her here and that she had the potential to do great things. I reminded her she was strong enough to weather this storm. Neysha had been through a lot growing up and had managed to make it through adversity with a very positive outlook on life. "Neysha," I said, "the department and your officers need you now more than ever."

She seemed to be coming around a little bit. Before she headed back to the SOD, we both promised to keep in touch.

But then, right around 11:00 p.m., just after Mendoza left my office, Lieutenant Schauf, the watch commander, came into my office and shut the door. "I've got bad news," he said.

What he proceeded to tell me was the news that every official dreads. He had just received a call from the Fairfax County Police, who had responded to the home of Officer Howard Liebengood. Howard had taken his own life.

I knew Officer Liebengood personally and considered him a friend. He and I went to the same gym and shared the same hobby. In our younger years, we had both raced cars. He was a rally racer, while I did quarter-mile racing, and we often shared racing stories and discussed working on cars. I was staggered by the news, and I was quite concerned about how it would hit the department, especially after what we all had been through. I knew this had to be handled with the utmost care. Resources needed to be made immediately available to the officers, who would be devastated by the news.

No one else at the department had gotten the awful tidings. Schauf had not yet informed Pittman. I told him I would call her. Pittman was at home when I broke the news to her. She, too, was shocked and saddened. She had never responded to an officer's suicide, and asked my advice. Sadly, I had dealt with police suicides before, twice just in my time at the USCP. I advised her that she and Thomas needed to go to Liebengood's home to meet with the police on the scene and do what they could to console his wife.

I knew it was going to be very difficult for Pittman, but it needed to be done. The agency needed to see the new acting chief actively dealing with the tragic incident so that the officers would respect her as a leader. "Remember what I told you at the demonstrations?" I said. "Seeing the chief in the field is important to the officers."

I told her I'd have Schauf send her all the information. She thanked me and ended the call.

Within the next minute, I got a call from USCP K9 officer Andy Maybo. Andy often assists the USCP and partner agencies during critical incidents. He was a former union chairman and had contacts with all the area police departments. He wanted me to know that he was en route to Liebengood's home. *That's good*, I thought. Andy would know what to do and could assist Pittman and Thomas. I had never met Howie's wife, and I felt it would be inappropriate for me to show up with Pittman already on the way. Besides, much still needed to be done for the officers here on the Hill.

Mendoza had just left my office, unhappy about my departure but also deeply upset about Sicknick's death. I knew this additional bad news would be devastating. So I called her cell phone and asked her to come back to the office. She walked in, and we sat down at the same spot where we were sitting just a few minutes earlier. I broke the tragic news to her. She was very stoical as she processed it. We sat in silence for a minute or two. She was unsure what to do next.

"Neysha," I said, "there's a lot that needs to be done to help the officers through this. I'm going to need your help to start coordinating notifications and assistance." It's important in this type of difficult situation to immediately start talking to the officers and addressing the evening roll calls. Mendoza and I decided we would go together. "It's important that we notify the Command Center officers first," I said. "They'll start getting media calls and other inquiries once word of this gets out."

Mendoza had previously been the watch commander of the Command Center and thought of the officers in the center as family. When we got to the USCP nerve center, I asked the Command Center staff to step into a back office. I wanted to brief them in private and away from any non-USCP personnel. (After January 6, we had various military and law enforcement liaisons staffing our Command Center around the clock.) The staff stepped into the sergeant's office and made a semi-circle around me. I knew every one of these officers well. They listened intently as I told them the news. It was hard on them. Many of them knew Howie well. I explained that they were likely to start getting media inquiries and just to refer them to the public information officer. The shock and grief lingered for a while until, almost simultaneously, they remembered their mission and went back to work. I saw many of them wiping their eyes as they returned to their workstations.

Mendoza and I then went out to lot 16 across the street from USCP headquarters to brief the Special Operations Division officers who were attending the midnight roll call. On the way, I called Inspector Amy Hyman, the commander of the Senate Division, where Liebengood had been assigned. More stunned silence when I broke the news to her.

Everyone who knew Howie liked him. He was just that kind of guy. Inspector Hyman was unsure what to do. I told her we could use her assistance in addressing officers in roll calls. "It'll be emotional and difficult for everyone," I said, "but the officers will need someone to listen to them. It's important that they see officials dealing with this right along with them and truly caring about them."

My biggest worry was that given the emotional stress the department was already under, we could have more officers harming themselves. I knew we had to do our best to handle this situation correctly. Since I was still on the phone with Amy, she told me a little bit about the last few days with Howie. She told me he had been involved in some of the fighting on Wednesday and had also worked a long shift on Thursday. She said that toward the end of his shift on Thursday, he had been involved in a minor traffic accident. Her voice was starting to falter as she talked about him.

"We need to be strong for the officers," I said. "I know you can make it through this." I told her I was going to call in some counselors from the USCP Employee Assistance Program to help, as well as the counselors at the MPD, but that I needed her to come in as soon as possible.

Mendoza and I then walked through the gate in the chain-link fence into lot 16. The various police, military, and command vehicles parked around the lot cast long shadows in the industrial lights placed there by the AOC. Mendoza called over the SOD officers, about twenty-five of them, and they surrounded me in a circle. They were members of the Special Operations Division—K9, CERT, and the Motor Unit. Dark silhouettes of silent police officers, some wearing helmets, some in tactical gear holding rifles. I couldn't see their faces, only their breath fogging in the cold January air. It was a very surreal moment.

"I am here to give you some very tragic news," I said, and then I told them about Howie's death. It's always so difficult to break the news of the loss of a fellow officer. But I wanted them to hear it from me—someone who knew Howie and who cared deeply for these officers. No one spoke. I asked them to be sure to look out for one another and to reach out to me if anyone needed anything. I gave them my personal cell phone number before leaving the lot.

Before stepping onto the elevator to go up to the Senate Division in USCP headquarters, I called the Metropolitan Police Department, requesting the assistance of their peer support and counseling program. I also put in a call to the employee assistance program for the House of Representatives.

As the elevator opened on the fourth floor, I stepped out into the lobby area. This was the home of the Senate Division, Howie's assigned unit. It was bustling with officers. Just days ago, I was their chief. Now I was just a regular civilian in plain clothes walking around the building. It all felt like a really bad dream.

As I headed to the roll call room, several officers came up to tell me they were sorry I was leaving and to ask how I was holding up. I chatted briefly and then asked if they would join me. I pulled aside the roll call officials and told them the news first. Then we walked into roll call together.

The room was packed with officers, many standing and some spilling out into the hallway. Officers who were getting ready to check off were directed to come back in and join those just coming on duty. I looked around the room at all the faces, still weary from the most brutal week they'd ever had. I thought to myself, *This is going to be tough as hell.*

Just a few short years earlier, I had been introducing myself to these officers in this very room as their new assistant chief. Now I was here to tell them of the tragic loss of one of their fellow officers. The officials completed roll call and turned to me, and one said, "Chief Sund has an announcement to make."

I stepped to the front of the room and said, "I know that everyone here has been through a lot this week. I am here to tell you some very sad and tragic news that I know is going to be very hard on all of you."

When I told them about Officer Liebengood's suicide, the news hit everybody like a load of bricks. Officers expressed sadness, confusion, and anger. Some sat silently, some put their head in their hands, and several got up and immediately walked out of the room. I remained in the roll call room and hallway talking to officers and officials. Around 12:30 a.m. on Sunday, while still in the roll call room, I was informed we had a very distressed officer. He was taken to a room by his official for privacy and emotional support. The official asked if I could speak with him as well. His union representative was also called in to sit with him. For me, assisting an officer is nonnegotiable, and I will always do everything I can to assist.

As I came to the door, the union rep looked up at me. Normally, he would stay with an officer, but in this case, he decided it would be best for me to speak with the officer privately. As the rep was leaving the room, he thanked me for taking the time to speak with the suffering officer. Then I sat with the officer for about forty minutes. Mostly I listened, but the conversation felt beneficial to both of us. I think we both just needed someone to talk to.

It seemed only yesterday that I was a young rookie officer sitting in the roll call room of the Sixth District at MPD. I can only imagine what this officer was feeling after the events of the past few days and then hearing about Howie's death. By the end of the conversation, I think we both were doing a little better. I had grown to truly love these officers, and it hurt like hell to see what they were going through. I stayed at headquarters and grieved and talked with officers for several more hours. I was exhausted and it was very early Sunday morning, but I didn't want to leave. I left my office, took one last walk through the Command Center, then walked down the long hallway past the official portraits of Stenger, Blanton, Irving, and me surrounded by large emblems of all our partner agencies—USSS, FBI,

MPD, USPP, DEA, ATF, Amtrak—and onto the elevator on the seventh floor. When I exited on the first floor, I again tapped on the security glass separating the screening area and acknowledged the officers. I walked by the plaque honoring the fallen USCP officers and down the hallway lined with the photos of the various USCP police units. As I approached the exit door, I stopped and paused briefly. I knew that when I walked out of police headquarters, nothing would ever be the same.

When I left my office around 5:00 a.m. on Sunday, I had packed up all but a few things. As I left, I placed on my old desk two books I thought the acting chief would find useful: *Crisis Leadership Now* and a pocket copy of the Constitution of the United States that I often carried with me. When I returned to pack up the rest of my belongings on Monday morning, I found everything stuffed in a box in the hallway, with the two books sitting at the top of the pile.

––––––––––

Just days after calling for my resignation, Pelosi announced the formation of Task Force 1-6, to be headed by retired lieutenant general Russel Honoré. The mission of Task Force 1-6 was to determine how this attack was successful and how to prevent such an attack in the future. Before being asked to head the task force, Lieutenant General Honoré had gone on television and Twitter and had passed judgment on me and the agency. He was far from an unbiased and objective choice for such a task after comments such as "I've just never seen so much incompetence, so they're either that stupid, or ignorant or complicit. I think they were complicit."[1]

The extremely vocal and public prejudicial comments by the task force commander did not instill a high level of confidence in many, including me. The team's obvious bias and the skewed angle of Pelosi's

1. Sabrina Wilson, "Gen. Honoré Blasts Security Failures at the U.S. Capitol Building; Says Some People Deserve Jail," Fox 8, updated January 8, 2021, www.fox8live .com/2021/01/08/gen-honore-blasts-security-failures-us-capitol-building-says-some -people-deserve-jail/.

partisan task force made for great television but did little to help the USCP or reassure the public that a thorough review was being conducted.

Less than two months after January 6, Task Force 1-6 released its findings. Its recommendations included increased intelligence analytical capabilities, better information sharing, and more integration of intelligence into operations. The task force called for changing the two laws that restricted my ability to bring in the National Guard, in order to give the USCP chief more options to call in additional resources. This was a recommendation that I absolutely agreed with.

The task force also identified what we already knew: that before January 6, the department was short 233 officers. The task force recommended hiring an additional 884 employees to help fulfill the increasing mission requirements and reduce overtime. The task force also recommended that the department establish dedicated civil disturbance unit platoons that would be on duty whenever Congress was in session. In other words, they were recommending that the department have anywhere from forty to eighty officers on duty and waiting for a demonstration to occur, anytime Congress is in session. No police department in the country has full-time dedicated CDU resources just sitting around waiting for a demonstration. This is an extremely costly and inefficient use of manpower.

The task force also recommended reestablishing the horse-mounted unit as an effective crowd management tool. I had reviewed and considered that when I first became chief. Having managed a horse-mounted unit at the MPD, I knew the benefits. I had recommended against it, however, due to the reduced effectiveness of horses on the various types and levels of hardscape around the congressional buildings. Limestone and marble surfaces are far from ideal for horses. I believed more effective capabilities would come from bicycle-mounted officers.

Overall, the recommendations from Task Force 1-6 read like one big wish list. Apparently, they believed that throwing money and bodies at a problem will fix anything. Their recommendations were an unobtainable and unsustainable plan that would reap minor benefits while turning the Capitol Police into one of the costliest departments in the country. It was also apparent that the task force interviewed a number of people to find their *wants* as opposed to their *needs* and then developed a pie-in-the-sky series of recommendations. Imagine if I had gone to Congress before January 6 and requested to increase my staffing by a thousand people and double my budget. They probably would have sent me for a psychological examination.

Clearly, the task force didn't try to identify the true root cause of what resulted in our lack of preparedness for January 6: a failure of intelligence. (I go into much more detail on this subject in chapter 4.) The remedy for an intel failure is proper management of intelligence, not a huge budget increase and stumbling horses. In October 2020, I published a five-year strategic plan for the department's operations and human capital, which specifically outlined a road map to integrate intelligence into operations.[2] The continued implementation of the strategic plan would be a much smarter process for enhancing the capabilities of the department. I'd hate to think how much this Task Force 1-6 cost the American taxpayer.

———————

I was growing increasingly concerned about the inaccurate and incomplete information being disseminated in the media. I needed to get the facts out ASAP, for two important reasons. First, I believed that true and accurate information needed to be provided to the public. The American people needed to know what really occurred and what hamstrung the Capitol Police's ability to respond to the attack on January 6. I also felt that no one was standing up for the officers who had fought so heroically to carry out their mission to protect Congress and defend the Capitol. Even some of the very people the Capitol Police swore an oath to protect had come out making disparaging public statements. Senator

———

2. Steven A. Sund, *Department Strategic Plan 2021–2025*, United States Capitol Police, n.d., www.uscp.gov/sites/uscapitolpolice.house.gov/files/USCP%20Department%20Strategic%20Plan%20for%202021-2025.pdf; Steven A. Sund, *Human Capital Strategic Plan 2021–2025*, United States Capitol Police, n.d., www.uscp.gov/sites/uscapitolpolice.house.gov/files/wysiwyg_uploaded/USCP%20Human%20Capital%20Strategic%20Plan%20for%202021-2025.pdf.

Lindsey Graham stated on January 7 that "anyone in charge of defending the Capitol failed."[3] Someone needed to let them know that these police officers had not failed in their mission and that against insurmountable odds, they had protected every member of Congress, every staff member, and the vice president of the United States. Because of these officers and the support we received from partner agencies, we got Congress back in session just hours after this horrific and deadly attack.

But even as we were battling on January 6, the media had already begun pushing an incorrect narrative regarding the Capitol Police. Initial reports included such false statements as the USCP was soft on the mob, USCP delayed calling in assistance, Capitol officers waved in and opened gates for the protesters, and USCP was somehow complicit in the attack.

One thing every cop knows is that initial information is usually incomplete and inaccurate and will likely change. Unfortunately, within hours of the attack, a slew of former law enforcement executives went to the media, jumping on the "Bash Sund/USCP" bandwagon. Even my former boss at the MPD, Terrance Gainer, couldn't pass up the opportunity to take a few potshots at me, stating, "If I was up there, I deserve to be fired for letting that happen."[4]

This was coming from someone who had firsthand knowledge of the complex nature of security on the Hill. Years earlier, when Gainer was chief of the USCP, he had recommended installing a permanent security fence around the Capitol. He was publicly lambasted by Congress for making such a recommendation. Congress was so opposed to a permanent fence, they introduced language into the 2004 appropriations bill forbidding the USCP from even spending money to evaluate the idea. But now Gainer was Monday-morning-quarterbacking me

3. Jordain Carney, "McConnell Ousts Senate Sergeant-at-Arms after Capitol Riots, The Hill, January 7, 2021, https://thehill.com/homenews/senate/533279-mcconnell-ousts-senate-sergeant-at-arms-after-capitol-riots/.

4. Tyler Clifford, "Ex-U.S. Capitol Police Chief Says He Would 'Deserve to Be Fired' for Capitol Takeover," CNBC, January 6, 2021, www.cnbc.com/2021/01/06/ex-capitol-police-chief-says-he-would-be-fired-for-capitol-takeover.html.

without all the facts, unaware that I had been denied key intelligence before January 6 and unaware that three days before the attack, I had been denied the necessary resources to support my perimeter—by Paul Irving, the same sergeant at arms who had refused to support Gainer's recommendation for a fence in 2004.[5]

For months following the attack, I heard from veteran USCP officers who informed me they had been telling the CPB for years that it would be impossible to protect the Capitol Building from a mob attack. Many officers felt that the CPB and congressional leadership had negligently let this security deficiency go unaddressed and that I was a casualty of their indecisiveness.

———————

The media descended like locusts on my family and me. We were receiving calls, emails, and texts at all hours from local, national, and international news outlets. The media would show up at the house, some days as early as seven in the morning, and stay as late as nine at night. I was on edge; my family was on edge; even our neighbors were on edge. Despite the barrage of attention, my interactions with the media were mostly uneventful, with one exception. I had just dropped off my police vehicle and was getting a ride home. On the way, I picked up some dinner for my family. I arrived home shortly before nine, and it was very dark outside. Although I had turned in my police vehicle, I still had my service weapon. I got out of the vehicle, slung my backpack over one shoulder, and grabbed the bag of food from the back seat. As I was closing the car door and about to walk into the house, I heard some car doors slam and saw figures running toward me. I dropped my bags on the ground and took a defensive position. With my left side toward the threat and my left arm extended, I put my right hand on my service weapon. I looked up and saw three men running toward me. "Stop!" I shouted.

5. Hannah Hess, "Gainer's Capitol Fence Is Not a Popular Concept," Roll Call, October 24, 2014, www.rollcall.com/2014/10/24/gainers-capitol-fence-is-not-a-popular-concept/.

They stopped in their tracks, eyes wide, surprised at my response. I then saw a camera, a person carrying lights, and another carrying a microphone.

"Who are you?"

"We're British press, sir."

"You should never go running up on somebody like that, especially at night! Can I see some identification?" When they complied, I ran the food inside to my family and then returned to talk to them.

I had a lot of press contacting me for interviews, but I didn't know a lot about them other than that there were some big names. Thank goodness I had a close confidante from a media family who was well versed in these things. One day, she asked me to put together a list of media that had contacted me. I had a list of about a dozen reporters who had reached out. She reviewed the list, pointed at Carol Leonnig's name, and said, "That is who you want to talk to. She's an award-winning reporter and she'll be fair. Talk to her."

Leonnig had emailed me twice on January 7, requesting an opportunity to talk. Although both emails were very respectful, I didn't feel like talking to anyone at that time. I emailed her back on Sunday, January 10, asking her if she was available for a call. She called me back a few minutes later. I was on my way back into work after a few hours of sleep. I had spent Saturday evening and early Sunday attending to the loss of Officer Liebengood. I was driving through McLean when I received Carol's call. I pulled over and parked in a church lot right down the street from CIA headquarters. I had never been one to reach out to the media in this fashion. The fact that I was now talking to the *Washington Post* while sitting in the far corner of a parking lot not far from Langley felt like something out of a spy novel. We spoke for over an hour as I told her about what really occurred on January 6 and the days leading up to it. She was kind, and I appreciated her consideration and in-depth interest. Carol told me she would need to validate some of the information I had provided and then get back to me.

The online article ran that evening, and the print article Monday morning. The story made the front page of the *Washington Post*, above the fold. On Sunday evening, I received two texts from Paul Irving. The first read, "Please call when you're available; just want to sync with press strategy." The second text that came in almost immediately read, "Just read the Post article. Please no worries from me."

Figure 3.4. Texts with House SAA Paul Irving

Shortly after the attack, I was also contacted by the producers of *60 Minutes*. I didn't respond at first to their requests for an interview, but after the recommendation from my friend Bryan Wittman and after consulting with my wife, I decided to call them back and discuss the possibility. When I called, I had the chance to speak with one of the senior producers, named Pat Milton. She could tell I had significant reservations about doing an on-camera interview for a major outlet like *60 Minutes*. She was very patient and polite in walking me through the process and ultimately made me feel comfortable enough to agree to do it.

Pat scheduled the interview to take place on Wednesday, January 13. When the day of the interview arrived, a week had passed since the attack. I still felt sick to my stomach. I wasn't eating or sleeping much and was still very apprehensive about doing the interview. But at about 11:00 a.m., a black Suburban pulled up in front of my home. A very polite driver stepped out and opened the door for me. It felt weird getting into the back of a black Suburban. I was usually the one providing security, escorting vehicles just like this, and now I was getting in the back of one and being driven to Washington, DC.

I arrived at the Embassy Suites on Twenty-Second Street in Northwest DC to conduct the first part of the interview in one of the conference rooms. I met the production staff at the entrance to the hotel, and they walked me down to a lower level and into a windowless conference room. It was dark except for the studio lighting. We were surrounded by several cameras and a lot of production equipment. In the center, surrounded by all this equipment, were two brightly lit chairs. I looked at the chairs and felt nervous, knowing that was where I would be sitting. I chuckled to myself, thinking, *Well, at least there's no plastic tarp under the chairs.*

The crew of two camera operators, a production assistant, and a producer introduced themselves. Then I met and spoke briefly to Bill Whitaker. He was a kind and soft-spoken gentleman. We were directed to have a seat. When Whitaker sat down in the chair across from me, he started to apply his own makeup. Due to COVID-19 restrictions, everyone was in charge of their own makeup. Mr. Whitaker pulled out his little kit filled with special brushes and powders. He seemed quite proficient in applying makeup and antishine powder here and there to his face. I looked at Whitaker and thought to myself, *Well, at least one of us will look good.* Then I reminded myself that I was here to do a job. I was here to stick up for my officers. I was not here for my looks.

Whitaker and I sat in the two chairs and had a brief friendly conversation as they set the lighting and audio levels. The time had come, and he started the interview. And it stopped as quickly as it had begun when the producer realized they had to make some more technical changes. This brief interruption occurred once more before we could finally settle in for the interview. About ninety minutes later, the interview had concluded, and as I looked around the room, several people were wiping their eyes. I, too, was very emotional. We gathered up our belongings and went down to the Capitol to finish the interview in the field.

We drove to Louisiana Avenue and D Street NW, not far from Union Station, to complete the interview. This was as close as we could get to the Capitol with its two rows of razor-wire-topped fencing surrounding the complex. I got out of the Suburban and met with Whitaker and the production team on Louisiana Avenue. We decided to finish the interview walking on the sidewalk, with the Capitol in the background and the security fence lined with National Guard troops. I could see the USCP officers who were handling the street closures looking at me as I was interviewed. They recognized me. Just as the interview began, an officer drove up to me in a marked vehicle to say hello. The camera crew saw this and wanted to record the interaction to be included in the interview. But I requested that they not, out of concern that the officer might get in trouble. The second part of the interview took about twenty-five minutes to complete. The producer turned toward us and said, "I think that's a wrap, gentlemen. That was great!"

It was done. I had spent two hours being interviewed, knowing this was going to be distilled down to about five minutes. I didn't know what to expect with the final version of the interview after the edits. As the rest of the production crew packed up and drove away, I asked my driver, Nasir, if he would wait a few minutes while I said hello to the USCP officers. I went over to the group of officers, who seemed genuinely happy to see me. It was nice to talk to them, even briefly. I spoke again to Pat Milton on the way home and thanked her for the kindness she and her production team had shown me. Pat told me that she expected my interview to run on the upcoming Sunday, January 17. I wasn't sure whether that made me feel better or worse. Either way, I was just glad the interview was over.

My family and I were already accustomed to the constant calls, texts, and visits from the media. I knew that the *60 Minutes* episode I filmed would be shown the coming Sunday and that with the inauguration coming, we were probably going to experience another spike in media inquiries. I really just wanted to get out of town for a few days, so on Sunday evening I checked into a hotel in Maryland with my family. We grabbed some food to go from the restaurant and headed to our room to watch *60 Minutes*. My wife and kids were sitting down, waiting for the program to begin, and I was up, pacing back and forth. When the segment started, my wife tensed. The first thing she noticed was how pale I looked. The stress and lack of sleep were clearly written all over my face. But I felt that the program did a good job capturing what I wanted to portray. I hadn't told anyone but close friends and family that I was going to be on the show. Immediately, people reached out to tell me they had watched and that they supported me.

I was spent and wanted to go to bed. Later, I would learn that the episode had 10.6 million viewers tune in and was the number one show in the time slot. My family and I spent the next couple of days decompressing and reconnecting with each other.

I woke up early the morning of January 20, Inauguration Day, with my wife asleep beside me and my kids sacked out in the adjoining room. I lay there reflecting. I had worked the past seven presidential inaugurations and had been the chief of the United States Capitol Police just days ago, planning for my eighth inauguration, and here I was on Inauguration Day, still in bed.

I was staring at a hotel ceiling, while the men and women of the USCP were on post in the cold, still reeling from the loss of two colleagues and having to deal with the physical and psychological injuries from the attack that had occurred just two weeks earlier. I wished I were there with them. To mourn with them, to cry with them, and to try to heal with them. I knew what I was going through and could only imagine what each one of them was dealing with that day. How worried their families and loved ones must have been as they watched them leave for work, with the indelible images of January 6 still clear in their memory.

I walked over to the sliding glass door and opened the curtain just wide enough to look out but not enough to flood the room with light and wake my wife. I looked out past the leafless trees and across the cold and deserted Choptank River, which flows past the hotel grounds. Looking in the direction of Washington, DC, I said a prayer for all the law enforcement, military, and numerous other agencies that I knew were working the day's events: *Please, let everyone be safe today.*

I sat in the darkened room for several minutes, then decided to go and find some coffee for my wife and me. I quietly got dressed, slipped out of the room, and headed for the lobby.

The hotel was mostly empty. It was the off-season and many of the shops were closed, but I finally found a small shop selling coffee and some limited Danish pastries and sandwiches. A couple in front of me was placing their order, and I got in line behind them. A short time later, a woman with her small children got in line behind me. I glanced back at them and noticed that one of the boys was wearing an MPD shirt. I turned to the family and, gesturing to the shirt, said, "I like the shirt. MPD is a great agency." I turned back to the barista.

After I placed my order, I stepped aside to wait for the coffee. The young woman then asked me, "Are you a police officer?"

I thought about the question for a second and decided not to say anything about my time at the Capitol. I said, "I was with MPD for over twenty-five years and retired a few years ago as a commander." I figured that answer was fairly innocuous, and besides, I was way out in Maryland—what were the odds of our having any acquaintances in common?

But then she mentioned her husband's name and said he was also a commander with the MPD. "Do you know him?" she asked.

Well, so much for the odds, because I had known her husband, Mike, for many years. In fact, Mike had reported to the USCP Command Center on January 6 and had talked to me numerous times late into the evening and early morning hours, coordinating MPD's support. "Yes, when I was the commander of MPD Special Operations Division," I answered. "I knew Mike well. He's a terrific commander."

She smiled at the accolades, even though this surely wasn't the first time she had heard them about her husband. She told me that she and the kids had decided to take a getaway out of town since Mike would be work-ing long hours for the inauguration. As I grabbed my coffees, I wished her a good stay and told her we might see each other again around the hotel.

"Who shall I tell Mike I ran into?" she asked me.

I hesitated. Then I took a deep breath and said, "Steven Sund."

I could tell she recognized the name. "Oh, you're . . ." she started to say. Then she caught herself and stopped.

"Yes, I'm that guy," I said, and I went on to tell her about the as-sistance Mike had given me on January 6 and how appreciative I was of the MPD.

"I'm Michele," she said. "I hope you're doing okay."

I thanked her and said goodbye to her and her family. But as I walked out of the shop with my two coffees, I thought to myself how much it sucks to be "that guy." I wondered if I would have to live with that for the rest of my life.

————

When we got back to Washington after our brief getaway, I received a call from a detective I had once worked with at MPD. I hadn't seen or heard from Avis King in years. It was a pleasant surprise. Avis informed me that after retiring from MPD, she had begun working for some legal teams. She told me about a firm she was associated with by the name of Katz, Banks and Kumin. She told me a little bit about the firm and said that if I was thinking about obtaining legal representation, she would highly recom-mend them. My wife and I had already talked about it, so I reached out to the firm. After a good discussion with Lisa Banks, I retained their services. Molly Levinson, a communication specialist, also became part of the team.

Everyone in the media was clamoring for a story, yet no one seemed to be getting accurate information. Since being unceremoniously asked to resign by the Speaker of the House on January 7, I'd had no further discussions with congressional leadership. I was concerned they were getting all their information from the media and needed to hear, as Paul Harvey used to say, "the rest of the story."

Lisa and Molly recommended that I consider writing a letter to congressional leadership to provide them with the facts. *What a simple yet brilliant idea*, I thought. We worked together over the next few days, going through several drafts. On Monday, February 1, I emailed a copy of my eight-page letter to the offices of all the congressional leadership. I didn't receive a response from any of the offices, so on Thursday, February 4, I sent a follow-up email to ensure they had received my document and to inform them that I would be sharing it with congressional oversight the next day. I received one response from Kevin McCarthy's office acknowledging receipt. The following morning, I shared the letter with my four former congressional oversight committees. True to Washington, DC, form, my letter appeared in the media just hours later, with all eight pages published on CNN.

On Wednesday, February 3, I drove up to the Capitol to pay my respects to Officer Sicknick. Less than a month earlier, I had been the chief, and now I had to get someone to grant me access through the two rows of fencing and armed National Guard soldiers. Not showing up to pay respects to one of my fallen officers was no option, but I didn't want my presence to distract from the official service with congressional leadership later that morning. My wife had been monitoring C-SPAN's live coverage of the event and determined that the media would not be back until around 7:30 a.m. to resume live coverage. We concluded that I needed to be in and out before then.

I arrived on the Hill at 5:15 a.m. and managed to get an official to arrange parking and help me get into the Capitol. I was glad I had come early. The main lights were off, and the rotunda was dimly lit. It was beautiful and peaceful. I stood in silent reflection in front of Officer Sicknick's remains, with a lone USCP Ceremonial Honor Guard member standing by. I have been to many police funerals in my career and have lost a few friends in the line of duty. Police funerals are always tough, but this one was especially difficult as I reflected on what Brian and all the other officers had gone through in this very room only weeks earlier.

The lone officer was aware of my presence. Although she did not move, we locked eyes briefly. We were both fighting back tears. I felt odd not being in uniform. This was the first police funeral I attended in a suit and as a civilian. After several quiet minutes in the rotunda, I stood at attention, slowly raising my right hand to my brow, rendering a salute to Officer Sicknick. My hand was trembling as I continued to fight back tears. I held the salute before slowly lowering my hand back to my side, turning away, and quietly departing. I felt so sad and empty.

As I walked from the rotunda, I ran into Officer Jodie Penny, who was assigned to one of the hallways. Jodie was a member of the executive board of the Police Labor Union. I had always thought highly of her and truly enjoyed working with her on a number of issues for the officers. We spoke for a few minutes, and she thanked me for coming and said, "We miss you, Chief. Please stay in touch." We embraced briefly, and I went on my way, reminding her to stay safe.

I decided to stop in to see the rest of the Honor Guard, who were in a break room nearby. I always appreciated the dedication and the efforts of the members of the Ceremonial Honor Guard, at both the MPD and the USCP. Most people don't know how difficult and physically demanding it is to stand an honor guard detail. They appreciated that I stopped in to see them. After chatting with some of the officers, I left the Hill and drove home to watch the memorial service on television. It was damned hard to watch that service and not be there. I missed my officers more than ever.

TESTIFYING BEFORE THE SENATE

In the first week of February, USCP General Counsel Tad DiBiase sent me a text saying he had heard there may be two hearings regarding January 6. The hearings were scheduled for February 23, 2021.

I knew I couldn't miss this opportunity to testify before Congress. So much had been screwed up that fateful day. I needed them to hear not only what went wrong but also what went *right*. According to Tad, the hearing was supposed to focus on only a select group: Capitol Police, DC Metropolitan Police, the Department of Defense, the FBI, and the Department of Homeland Security. Then, to my great surprise, he told me he didn't expect them to call me as a witness. "The committees are not going to call anyone who is no longer employed by the agency they reported to on January 6."

I thought that was crazy. That would exclude all those at the center of Capitol security: Mike Stenger, the Senate sergeant at arms; Paul Irving, the House sergeant at arms; and me. Why would they want to exclude us? Tad agreed this was odd.

I stewed on this for a day or two and decided I wasn't going to accept this without giving them some pushback. I called Rachelle Schroeder on the Senate Rules Committee. She was always personable and easy to work with, and I believed she would be the best person to query about the upcoming hearings. She confirmed that the committee would be holding the first hearing on February 23 and that the hearings would probably be restricted to current employees. I told her that I'd hoped to be able to testify.

"Chief," she said, "are you telling me you would be willing to voluntarily testify?"

"Yes, I would like to testify."

She seemed surprised by this. She then asked me if I thought Stenger and Irving would be willing to. I told her I couldn't speak for them and that she would have to find a way to reach them. After the three of us resigned, Stenger and I remained in Virginia, while Irving left the area and effectively disappeared off the radar. Although Irving and I hadn't communicated much since January, Stenger and I had spoken regularly and gone out to lunch a few times.

As more days went by, the upcoming Senate hearings continued to occupy my thoughts. I determined that if they excluded those of us at the center of the security apparatus on January 6, they must not be truly interested in finding out what occurred that day. Anyone currently working security on the Hill and being asked to testify would probably be looking to save their job and hence would answer questions in CYA fashion.

But I was pleasantly surprised when the congressional committees had a change of heart. On February 11, I received my invitation to testify at the US Senate Committee on Homeland Security and Governmental

Affairs and the Committee on Rules and Administration's joint hearing titled, "Examining the January 6 Attack on the US Capitol."

I didn't know what had changed or why, but I was happy to be included. I immediately began to prepare my testimony with my legal and media team, Lisa Banks and Molly Levinson.

Due to COVID-19, I had been given the option to testify remotely. But I felt strongly that I had nothing to hide, nothing to be ashamed of, and I wanted Congress and the nation to see it. I wanted to be there in person, to answer their questions directly. The committees were surprised that I was so interested in testifying in person.

The hearing was to take place in the Dirksen Senate Building, in hearing room SDG-50, a very large and grandly appointed room that I knew well from my time with both the MPD and the USCP. Shortly beforehand, I was informed that I would be testifying along with Stenger, Irving, and Acting Chief of the Metropolitan Police Department Robert Contee. But I would be the only one testifying in person.

My legal team insisted that they pick my suit and tie. They wanted a photograph of options, but I just couldn't seem to get the lighting right. The grays and blues wouldn't come out in the pictures. I wanted to wear a light-colored tie, but they told me to go with a red power tie. I was going to pick the standard government gray suit but ultimately decided to wear my boldest blue suit and my favorite Allen Edmonds wingtip oxfords, which a friend had given me as an MPD retirement gift. I thought the suit looked good, but it wasn't what I was used to wearing before Congress.

On the morning of February 23, 2021, I woke up early as usual. I had my coffee and did my best not to wake anyone. (Putting on a suit is a lot quieter than putting on a police uniform!) I took the dogs out for a quick walk. As much as I wanted to talk to my wife, I didn't want her to wake up too early because the longer she slept, the less time she would spend worrying over me. I made her a cup of coffee in an insulated travel mug and put it on her bedside table, kissed her, and quietly left the house.

My legal team had said that having a warm liquid on hand would help when speaking for a very long time. I believe they had learned that from a previous client who testified on the Hill. I grabbed my usual Venti drip coffee at Starbucks and went to pick up my attorneys.

The Capitol Building was surrounded by two layers of tall fencing with concertina wire on top. There were also checkpoints everywhere staffed by armed National Guard troops standing with USCP officers. I knew that navigating the new perimeter would be complicated, especially in a civilian vehicle and with no police credentials. I had coordinated with Lieutenant Michael Weight to get me through the barricades. Michael was kind enough to find me a parking spot close to the Dirksen Building. That's why I had told my attorneys I would pick them up at Union Station, so that I could get them through the perimeter. Due to COVID-19, I had never seen my legal team in person until that morning.

We proceeded to the first perimeter check, where USCP officers greeted us. "Chief, good to see you, sir!" At the second perimeter, the same thing: "So glad to see you, sir. How have you been? We miss you, Chief!"

As I was driving, I realized I didn't have my favorite USCP lapel pin. The pin has the Capitol badge with the US and Capitol flags on either side. But I knew that Kerry, my former executive assistant, always kept a bag of lapel pins behind her desk. Like Salley, she had been an integral part of my talented team. She was well organized, professional, friendly, and always ready to do anything for me and the team. Initially, after the previous chief, Matt Verderosa, retired, she wanted to transfer somewhere else on the Hill, but as the weeks went by, she realized she wanted to stay because she enjoyed working with me and liked what I was doing for the department. Kerry took my abrupt departure hard, and when I texted her about a lapel pin, she was more than happy to do one more thing for me. She sneaked out of the building and gave the pin to Lieutenant Weight to pass along to me. I put it on, and we began walking toward the Dirksen Building. In the parking lot, a few officers intercepted us. They each wanted to see how I was doing and to tell me they missed me.

As we approached the prescreening area of the Dirksen Building, the officer at the post, whom I had regularly talked to in the field, came up to me and said, "Chief, so happy to see you, sir! Would a hug be appropriate?"

"Absolutely, Lisa," I said. We passed a few more officers inside the building who expressed how glad they were to see me. One even asked me when I was coming back. Debra, Lisa, and I walked down a long series of hallways with a number of doors. I always open doors for women. It's how I was raised and how I raised my son. They seemed uncomfortable with it at first, but by the fifth or sixth door, they didn't seem to mind. I believe there's even a press picture of me opening the door for Lisa. At the end of one corridor, we turned the corner into a sea of reporters. The cameras started to go off. Lisa and Debra flanked me as we made our way through. I had the impression they both got a kick out of it.

We entered the hearing room. I thought, *Here we are.* I was looking sharp but feeling like crap. Senator Amy Klobuchar immediately recognized Lisa and Debra from the Kavanaugh hearings. She made a beeline to them, and they spoke for several minutes. She then came over to me to thank me for coming in person. Captains Neysha Mendoza and Jeanita Mitchell came up, and Jeanita announced, "We're here to be your cheerleaders, Chief!" Neysha then told me she would be speaking first and that she wanted to stay and hear my opening statement before she went back to work.

Neysha delivered a very heartfelt statement, and toward the end of her speech, she said, "I want to acknowledge Chief Sund's leadership." I did not expect this. She had stated earlier she would mention one of her supervisors but hadn't said it would be me. "I served under his command as a watch commander for three years and was able to personally see his hard work and dedication," she went on. "He was fully dedicated to the US Capitol Police, and he cared about every employee on the department. I often hear employees on the department praise his leadership and his ability to inspire others."

I was sitting there thinking, *Here's an individual who has gone through significant trauma, was asked at the last minute to come in and talk about her experience on January 6, and yet is taking the time to praise me as a leader.*

It was difficult for me to listen without feeling emotional. "He has made a significant impact on our agency," she concluded. "Thank you, Chief."

I was fighting back tears and had to remind myself that I would be speaking shortly and should probably hold it together. After Neysha delivered her remarks, MPD Acting Chief Contee was called to speak next. As he spoke via Zoom, I began to feel a tightness in my chest. I started thinking, *This would really suck if I passed out on national TV.* I started wondering where the nearest automated external defibrillator was. How long would it take for one of my officers, whom I knew to be pretty good with those things, to get to me with an AED? I took a few sips of water and told myself to calm down. *It's not a heart attack—just nerves.*

Staffers and senators kept shuffling in and out, and I could see officers periodically peeking in and looking at me through the tiny round windows in the doors. Lisa sat right behind me, and Debra sat at the advised social distance of six feet to Lisa's right. They had already given me one final pep talk: "Steve, we support you. We prepped. You got this. We will step in if things look like they are going sideways."

As I sat down, I looked at the little note my wife had written in my binder: *I Love You.* She didn't want it to be easily seen by cameras or onlookers, so she had written it very faintly in pencil at the top corner of my opening statement. Before and after the hearing, senators from both sides of the aisle came up to thank me for coming in person. Everyone was very respectful, and Senator Klobuchar seemed especially happy to see me. We joked about how I had become her best friend over the summer when she needed assistance with a security issue. During that time, she had called me fairly often, and my office would joke that Ames was "my new bestie."

The almost four and a half hours of testimony felt as though it went by quickly. I felt very comfortable with my testimony and my answers. I was a little perplexed at Irving's lack of recollection, and I couldn't believe I had blanked out on the specific statute requiring CPB approval to request the National Guard. But all in all, I thought it went well, and for the first time since January 6, my stomach wasn't hurting.

On the way back to the car, more officers stopped us, wanting to talk to me. Debra, Lisa, and I got into my car as yet another officer walked up. It was Inspector Erickson, commander of the Inaugural Task Force for USCP. I stepped out, and Erickson told me he wanted to give me a few things on behalf of the officers in the task force. He gave me two personalized inaugural license plates and an Inaugural Task Force polo shirt with "Chief" on it. We kept talking until I jokingly told John, "I've got two attorneys in the car, and they charge by the hour. I've really got to go!"

After I dropped Lisa and Debra off at Union Station, I met with some members of the USCP Special Operations Division (SOD). I had renamed the unit, which had previously been called the Patrol Mobile Response Division (PMRD). No one had liked the original name, so it was a welcome change. Captain Mendoza and SOD had put together a photo book of emails and messages from various officers and officials. Even Robert Glover, the MPD official who had overseen the CDU response on the West Front on January 6, made an entry. I started looking through the book, reading the entries, letters, and poems. As I flipped through the pages, surrounded by officers, I began to get choked up. "Guys, I've had an emotional day," I said. "At this point, I think I can only look at the pictures."

Jeanita gave me a glass apothecary jar of blue plastic starfish with a blue bow, which corresponded to a poem she had included. I still read this poem and the notes from the officers regularly. Some other officers put together another jar filled with chocolates. They said they wanted to do something to make me feel better and had decided chocolate couldn't hurt. They added that they all wanted to do something because they felt I didn't get a proper send-off. The large glass lid on the jar rattled in the back seat of my car all the way home.

As soon as I was alone, I called my wife. She told me she was very happy with how I looked and sounded and that she was proud of me. She was relieved it was over because the night before, when I was practicing my opening statement, it wasn't going well. I was either going too fast or losing my place, or I kept stumbling over the words.

I had my phones turned off during my hearing. When I turned them back on, I was bombarded with texts and emails from law enforcement personnel and civilians. USSS Chief Tom Sullivan texted, "Well done today, so when are they bringing you back?" Even Officer Vince Summers, the number two at the USCP labor union, along with the secretary of the union, sent me positive texts about my testimony.

Neither my wife nor I felt like cooking, so we decided to go out for dinner that night. We went to a restaurant where my son had started working a few months earlier to help pay for his flying lessons. We sat near the bar and had dinner, surrounded by large-screen televisions mounted all around the restaurant. Tiger Woods had been involved in a serious single-car accident earlier that afternoon, and the coverage was dominating the news. Following that story, the news switched to the hearing. Images of me testifying appeared on the large screens. My wife looked at me and wondered if anyone would notice me. Happily, they didn't.

The next day, I received a text from an officer stating that Mendoza and I were on the cover of the *Washington Post*. I drove to the grocery store in my neighborhood to get a copy or two of the paper. I texted Mendoza and sent her a picture of the front page. The front cover of the *Washington Post* pictured the two of us hugging at the hearing.

For most of that Thursday and Friday after the hearing, I worked on my supplementary testimony, which I submitted on Friday, February 26, around 7:00 p.m. The testimony detailed the exact times I had requested the National Guard, and I provided attachments of my phone records and video evidence provided by the USCP.

This supplemental testimony corrected such critical information as when I first approached the House and Senate sergeants at arms to request the support of the National Guard on the morning of Sunday, January 3, and the numerous calls I had made to Irving and Stenger making the urgent request for the National Guard as we were under attack on January 6. These were critical events that I could narrow down to the minute using video transcripts and my phone records, which the department had provided. All this evidentiary information was provided to the committees as attachments to my testimony.

By the end of February, things seemed to finally settle down a bit. I

watched the department's and the Architect of the Capitol's appropriations hearings at the beginning of March. They both requested significant
budget increases to address the shortfalls that were brought to light as
a result of January 6. I received an occasional call from the press, following up on my testimony or asking questions about some lead they
had heard about. I also received an occasional call from staffers from
some of the committees on the Hill. Usually, these calls were just personal inquiries to see how I was doing. Things seemed to be starting to
calm down, and I began thinking about what I was going to do in my
next chapter in life. The second row of fencing topped with razor wire
was brought down toward the end of March. The Capitol complex was
starting to return to normal.

Then on Friday, April 2, without warning, Noah Green, a twenty-five-
year-old Black nationalist, drove his car at high speed from Constitution
Avenue, turned onto Delaware Avenue, and rammed his vehicle into
the north barricade, striking two officers. Green then jumped out of
his vehicle with a large butcher-style knife and lunged toward one of
the injured officers. Another USCP officer at the barrier shot and killed
the assailant before he could attack anyone else. Within minutes of the
north barricade attack, I received a spate of calls and texts from officers
and officials on the scene. It was heartbreaking, talking to these men
and women and being asked to guide them. A few minutes later, the
media started reporting on the incident, and "special reports" began interrupting programs on television.

Just a short time before the attack, the assailant had visited a specialty
knife shop just blocks away at Union Station, where he had reportedly
purchased the custom-made Japanese knife he used in the attack for three
hundred dollars. Tragically, USCP Officer William "Billy" Evans died of
injuries he received in the attack. The second USCP officer, Ken Shaver,
was hospitalized as a result of his injuries. I had gotten to know both
officers during my time with the Capitol Police, and I recalled friendly
conversations with Billy about the small garden gnome they had put in
a planter near the barricade. I had found it humorous to pull up to the
barricade in my unmarked police vehicle and see this little gnome with

a red hat peeking at me as I waited to enter the security barrier. Around Christmastime, Billy and his partners at the north barricade would put a small battery-powered Christmas tree in the planter next to the gnome. I used to ask him, "When is the official tree-lighting ceremony?"

I will always remember Billy's characteristic greeting whenever I approached the north barricade: "Going all the way up, boss?" He was a good man and a good cop. I will never forget him.

The very next day, Billy's partner, Ken, came home from the MedStar Washington Hospital Center. Mendoza and some officers were going there to greet him when he was released and asked me if I'd like to join them.

"Absolutely," I said.

When I arrived, there were officers not only from the USCP but also from the Metropolitan Police Department, the United States Park Police, and the Secret Service Uniformed Division. I arrived and parked in the visitor lot right where the officers were standing in a few small groups, deep in conversation. Some MPD officers came over to me. Several of them worked at my old command, the Special Operations Division. I made it a point to let the MPD officers know how much I appreciated their support on the sixth and how sorry I was for what they had to go through. I had not seen many of the USCP officers since that day, so I wanted to make sure I got around to each of them to say how I wished I could have done more to assist them during the fight. I also spoke with the officers from the USPP and the USSS and expressed my appreciation for their assistance.

A short time later, we got word that they were getting ready to bring Ken out of the hospital. He was brought out in a wheelchair and got a big round of applause from all the officers. He was overcome with emotion. It was hard for anyone to imagine what he had been through in the past twenty-four hours. Once Ken and his wife were in their car, I took a minute to talk to them. We exchanged contact information, and I told him I was there for him if he ever needed anything. We are still in contact to this day.

On Tuesday, April 13, I again found myself heading to the Capitol to pay respects to a fallen officer. I arrived early and was on the East

Plaza for the arrival of the hearse and Billy's family. I stood at attention with hundreds of others as we watched the Honor Guard carrying the casket bearing the remains of Officer Billy Evans, stepping in unison up the center steps of the Capitol and into the rotunda as a member called out cadence: "Step . . . Step . . . Step." Although I had been offered VIP seating to watch the official ceremony, I preferred to sit in the Capitol Visitor Center's auditorium and watch the service with the officers. I felt that I needed the time to grieve and heal with them.

Watching the service with all the officers and standing in the reviewing line as it worked its way through the CVC to the rotunda gave me the opportunity to talk to many of the officers I missed so much. I stayed well into the evening until the end of the service. At the conclusion of the ceremony, I again joined the hundreds of officers on the East Plaza. This time, I was asked to participate in the formation of Capitol Police officers lining up to honor Officer Evans during his departure from the Capitol. As I watched Billy's casket being carried down the rotunda steps and loaded into the back of the hearse, I looked around at the faces of all the officers around me. I could see that while they were still in shock from the attack in January and numb from this most recent loss, there was still great courage and dedication in all of them. I realized that very few people understand what police officers must face in their line of work.

I felt the rumble of the four Harley-Davidson police motorcycles, one at each corner of the hearse, as they slowly drove past.

They were escorting Billy one last time through the north barricade where he had bravely stood guard, and past the little gnome in the red hat.

THE SENATE ISSUES ITS REPORT

Following my testimony, the Senate committee held several more public hearings with testimony from the FBI, Department of Defense, Department of Homeland Security, and DC National Guard.

I felt that the hearings supported my testimony but also raised a number of serious concerns regarding the impact of January 6. The committees also interviewed Architect of the Capitol Brett Blanton and several USCP officers and an inspector. They also heard from Yogananda Pittman, one of my old assistant chiefs and now the acting chief of police, but oddly, they didn't interview Chad Thomas, my other assistant chief.

In mid-May, I was informed that the committees were wrapping up their report. I had heard that both committees wanted to conclude their combined work in order to pursue their individual investigations regarding January 6. On Tuesday, June 1, the Senate Rules Committee emailed me a heavily redacted portion of a draft of the upcoming Senate report. According to the accompanying note, this was the only portion of the report that was pertinent to me. They sent me thirty-four pages that included only those sections where I was mentioned or quoted. The pages were over 90 percent redacted, often providing only one or two sentences of text per page to review.

I could look at only a couple of sentences per page, yet I was supposed to validate the accuracy of the information and understand the context in which my information was used? I found this ridiculous because I was allegedly being given this document so I could provide additional information if needed. With such highly redacted pages, I wasn't sure how they expected me to know when additional information would be necessary. The accompanying email chain indicated that the excerpts were being provided "as a courtesy, so that you have advance notice of the content related to Mr. Sund."

The committee gave me until 9:00 a.m. on Thursday, June 3—less than two days—to offer any corrections, which would be considered at the discretion of the committees. I reviewed the documents as well as I could and noted several areas that required corrections. In the end, I provided an additional three-page response with a number of recommended corrections, citing corroborating evidence and previously submitted testimony. (This was on top of the five pages of supplemental testimony I had already submitted to them on February 26, three days after I testified in person. Also, on April 2, I had responded to several *questions for the record* from the senators on the committees. In my response, I had submitted twenty-five pages of detailed answers.) As I was preparing my edits, I worked closely with my personal legal counsel, who also found the highly redacted pages a little peculiar. I waited for the next correspondence from the committees since they had informed me that I would receive a complete unredacted copy the day before its public release.

Six days later, on the morning of Tuesday, June 8, my wife and I were having coffee as she reviewed the morning news on her phone. She paused and looked at me, a little perplexed. "Did you ever get the copy of the Senate report they promised you? Because it's out in the media."[6]

I checked my email. No report. They never sent me the final version before it was made public, as they had promised. I was stunned. I could have been approached by the media that morning and questioned about the report, and I would have been caught off guard.

I reached out to Salley Wood, my old chief of staff at the USCP, and inquired whether the department had received an advance copy of the report. Salley said they had received it a few days ago and that she could provide me a copy. I thanked her but told her I'd be reaching out to Senate Rules to ask why I didn't get a copy. I emailed the Senate Rules Committee and received a copy later that day. The email response they sent me with the attached full unredacted report stated that they had made an "unforgivable oversight by not providing it to you in advance as discussed." It might have been unforgivable, but as far as its being an "oversight," I rather doubted it.

When I first heard about the combined committees' scheduled hearings, I believed this would be my opportunity to tell my side of the story to Congress and the American people. I thought this would be a fair and bipartisan platform, and that's why I readily volunteered to testify. It was the first public testimony on the attack on the US Capitol, and I knew the world would be watching. I had poured my heart out and

6. Gary Peters, Rob Portman, Amy Klobuchar, and Roy Blunt, *Examining the U.S. Capitol Attack: A Review of the Security, Planning, and Response Failures on January 6*, Senate Committee on Homeland Security and Governmental Affairs and Senate Committee on Rules and Administration, n.d., www.rules.senate.gov/imo/media/doc/Jan%206%20HSGAC%20Rules%20Report.pdf.

testified before the committees for over four hours, answering every question posed to me, only to see my lengthy oral testimony and all my supplemental testimony distilled into minor bits of the final report. Although I had already submitted video and phone records and provided highly credible witnesses in my supplemental testimony, the Senate's final report contained only a single reference to my corrected testimony.

President Biden had called January 6 "the worst attack on our democracy since the Civil War." Given that, I would have expected Congress to do a more thorough job of reviewing, corroborating, and presenting its findings. There were a number of errors and contradictions throughout the document, and several of my statements for which I had supplied supporting documentation (the phone records and video evidence that corroborated my requests to the sergeants at arms for National Guard support on January 3, as well as my many urgent requests on January 6) were not reported as having been conclusively substantiated. In fact, the report started off in "Section III: Background, A. Agencies Responsible for Protecting the Capitol Complex" describing the Capitol Complex as including the US Supreme Court.

It appeared that the committees either forgot or were unaware of the fact that the Supreme Court, part of the judicial branch of government, has its own police force, the US Supreme Court Police. A report that starts that poorly doesn't inspire much confidence in the rest of the document.

The Senate report, like the hearings, was riddled with serious discrepancies and blatantly untrue statements—issues that if openly and honestly addressed would have provided a much clearer picture to the American public of what *really* led up to, and occurred on, January 6. Instead, certain inconvenient topics and questions were avoided, dismissed, or downplayed, including answers to such pertinent questions as these:

- Did the chief of the Capitol Police seek the support of the National Guard in advance of January 6?
- What specifically, were the concerns for "optics" that HSAA Irving expressed over the use of the National Guard?

- Who had what intelligence, and how did this influence planning for January 6?
- Who was involved in the seventy-one-minute delay in approving the use of the National Guard during the attack?
- What was the impact of the political conflict between the DC city government and the executive branch on security in the city?
- What intelligence did the Department of Defense have, and how did the unprecedented restrictions placed on the National Guard by the secretary of defense affect USCP?
- What impact did the oversight structure and budget that Congress provided for the USCP have on the agency's preparedness on January 6?

None of these questions were seriously addressed by the Senate committees.

The narrative in the media, and the opinion of much of the public as they watched that day, was that the Capitol Police was an ill-prepared, ill-equipped force that missed or ignored intelligence regarding this event and then easily gave up their perimeter. As a result, Speaker of the House Nancy Pelosi told the nation that I had failed as a leader. I had failed to keep a mob of more than ten thousand from breaking into the Capitol Building with the resources I was provided. Because we couldn't physically hold back a mob that outnumbered us 58 to 1, I had to resign.

This deeply offended many of my officers, who felt that their efforts weren't appreciated. The congressional leadership had removed all three top security personnel and then proceeded to put up two layers of fencing topped with concertina wire and supplement the police force with twenty-five thousand armed troops so that the department would be prepared and equipped and wouldn't "fail" should the mob return and try again. It was an unprecedented attack followed by an unprecedented solution. The Capitol had never in its history been surrounded by such fencing with armed National Guard.

My personal and law enforcement family know what odds we faced and what we were up against. That was a horrible day for everyone on the Hill and for those watching on television. The public criticism of my officers after their ordeal was deeply upsetting and unwarranted. The stinging criticism and attacks on my leadership were painful and life altering. I had gone from thirty years in DC as a decorated, widely respected leader to suddenly being publicly humiliated and forced to resign on national television.

THE LASTING EFFECTS

January 6 wasn't the kind of traumatic incident that affects only a limited number of employees. It wasn't just one shift or one section of the department. January 6 affected every single employee of the USCP, both sworn and civilian, and even contract workers. My chief of staff, Salley, my public information officer, Eva, my office staff, my fleet services, and property division personnel—none of them were involved in the fighting, but all were deeply scarred by the event. Even the human resources department, which had to deal with all the injury claims and resignations—*everyone* was hit hard in some way. And with all their difficulties compounded by the pervasive news coverage, the families of USCP employees experienced a lot of stress. Many employees I've spoken with have told me their personal stories of physical illness and mental anguish, often describing issues with sleeplessness, anger, and depression.

For me and my family, the impact of this event has been far greater than I could ever have anticipated. Some days, I feel as if I were amped up on six cups of coffee and have the sensation of an electrical current surging through my body. While these feelings have eased slightly over time, they're still very much with me. I still continually run through the events of January 6 in my head, subjecting myself to "What if" over and over again. But no matter how many times I try to rewrite the script, there is never a good outcome.

Friends and acquaintances often ask me, "How are you sleeping?" My standard response is to say I'm doing well and sleeping fine. But the truth is, at first I couldn't sleep at all, even though I desperately wanted to and was beyond exhausted. After about a week, the initial shock of the attack and being forced to resign wore off, and I could finally sleep. And I slept as much as I could because when I was awake, my mind was constantly racing and reliving the events of January 6 and 7.

I experienced temporary vision loss in one eye and found myself often breaking down crying when I was by myself. I did my best to hide this from my family, but one day when I was driving home from the gym with my son, I just broke down crying. There was nothing I could do about it. My son was calmly trying to comfort me. He had never seen his father this way. This occurred a second time, not long after, when I was out with my two daughters. I don't know what triggered it. It just happened.

My wife was devastated, not only by the impact on the family but also by what she saw happening to my reputation in the press and on social media. She saw and read the viral outbursts against me. The allegations calling me complicit, a criminal, and a racist were especially painful to her. Maria has been with me from the very beginning of my career in law enforcement and knows what kind of cop and what kind of man I am. While we received a lot of support from friends and neighbors, I knew that my wife was internalizing a lot to protect me. She wouldn't discuss what was being reported and kept reminding me to focus on myself and not on what others were saying.

I have come to realize how important it is never to underestimate the impact an event like this can have on a spouse. The constant media attention and the concern about someone possibly retaliating against me or the family made her anxious and jumpy. I knew this was the case when I received a frantic call from her telling me a man was at the door with a baseball bat. She sent me a screenshot from one of our security cameras showing a large man at our door, holding what appeared to be an aluminum baseball bat. As the guy kept pounding on the door, my middle daughter was able to determine it was not a baseball bat after all, but a metal microphone boom.

While my wife was upset and heartbroken about how my career ended, my two daughters were angry more than anything else. Angry that

Trump grossly mishandled his election loss and placed himself above the country. Angry that people were hurt and killed because partisan politicians were pushing division and hatred. Angry that Pelosi fired me while publicly citing false information. Angry that Congress and the media immediately made the police out to be the bad guys—racist, complicit, and God knows whatever else. It all just reinforced my kids' negative view of politics and politicians. But it was my son who, I believe, took it the hardest. He had looked up to me as a cop his whole life. He had been to my work at the MPD many times and had grown up riding in police motorcycle sidecars and going out on police boats and helicopters. He wasn't angry like the girls. He just became withdrawn and quiet.

In fact, not until sixteen months later did my son finally open up to me about how he learned of the attack at the Capitol. As we were riding in the car together one day, he began to tell me his very emotional story. It was early in the afternoon on January 6, and my son was attending his tenth-grade classes virtually, due to the COVID-19 pandemic. He was alone in an upstairs bedroom, lying on the floor in front of his laptop for his English class, where they were discussing George Orwell's classic novel *Nineteen Eighty-Four*. His English teacher kept glancing over at something next to her computer. She was visibly distracted and appeared distraught. "Are you guys seeing this?" his teacher asked. "Are you seeing what is happening at the Capitol in DC? It's terrible, just terrible!"

My son's thoughts instantly went to me and my work. He knew I had been anticipating a large demonstration that day. But now several of his fellow students were commenting online about the horrific attack on the Capitol. Some said that protestors had smashed out windows and were inside the building. Others were instant-messaging the rest of the class, talking about how bad the fighting was.

The teacher, now on the verge of tears, turned her laptop camera toward her TV. The screen showed disturbing images of protesters smashing windows and breaking their way into the Capitol and others battling with police on the West Front.

As we drove on, my son turned to me with his voice starting to shake as he said, "Dad, I was watching officers wearing MPD and Capitol police uniforms fighting for their lives." My son had grown up around these familiar uniforms. He said he even recognized some of the officers. He recalled, as he was seeing these images on his laptop, that his heart was racing and he felt sick to his stomach. Thousands of rioters were attacking the police. The officers he knew would be doing everything they could to defend the Capitol. He hoped they would all make it home.

He told me he couldn't watch it anymore, so he closed his laptop and ran downstairs, where he found Mom sitting in the basement, watching the TV. She was crying as she sat there speechless, watching the same images. One of my daughters was sitting on the stairs leading to the basement, silently watching the TV from there.

My son told me that he took a seat on the stairs next to his sister. Neither of them said a word. They just kept watching. And he never did return to his virtual classroom that day.

I called him on the night of January 6, right around eight, just to see how he was doing. But it took him sixteen months to finally tell me how that day had really hit him.

That's just one of the stories I think about now as I look back on everything we've been through since January 6. It is during difficult times like these that you find out who your true friends are.

One day, when my son was at work at a local restaurant, several of the television sets were showing Speaker Pelosi. The manager saw this and immediately had the stations changed to spare my son any added grief. It is little kindnesses like this that have meant so much to me and my family.

It means a lot to me when people take the time to call and ask how we're doing. I am usually the one calling to check on a friend or colleague, so it was a little strange being the one on the receiving end. Seeing my name and picture beside some terrible headline on national and local news made it seem as if the entire nation had turned on me and my department. But despite all the headlines and the smears, my officers did not. Their outpouring of support brought me great comfort. The outreach from USCP members, the texts, calls, emails, letters, and postcards from sworn officers and civilians, have meant a great deal to me and have helped me greatly through this process. I still get multiple texts and calls each day from current and former USCP employees. I cannot thank my friends and former colleagues across several agencies enough for their continued friendship and support. Without them, it would have been much harder.

I would be remiss if I did not acknowledge the positive impact my faith and my church have had on me. Within hours of Speaker Pelosi's press conference, Father Victor and other members of the clergy reached out to see how I was doing and to offer prayers and support. My family and I will forever be grateful for the constant support we have received from them all.

CHAPTER 4:

WHAT WENT WRONG, AND LESSONS TO LEARN

During my almost thirty years in law enforcement, I have been involved in many critical incidents and responded to some horrific scenes. The events on January 6, 2021, were far and away the worst mass attack on law enforcement I have witnessed in my entire career. As I watched the attack unfolding, I saw first hundreds, then thousands, of people besieging the Capitol and violently attacking my officers. At the height of the attack, on the West Front alone, close to ten thousand rioters had advanced into our closed and restricted perimeter. Thousands more were on the East Front of the Capitol. It quickly became evident to me that many in this crowd had planned and had come equipped for this attack.

Why weren't we better prepared? Where to start when I had tried to increase the intelligence and operational capabilities of an agency for years, only to have it all unravel when faced with the challenges of January 6? When I dissect the events of that day, I start to see the issues that have plagued security on the Hill for decades and directly contributed to the horrific events. This was the perfect storm of ill-informed planning, preparation, and response, involving many more players than just the United States Capitol Police. Issues involving intelligence, the Capitol Police Board and congressional leadership, and the Department of Defense, combined with deficiencies in the USCP's response and management of the situation, all contributed to the vulnerabilities we faced when a mob of thousands, enraged by a sitting US president's claim of a stolen election, descended on our Capitol.

This is not an attempt to cast blame on others or to avoid accepting my own responsibility. No one holds themselves more accountable than I do for what my officers and all the responding officers went through that day, and I wish I could have done more. January 6 was an important day in American history, and it is time the American people know the truth behind some key issues that made this horrific attack possible.

INTELLIGENCE

The most significant shortfall that impeded USCP preparedness on January 6 was intelligence. Complete, accurate intelligence is critical in law enforcement, especially for an agency like the United States Capitol Police. Intelligence not only drives our deployment and protection strategy but also informs critical decisions. The intelligence pushed out by the Intelligence and Interagency Coordination Division (IICD) drives much more than just my decisions as the chief of police. The IICD's products inform the Capitol Police Board, congressional leadership, members of Congress, and my oversight committees. Each of these recipients uses this information to make critical decisions regarding security on Capitol Hill. These decisions include staffing, budgeting, training, and the relative ranking of physical security and infrastructure programs. All these critical decisions rely on complete and accurate information provided by the IICD. Incomplete or misleading information can have a disastrous cascading effect across the Hill.

Since leaving the department on January 8, I have learned that the intelligence the IICD provided to assist in our planning and preparations for January 6 was neither complete nor accurate. Indeed, it was seriously flawed. In our planning for January 6, the USCP relied on intelligence and information from both internal and external sources. While there were things I wished our federal partners at the FBI and DHS had done better, the handling of intelligence by my own intelligence unit was by far the biggest factor contributing to our lack of preparedness on that day. *This was a colossal USCP intelligence failure, plain and simple.* The failure of the Protective Services Bureau and IICD leadership to present a complete and accurate depiction of the intelligence they possessed created false expectations about the event for the USCP, the CPB, and members of Congress. These false expectations had a disastrous effect on the planning and preparations for January 6. In fact, knowing what I do now, we are lucky things didn't turn out far worse.

With the director of the IICD retiring in November 2020, we initiated a nationwide search for a replacement. I had recused myself from the review panel and brought in a representative from the USSS intelligence unit to sit on the selection committee with Pittman and Gallagher. Following an extensive interview process, retired NYPD official John "Jack" Donohue was selected as the new director. Donohue had thirty-two years of experience with the NYPD and at one time had been their assistant chief in charge of intelligence. He was considered an expert on domestic extremism. During the interview process, Gallagher and Pittman also identified another candidate whom they felt would be perfect to oversee our analytical capability and act as the assistant director of IICD. Based on their recommendation and a vacant civilian position, I was able to hire both a director and an assistant director. Julie Farnam began working at IICD as the assistant director the last week of October 2020, and Jack Donohue started as the director the first week of November.

Weeks before January 6, the new IICD leadership began a massive reorganizing of the intelligence unit. They began shuffling analysts' responsibilities around, creating what analysts described as a lot of confusion within the unit. The Open Source Section, one of the most critical intelligence assets for monitoring demonstrations and online threats against the Capitol and members of Congress, was decimated, with many of the analysts being directed to clear backlogs of assignments for investigations instead of monitoring open-source information. The IICD was a unit that had provided effective and actionable intelligence on many occasions in the past. During my four years with the USCP, we had dealt with several very contentious, high-profile events, including two Supreme Court nominations (Brett Kavanaugh and Amy Coney Barrett), some heated health care and immigration demonstrations, and a presidential impeachment trial. During these events, thousands of people protested, sometimes in several locations at the same time, inside and outside the congressional office buildings. These events were successfully managed with operational plans that were developed based on good intelligence. During some of these protests, USCP locked up hundreds of protesters in a single day without incident or injury. The IICD had provided accurate and actionable intelligence regarding these events. But now the IICD was facing an organizational crisis, all while the events of January 6 were fast approaching.

As the planning for January 6 continued, there seemed to be no extra coordination, preparation, or sense of urgency from the leadership at the IICD. Analysts were giving IICD leadership concerning intelligence they were receiving, but the information was not included in the assessments. The analysts were not receiving feedback or additional direction regarding January 6.

Since December 14, when the department first became aware of the rally and demonstrations coinciding with the joint session of Congress, the IICD produced a total of four special event assessments for the January 6 joint session. The first three assessments were published on December 16, December 23, and December 30. All three of these assessments indicated that there was no information regarding specific disruptions or civil disobedience targeting this event, and none of the critical bottom-line-up-front (BLUF) bullet points indicated any expectation of violence targeting Congress or the Capitol.

The next and final intelligence assessment, IICD Special Event Assessment 21-A-0468 v.3, dated January 3, 2020, was a fifteen-page document distributed about forty-eight hours before January 6.[1] The fifteen pages that made up this final assessment provided a more detailed description of the various demonstrations expected to occur both

---

1. Bolton, *Review of the Events Surrounding the January 6, 2021, Takeover of the U.S. Capitol.*

downtown by the White House and on Capitol grounds. The critical BLUF included four points:

> *On Wednesday, January 6, 2021, the 117th United States Congress will gather for a joint session in the chamber of the House of Representatives to certify the counting of the electoral votes.*
>
> *There are some representatives and senators who plan to challenge the votes during this session, which will allow the objection to move forward.*
>
> *The Intelligence and Interagency Coordination Division is currently tracking several protests slated to take place on Capitol grounds and elsewhere in Washington, DC, on January 5, 2021, and January 6, 2021, and some protesters have indicated they plan to be armed. There is also indication that white supremacist groups may be attending the protests.*
>
> *Detailed information concerning potential counterprotest activity is limited.*

The final IICD intelligence assessment indicated that the January 6 protests and rallies were "expected to be similar to the previous Million MAGA March rallies in November and December 2020, which drew tens of thousands of participants." The assessment also stated, "No groups are expected to march and all are planning to stay in their designated areas."

I reference the BLUF section of all the assessments because of the importance that IICD leadership had placed on them. On December 8, just a week before releasing the first special event assessment for the joint session of Congress, the new IICD assistant director had sent an email to all IICD personnel, coaching them on the purpose and importance of the BLUF and directing them to include it on all future IICD products. The email read in part:

> *BLUF is an Acronym for Bottom Line Up Front. This is a term frequently used in the intelligence community, in the military,*

and elsewhere. The majority of the documents we produce in IICD should have a BLUF so the reader knows the most important details of the document at the very beginning. The BLUF should be very brief—one or two sentences—and should succinctly note the main or most salient points of the document . . .

However, none of these BLUF bullet points—"the most important details of the document"—mentioned any high level of concern for violence or threats against the Capitol or members of Congress. Inconsistencies in the reports were noted both by the Senate committees and by the USCP Office of the Inspector General in their reports.

The last paragraph of the final assessment, located after several pages of traffic closures and peppered with qualifiers, was the IICD's overall analysis of the event:

Due to the tense political environment following the 2020 election, the threat of disruptive actions or violence **cannot be ruled out**. Supporters of the current president see January 6, 2021, as the last opportunity to overturn the results of the presidential election. This sense of desperation and disappointment **may lead** to more of an incentive to become violent. Unlike previous post-election protests, the targets of the pro-Trump supporters are **not necessarily** the counter-protesters as they were previously, but rather Congress itself is the target on the 6th. As outlined above, there has been a worrisome call for protesters to come to these events armed and **there is the possibility** that protesters **may be inclined** to become violent. Further, unlike the events on November 14, 2020, and December 12, 2020, there were several more protests scheduled on January 6, 2021, and the majority of them will be on Capitol grounds. The two protests expected to be the largest of the day—the Women for America First protest at the Ellipse and the Stop the Steal protest in Areas 8 and 9—**may** draw thousands of participants and both have been promoted by

President Trump himself. The Stop the Steal protest in particular does not have a permit, but several high profile speakers, including Members of Congress are expected to speak at the event. This combined with Stop the Steal's propensity to attract white supremacists, militia members, and others who actively promote violence, **may lead to a significantly dangerous situation** for law enforcement and the general public alike. (Emphasis mine.)

Reviewing the final assessment, I didn't note any new or concerning information. Everything listed in the report was information I had seen before. I remember reading through it and getting to the pages of the traffic closures and thinking this was going to be just like the previous two events. I don't recall much of my review of the final paragraph before January 6, other than that it was nothing extraordinary, nothing that caused me alarm. However, since January 6, I have spent a lot of time reviewing and rereviewing this document. While it still doesn't scream DEFCON 1, that last paragraph has always seemed odd. The previous assessments were more definitive and concise in the final paragraph, which was the IICD overall analysis section. They included definitive statements about the upcoming event and the intelligence that IICD possessed at the time. But this assessment had peppered the last paragraph with qualifiers. In fact, *every* sentence in the final paragraph that raised a concern also included qualifiers. For example: "This sense of desperation and disappointment *may* lead to more of an incentive to become violent . . ." The overuse of qualifiers by a writer does not convey a degree of certainty or a high level of concern but, rather, creates doubt about the veracity of the writer's information. The offhand tone and the use of qualifiers in this final paragraph gave the appearance that it was written by someone other than the author of the rest of the document and the other assessments.

Months after I left the department, I learned that the final paragraph of the assessment was indeed rewritten by Farnam, the assistant director of the IICD. However, the concerns she was apparently trying to relay in the final paragraph were never clearly portrayed or translated into the critical BLUF section. After updating the last paragraph of the assessment, the IICD distributed it late on January 3.

Weeks after January 6, Donohue stated that he had thought that day was "going to be bad" and that he was surprised I wasn't getting briefed on all the information. If IICD leadership was so worried about January 6, why wasn't that level of concern effectively portrayed in any of its intelligence assessments or briefings? We had known about the planned demonstrations for almost a month in advance, with the first assessment produced on December 16. If we'd had advance knowledge of concerning intelligence then, the department would have had plenty of time and opportunity to plan effectively for the event. I have a hard time comprehending why the new leadership in the IICD, when faced with its first major event at the Capitol and feeling that it was going to be bad, did not publish a series of assessments indicating that Armageddon was coming.

In addition to the special event assessments, the IICD also distributed several daily intelligence reports. The DIR dated January 4 has been the focus of a lot of scrutiny and comments from investigators and the department alike. The DIR assessed *"the level of probability of acts of civil disobedience/arrests occurring based on current intelligence information"* for all the groups expected to demonstrate on Wednesday, January 6, as "remote" to "improbable."

This report was also distributed to the offices of the sergeants at arms and members of the Capitol Police Board and would play a significant role in their assessment of January 6. Pittman tried to downplay the credibility of this report to the Senate committees, stating that it was developed by a "single analyst" and not reviewed by the supervisors within the IICD.[2] But it is important to note that these reports were published under the same IICD heading as the assessments, and the same findings were reported in the January 5 and January 6 DIRs.

---

2. Peters, Portman, Klobuchar, and Blunt, *Examining the U.S. Capitol Attack.*

I read these reports daily and relied on the information they contained to be complete and accurate. Why would an intelligence division be publishing a report that its own officials neither review nor feel is even accurate? I find it extremely concerning that no one within protection and intelligence operations appeared to be reviewing these documents and validating the contents. Both the special event assessments and the DIRs are critical intelligence documents that the USCP and the CPB rely on when preparing for events.

The rewrite of the final paragraph did not appear to have the intended effect of making it sound more concerning and only added confusion to the expectations for the day. The final assessment, combined with the multiple daily intelligence reports assessing a low probability of civil disobedience, gave the operational leaders a false sense of expectations for the event and seriously hindered our preparations. In reference to the final paragraph of the assessment, Deputy Sergeant at Arms Blodgett testified, "Warnings should not be qualified or hidden."[3]

As noted by the Senate investigative report, the inconsistencies in the final assessment and the various IICD intelligence products led to a serious misunderstanding by many within the department regarding the threat posed on January 6. But Pittman would not acknowledge the internal inconsistencies, telling the committees, "I think the report itself captures what [IICD] was trying to share with [USCP] in terms of what we may have been facing regarding the violence."[4]

On January 26, Pittman testified at a closed-door hearing before the House Appropriations Committee, stating, "I am here to offer my sincerest apologies on behalf of the department." She went on to advise that the USCP had been aware of a "strong potential" for violence on January 6. Pittman further testified, "Let me be clear: [USCP] should have been more prepared for this attack. By January 4th, [USCP] knew

3. Timothy P. Blodgett, *Testimony of Timothy P. Blodgett Acting Sergeant at Arms U.S. House of Representatives before the Subcommittee on Legislative Branch Committee on Appropriations*, February 25, 2021, https://www.congress.gov/117/meeting/house /111235/witnesses/HHRG-117-AP24-Wstate-BlodgettT-20210225.pdf.

4. Peters, Portman, Klobuchar, and Blunt, *Examining the U.S. Capitol Attack*, 46.

that the January 6th event would not be like any of the previous protests held in 2020."[5]

But wait—this contradicts *everything* in the intelligence assessments.
All four intelligence assessments produced for this event presented January 6 in the same terms as the previous two MAGA events. In fact, the
final assessment, produced by Pittman's intelligence division late in the
evening on January 3, specifically stated: "The protests/rallies are expected
to be similar to the previous Million MAGA March rallies in November
and December 2020, which drew tens of thousands of participants."[6]

Although Pittman testified, *"By January 4th, [USCP] knew that
the January 6th event would not be like any of the previous protests held
in 2020,"* her actions and those of her subordinates leading up to the
event indicated nothing remotely near this level of concern. Their actions clearly showed a lack of urgency or even concern regarding the
expectations for this day:

- Just hours before the final January 3 assessment was distributed on Sunday, Gallagher briefed the House sergeant at arms
  and staff regarding January 6 and the department's plans. The
  briefing mentioned no high level of concern and gave assurance that the event would be similar to the two previous
  MAGA rallies. Tim Blodgett, the deputy House sergeant at
  arms, testified on February 25 regarding this briefing: "This
  characterization of the threat posed by these protests only reinforce the notion and thinking that these were similar to the
  two previous demonstrations and not the violent insurrection
  that we experienced." Blodgett further testified, "Intelligence
  missteps cascaded into inadequate preparation, which placed
  the health and lives of front-line officers at risk."[7]

5. Peters, Portman, Klobuchar, and Blunt, *Examining the U.S. Capitol Attack*, 48.
6. United States Capitol Police, *Special Event Assessment 21-A-0468 v.3*, January 3,
2020, 2.
7. Timothy P. Blodgett, *Testimony of Timothy P. Blodgett*.

- On January 4, Pittman, as the head of intelligence, submitted information to my chief of staff to be used to brief members of Congress about expectations for January 6. The information she provided did not express any new concern or high level of concern for that day.

- Both Deputy Chief Gallagher and Assistant Chief Pittman signed off on all the permit applications for groups to demonstrate on Capitol grounds, recommending that I approve all of them. Pittman signed off, recommending approval of most of the permits on January 4 after the final intelligence assessment was published. This directly contradicts Pittman's testimony when she said, "*By January fourth, [USCP] knew that the January sixth event would not be like any of the previous protests held in 2020.*" If Gallagher and Pittman had a high level of concern for violence on January 6, why would they recommend approval for the permits? They could have recommended disapproval, noted their concerns, or come to see me. But they didn't. They approved the permits as they were and pushed them up to me for approval. It should also be noted that each of the demonstration permits contained an assessment from the IICD about the probability of civil disobedience, and all listed the probability as low.

- On January 4, at 1:00 p.m., Gallagher had an intelligence briefing scheduled for USCP leadership to discuss January 6 and the final assessment. Donohue provided the briefing on a conference call. Oddly, however, they failed to invite me. I only learned about the briefing after my resignation. The recollections of the call by many who participated indicated that Donohue did not present any new or concerning intelligence about January 6. No one got off the call with any sense of alarm. When the media asked why the chief was not invited, a spokesperson for the department stated, "The meeting was for operational commanders and was not a meeting Sund would normally attend."[8] I found that response baffling. I regularly attended intelligence briefings. And if the assistant chief and intelligence leadership believed they had critical information indicating that [USCP] *"knew that the January sixth event would not be like any of the previous protests held in 2020,"* and they possessed intelligence that could affect the safety and security of Capitol Hill, members of Congress, and my officers, you sure as hell would expect the chief of police to be invited.

- On January 4, the director of the IICD sent an email to his unit regarding January 6. In the email, the director assigned a *single* analyst per shift to monitor the critical open-source information related to the January 6 demonstrations. He then reminded the rest of the staff that there was still a backlog of cases (not related to January 6) and directed them to help clear those cases throughout the day.

- The same day, January 4, the assistant director of the IICD sent an email to the IICD team, also advising them of the backlog of cases, and directed them to work on the backlog unless assigned otherwise.

- At 7:21 p.m. on January 4, Deputy Senate Sergeant at Arms Ronda Stewart sent a copy of the Senate's "Dear Colleague" letter to Pittman. In this letter, which was distributed to the entire Senate community, including Senate leadership and every senator, the SSAA indicated that expectations for January 6 were for "several First Amendment activities that will take place throughout the District of Columbia." But Pittman offered no disagreement with their assessment, nor did she provide alternative language that would better prepare the Senate for what might occur on January 6.

- On January 5, Deputy Chief Gallagher briefed Congressman Rodney Davis and his deputy staff director, Tim Monahan,

---

8. Jacqueline Alemany et al., "Red Flags," *Washington Post*, October 31, 2021, www.washingtonpost.com/politics/interactive/2021/jan-6-insurrection-capitol/.

regarding the expectations for January 6. According to both Representative Davis and Monahan, Gallagher expressed no serious concern and portrayed the event as being "just like the previous two MAGA events." At no time did Gallagher give Davis or Monahan the impression that he was concerned about the demonstrations creating a significantly dangerous situation for law enforcement.[9] According to Davis and Monahan, they didn't walk away from the briefing with a feeling of concern about the demonstrations scheduled to take place the following day.

- On January 5, Pittman participated in briefings with members of Congress, both sergeants at arms, and law enforcement and military partners in reference to January 6 and never expressed concern for the following day in any of the briefings.

- On January 6, IICD leadership had two-thirds of the intelligence staff working from home. The directive I had issued to the department to have all hands on deck (AHOD)—that I wanted everyone working on campus and focused on the event on January 6—clearly was not followed within the IICD, further removing any sense of urgency within the unit regarding January 6.

All these actions are in stark contrast to the statement Pittman made before the House Appropriations Committee on January 26, 2021. A lot of CYA was going on after the fact, especially when it came to intelligence. Acting on the intelligence given to me at the time, I had anticipated and planned for an event similar to the MAGA I and MAGA II demonstrations. My concern for the large number of attendees and the size of our perimeter prompted me, on January 3, to seek approval for bringing in the National Guard. The request for the National Guard would have been specifically for unarmed troops to help fill the gaps on

---

9. Rodney Davis, telephone call with author, October 14, 2021; Tim Monahan, telephone call with author, February 23, 2022.

our perimeter. But the House sergeant at arms immediately denied this request out of concern for the "optics" of having the National Guard on Capitol Hill and because he felt the intelligence did not support it. Even the IICD briefing and assessment he received later that day did not change his position.

Following the events of January 6, many in the department were terribly demoralized by the acting chief's apology and statement that the department knew in advance this event was going to be gravely dangerous. They felt the department had thrown them under the bus and left them ill-prepared for what had been anticipated. Many had felt early on that this was, above all, an intelligence failure, but now Pittman was apologizing for the department's failure to properly plan for the event. She made it into a planning and operations failure. Officials like Chad Thomas, as well as Waldow and Loyd (who were both out fighting in the field), were vilified as having failed to plan for and manage the event properly. But there was no similar public ridicule or punitive measures surrounding Pittman's intelligence unit's failures associated with January 6.

Even the intelligence analysts felt that IICD leadership failed to portray the level of intelligence and the concern for violence in the assessments. For weeks, the IICD analysts had been flagging concerning intelligence and sending it to their leadership in anticipation of its being included in the intelligence assessments. Following the attack on January 6, one of the intelligence analysts, turned whistleblower, sent an email to IICD leadership stating, "We analysts have been reporting for weeks that Patriot groups are commenting on social media their intentions to storm the US Capitol with overwhelming numbers. I don't know what was occurring behind the scenes, but I hope this information was briefed with the veracity it deserves, and not just a one-time Event Assessment."[10]

10. Eric A. Hoar, "1/6 Intelligence Failures" (memo to IICD leadership), January 9, 2021, https://justthenews.com/sites/default/files/2022-09/EricHoarIntelligenceFailures Memo1-9-21RedactedAddresses.pdf.

Another analyst's after-action report (AAR) stated that the analyst had received intelligence on December 21 indicating that people were coming armed and that they planned to overtake the Capitol and target members of Congress. But when this was translated into an assessment, it indicated only that "protesters may be armed." The analyst asked leadership, "Why is a generic statement to cover yourself used, and not the facts?" The analyst continued, "A generic, all-encompassing quote was put in the assessment which apparently the IICD director and assistant director felt was sufficient. This is inexcusable. Five people lost their lives. Two officers took their own lives and numerous injuries to officers have left some permanently disabled."

According to Kimberly Schneider, commander of the Dignitary Protection Division (DPD), the unit responsible for protecting congressional leadership, she never received any information from Pittman, Gallagher, or the leadership at the IICD indicating any serious concerns over violence directed at her protectees on January 6. The DPD is part of the Protective Services Bureau, and Inspector Schneider's office is just a few feet away from the IICD leadership's offices. I would think that if Gallagher and the IICD leadership had such serious concerns about violence on January 6, they might have walked across the hall to warn her.

I can now understand why many of the IICD intel analysts were so angry. Many of them blasted their leadership in the official USCP after-action report and their individual AARs and filed complaints with the USCP's Office of Professional Responsibility, the USCP's inspector general, and the Office of Congressional Workplace Rights over the mismanagement within the IICD, and the intelligence that the IICD had and failed to share.[11] Many of the analysts have also

11. United States Capitol Police, "Capitol Police After-Action Report Regarding January 6, 2021," Project on Government Oversight, June 3, 2022, www.pogo.org /document/2022/06/capitol-police-after-action-report-regarding-january-6-2021; Nick Schwellenbach and Adam Zagorin, "Inside the Capitol Cops' Jan. 6 Blame Game," Project on Government Oversight, June 9, 2022, www.pogo.org/investigation/2022/06 /inside-the-capitol-cops-jan-6-blame-game.

filed whistleblower complaints with the Committee on House Administration regarding the actions of the intelligence leadership. The whistleblower complaints against IICD leadership were so numerous that members of Congress were prompted to write a rare bipartisan letter to the USCP inspector general, urging that these allegations be fully investigated.[12]

Since I left the department, I have become aware that both PSB and IICD leadership possessed extremely concerning intelligence regarding the likelihood of attacks on my police officers, members of Congress, political figures, and the United States Capitol. Yet they did nothing to prepare the department for the onslaught of violence that was coming. For weeks, the IICD had been gathering concerning intelligence provided by the FBI, DHS, and other sources, but none of it was conveyed to the department or my oversight.

Below is just a sampling of intelligence excerpts that I later learned existed within the PSB and IICD before January 6:

December 17: A report from the FBI noted a tip of online activity calling for people to come to Washington, DC, on January 6, armed and promoting violence to save the country and indicating that "*You might have to kill the palace guards. Are you ok with that?*" This is a likely reference to my USCP officers protecting the Capitol. The posting goes on: "*In order to protect our wonderful country, I am ready to do whatever it takes.*" The online communication continues, again apparently referring to Capitol Police officers: "*They're also chickenshit cowards who are just there for a check. Drop a handful and the rest will flee. They won't die for this.*" The online discussion also refers to planning, stating, "*We need to start prepping secure lines of communication, because it's pretty likely to happen.*"

12. Amy Klobuchar, Roy Blunt, Zoe Lofgren, and Rodney Davis, "December 2021 Congressional Letter to USCP Inspector General," Project on Government Oversight, June 3, 2022, www.pogo.org/document/2022/06/december-2021-congressional-letter-to-uscp-inspector-general.

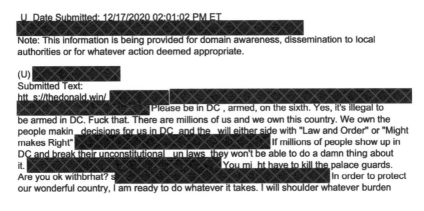

UNCLASSIFIED//FOUO

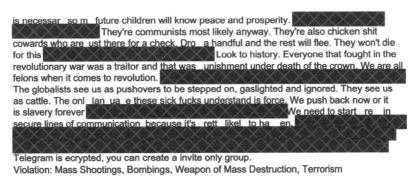

Telegram is ecrypted, you can create a invite only group.
Violation: Mass Shootings, Bombings, Weapon of Mass Destruction, Terrorism

Figure 4.1. FBI intelligence regarding online activity

December 21: The IICD received information from the DHS about individuals on a website chat room discussing a coordinated attack on the Capitol and the tunnel system. The website had specifics such as the layout of our building entry checkpoints and the number of officers assigned to them. This level of information about our security indicates that the writer had done some preattack research. The posting discussed focusing on garage exits and mixing specific commercially available chemicals to make lethal gas. The site also mentioned going to the homes of Pelosi, Schumer, McConnell, and Justice Roberts and burning down the Supreme Court. This intelligence regarding the garage exits became far more concerning after January 6, when the Architect of the

Capitol testified in an appropriations hearing that some of the garage doors could not be closed and secured on January 6.[13]

On the same day as the email about the tunnels, December 21, the IICD produced *internal* (meaning it did not leave the IICD office) Investigative Research and Analysis Report 21-TD-159.[14] The seven-page research report highlighted the ways individuals wanted to attack members of Congress and try to get into the underground tunnel system that connects the congressional buildings. Numerous people were in the online chat room, calling for getting together and bringing weapons and tools to storm the Capitol buildings, tunnels, and garages and to break into the homes of members of Congress and Supreme Court justices.

The December 21 IICD report attached a map of the Capitol campus that was posted to the blog, and flagged around thirty screenshots of comments on the website, including these:

- **"Exactly, forget the tunnels. Get into Capitol Building, stand outside Congress. Be in the room next to them. They wont have time [to] run if they play dumb."**
- **"Go to their homes and be in the kitchen with their wife and kids."**
- **"Let's burn down Pelosi's and McConnell's homes."**
- **"Burning the Supreme Court down."**
- **"Anyone going armed needs to be mentally prepared to draw down on LEOs. Let them shoot first, but make sure they know what happens if they do."** (I found this statement particularly alarming. I had several of my officers tell me that there were people in the crowd on January 6 who were armed and who appeared to be waiting for the police to shoot first.)

13. House Committee on Appropriations, "FY 2022 Budget Hearing for Architect of the Capitol and Government Publishing Office," March 11, 2021, https://appropriations .house.gov/events/hearings/fy-2022-budget-hearing-for-architect-of-the-capitol-and -government-publishing-office.

14. Bolton, *Review of the Events Surrounding the January 6, 2021, Takeover of the U.S. Capitol.*

- "Nerve gas. That is all"
- "If they don't show up, we enter the Capitol as the Third Continental Congress and certify the Trump Electors."
- "The world is watching. This is where we do that thing that will have the whole world still talking about the United States of America in 1000 years."
- "We can't give them a choice. Overwhelming armed numbers is our only chance."

Pittman, the assistant chief for protection and intelligence operations, would later inform the Senate committee that internal IICD Report 21-TD-159 was "distributed to officials the rank of deputy chief and assistant chiefs." But this was not the case. This was an internal IICD report that was not distributed outside the IICD. Even more concerning, this report was never included in any of the subsequent intelligence assessments or even footnoted in any of the reports.

Just two days after preparing the report on the DHS information, the IICD published the second special event assessment for January 6. The assessment didn't contain any of the information from the December 21 IICD case report or any other new concerning information. There were serious discrepancies between the intelligence that the IICD had at the time and the December 23 special event assessment for the joint session of Congress. When asked by the Senate committees, Pittman agreed there were discrepancies but could not explain why they existed, stating, "I cannot go into detail without having further discussion with those individuals [who wrote the reports]. I think that [at] US Capitol Police, my focus was always on the January 3rd final assessment."[15]

I'm not even sure where to start with this explanation. Whatever intelligence assessment you are publishing, it should be based on the most up-to-date intelligence. Your focus should always be on providing the latest and most relevant intelligence in your current assessments so

---

15. Peters, Portman, Klobuchar, and Blunt, *Examining the U.S. Capitol Attack*, 42

that those doing the planning have the information to base that planning on. Why, in December, would your focus be on the January 3 final assessment? We initially found out about the Stop the Steal demonstrations on December 14. If the December 23 special event assessment had painted a more realistic picture of the intelligence the IICD had at that time, this could have helped me obtain advance approval for the National Guard or even mutual aid from the surrounding law enforcement agencies. And with that more realistic picture of the intel the IICD had at the time, Irving may have been more inclined to agree that the intelligence *did in fact support requesting the National Guard.* This intelligence would have driven critical planning decisions, such as directing a stoppage of all construction on the campus on January 6 and the advance cleaning and clearing of the inaugural platform of all workers and the various construction tools and loose materials that were subsequently used as weapons against law enforcement.

It is important to understand that Pittman was in charge not only of intelligence but also of the Security Services Bureau, which handles all the physical security initiatives for the department, including recommending the appropriate physical barriers or fencing for demonstrations. These two bureaus, the IICD and SSB, were specifically placed under the assistant chief for protective and intelligence operations, precisely so that physical security would be based on intelligence. If the intelligence assessments had accurately portrayed the level of threat that the IICD possessed at the time, the SSB would have recommended a larger physical barrier, such as the eight-foot antiscale fence. The intelligence assessment would have warranted such a response, and the Capitol Police Board would have approved it, citing the threat.

December 23: A report from the FBI noted a tip about a person on social media calling for sniper attacks on law enforcement in DC on January 6. That same day, the PSB received an email from the US Marshals Service with information on a social media user calling for the use of snipers against police officers during the planned march on January 6.

December 23: The IICD received an email from the DC Homeland Security and Emergency Management Agency about a group talking about shooting and killing counterprotesters. The social media thread also contained threats toward members of Congress and other elected officials.

December 28: A report from the FBI described a tip that armed people were coming to DC and planning to overtake the government on January 6. The person who submitted the tip indicated, "Their plan is to literally kill people. Please take this tip seriously and investigate further."

December 28: The FBI received a tip about violent threats made by a deputy sheriff in Prince William County, Virginia, calling for people to travel to DC on January 6 with weapons and hunt down governors, mayors, members of Congress, and judges and kill them in their homes.

December 28: A report from the FBI described a tip from an individual who stated he had been informed there would be attacks on January 6 in Washington, DC, and to avoid the city in the afternoon and evening.

December 28: The USCP public information office received an email from an individual warning of countless people on social media saying they would be armed in the city on January 6. The email also referenced a large number of social media posts from people organizing to storm the Capitol on January 6.

December 31: An email to the IICD indicated that a user on a social media site was calling for individuals to "storm the capital building," adding that "it's our right to hang the politicians."

January 1: The IICD received an email from the MPD advising of a call into the tip line that said people were developing detailed plans to storm federal buildings on January 6.

January 4: The FBI received an email regarding social media postings about people bringing weapons to Washington, DC, to shoot police officers.

January 5: A USCP task force agent embedded with the FBI received a copy of a situational information report from the FBI Norfolk Office indicating that violent threats were made on social media referencing Washington, DC, on January 6. The memorandum indicated that in a social media thread, one user stated, **"Be ready to fight. Congress needs to hear glass breaking, doors being kicked in, and blood from their BLM and Pantifa slave soldiers being spilled. Get violent . . . stop calling this a march, or rally, or a protest. Go there ready for war. We get our President or we die. NOTHING else will achieve this goal."**[16]

Again, this is only a partial sampling of the intelligence they possessed. This list doesn't even include communications that occurred between the IICD and the Washington, DC, Fusion Center (NTIC) or other fusion centers around the country that reported seeing alarming levels of online posts calling for violence in Washington, DC, and for the storming of federal buildings.

None of this extremely concerning intelligence that the PSB and IICD had in advance of January 6 was included in their intelligence assessments. Nothing concerning the alarming statements, no threats to my officers and political figures. Nothing from the internal seven-page IICD report published on December 21 (21-TD-159) regarding the numerous online threats of surrounding and breaking into the congressional buildings and tunnels, attacking members of Congress in their homes, or using chemical weapons was included in any of the assessments.

There were significant threats to storm buildings and harm members of Congress and other prominent government officials, yet my

16. Bolton, *Review of the Events Surrounding the January 6, 2021, Takeover of the U.S. Capitol.*

intelligence leadership wasn't making this knowledge available to us to assist in our planning or to our stakeholders to support critical decision-making. The IICD had this information for weeks. It could have been a game changer for our preparedness on January 6. Instead, we received a single inconclusive paragraph riddled with qualifiers at the end of a fifteen-page document, a little over forty-eight hours before the day of the event. And from this single paragraph, I was expected to extrapolate this level of concern and overhaul three weeks of ill-informed planning? All while the assistant chief and deputy chief were participating in briefings with the sergeants at arms, members of Congress, and our military and law enforcement partners, *none* of whom were sounding the alarm?

The combined Senate committee investigating the failures of January 6 nailed it when it stated:

> The United States Capitol Police's ("USCP") Intelligence and Interagency Coordination Division ("IICD") possessed information about the potential for violence at the Capitol on January 6 but did not convey the full scope of information, which affected its preparations. Internal records and USCP officials' testimony confirm that USCP began gathering information about events planned for January 6 in mid-December 2020. Through Open Source collection, tips from the public, and other sources, USCP IICD knew about social media posts calling for violence at the Capitol on January 6, including a plot to breach the Capitol, the online sharing of maps of the Capitol Complex's tunnel systems, and other specific threats of violence. Yet, IICD did not convey the full scope of known information to USCP leadership, rank-and-file officers, or law enforcement partners.[17]

17. Bolton, *Review of the Events Surrounding the January 6, 2021, Takeover of the U.S. Capitol*, 5.

The inspector general for the USCP would later concur with the findings of the Senate committee, indicating that the Senate report was "spot on."[18]

Although Pittman testified that she felt the final assessment *"captures what [IICD] was trying to share with [USCP] in terms of what we may have been facing regarding the violence,"* there are ample conflicting positions regarding how the intelligence was handled between the analysts and intelligence leadership. The intelligence leadership at the USCP was aware of the concerning information regarding January 6. Why they chose not to include it in their assessments and briefings is still a mystery.

When I testified before the American public on February 23, I said I felt that the attack was the result of an intelligence failure. What I didn't realize at the time was that the biggest intelligence failure was within my department. A unit that had never experienced an intelligence failure had begun to fail as January 6 and the inauguration was approaching. Hell, even the date was wrong on the final assessment, and none of the IICD or PSB leadership caught it during the critical review stage.

The irony here is that except for Donohue, who resigned a few months after the attack, at the time of this writing, all the people who were in charge of intelligence on January 6 *are still in the same positions overseeing intelligence for the department.* Even Pelosi and Schumer, during their thirty-minute call with military leaders at the Pentagon while the attack was still underway, discussed the "obvious intelligence failures that led to the insurrection." Yet the intelligence apparatus on the Hill remains unchanged and unquestioned, all with the approval of departmental and congressional leadership.

18. United States Senate Committee on Rules & Administration, "U.S. Capitol Police Inspector General Praises Joint Report of Rules and Homeland Security Committees on Security, Planning, and Response Failures on January 6th," June 16, 2021, www.rules.senate.gov/news/majority-news/us-capitol-police-inspector-general -praises-joint-report-of-rules-and-homeland-security-committees-on-security-planning -and-response-failures-on-january-6th.

THE FBI

The FBI, especially the Washington Field Office (WFO), has always been a good partner to law enforcement in DC. When I was with the Metropolitan Police Department, we would regularly partner with the FBI on various initiatives to fight crime in the neighborhoods. For everything from identifying violent repeat offenders and gang and criminal organizations to investigating homicides, the FBI had the ability to bring in experts and resources to help the city address these issues plaguing the community. When I commanded MPD's Special Operations Division or when I was working with Cathy Lanier to develop the department's Homeland Security Bureau, we would regularly meet with the FBI's WFO to discuss threats to the city, investigations, and initiatives. It was always a pleasant break to get out of MPD headquarters at 300 Indiana Avenue and walk the two blocks down Fourth Street, past the US Attorney's Office, to the Washington Field Office. The WFO was always such a nice, new, shiny facility compared to the MPD's World War II–era headquarters.

On many occasions, I would go to the WFO to participate in briefings and executive meetings for the Joint Terrorism Task Force (JTTF). In addition to in-person meetings, the FBI would also host regular calls with the executives from the law enforcement agencies in the National Capital Region. The NCR is made up of the District of Columbia and its suburbs in Maryland and Virginia. The purpose of the conference calls would usually be to discuss upcoming major events or emerging threats that could affect the region. The head of the Washington Field Office would usually kick off the call and then have an FBI analyst provide an overview of concerns associated with the event or possible threat. Then they would open up the call to questions from agency executives. I always found these calls very helpful and an efficient way to share information across the region. When I began working for the United States Capitol Police, I continued to participate in these meetings and conference calls. Over the years, I have developed many close friendships within the Bureau, and I always appreciated getting the opportunity to visit with them. One of the last meetings I had at the WFO was the executive meeting in October 2020 with the region's top cops and the FBI to discuss the upcoming election.

Since January 6, I have learned that private investigative and research intelligence firms, other law enforcement agencies, and many fusion centers around the country flagged concerns regarding that day. Yet there was no call from the FBI for an executive meeting or a regional conference call to discuss the profusion of online threats to the city and law enforcement. I find this surprising, given the times in the past they had called us for events or threats of far lesser magnitude. But the FBI never made the call, nor did they produce an assessment specific to this event.

The handling of a piece of FBI intelligence that has since garnered a lot of attention is the January 5 FBI Norfolk Division Situational Information Report. The January 5 SIR advised of the potential for violence in the Washington, DC, area in connection with the planned Stop the Steal protest on January 6. The report was emailed from the FBI's Norfolk Field Office to the Washington Field Office at 6:52 p.m. on January 5. At 7:37 p.m., an analyst at the FBI's WFO emailed a copy of the report to the intelligence units of the USCP, MPD, US Park Police, and others. The contents of the report were briefed at 8:00 p.m. at the WFO Command Center, which included a USCP task force officer. The information was shared within the IICD and PSB, but nowhere else within the department.

While I acknowledge that there were opportunities for this information to be processed better internally by the USCP, I also think there was an opportunity to handle it more effectively at the FBI's level. Perhaps, if the FBI had conducted an intelligence assessment for the event, such critical last-minute information as the Norfolk memo would have triggered a reassessment or, at a minimum, an update to the intel. A reassessment would have been broadcast at a much higher level, and police leaders such as Chief Contee and me would likely have been contacted.

Although the Bureau didn't conduct an intelligence assessment for the event, they made collecting intelligence concerning *possible violence* associated with the joint session of Congress a priority. If this was the case, why didn't the late-breaking intel regarding violence in the Norfolk report garner more attention and elicit a higher-level response from the Bureau?

Equally concerning was the fact that the FBI was tracking numerous individuals who were planning to come to DC on the sixth. In her testimony, Jill Sanborn, assistant director of the Counterterrorism Division of the FBI, noted that they took "overt" action by contacting individuals of concern to dissuade them from attending the events in Washington on January 6. If the FBI was tracking these individuals and felt the need to take overt action, then it's clear they weren't tracking them simply for First Amendment activity. (In the past, the Bureau, to its credit, had always been staunchly against initiating investigations related solely to First Amendment activity.) If the FBI is tracking someone and is concerned enough to take overt actions, it's because there is some kind of predicate criminal activity, or even a concern over domestic terrorism.

Shortly after January 6, the media approached me with allegations that the FBI had been tracking domestic violent extremists who planned to come to DC on the sixth. At the time, I didn't give it much consideration because I thought for sure the FBI would have given me a heads-up. But additional media reporting on this allegation, along with Jill Sanborn's testimony, proved the media correct. While I certainly would not have wanted to jeopardize a criminal investigation, it would have been helpful to know that the Bureau was tracking individuals and to be aware of what their concerns were as well as what types of groups these individuals were associated with. This background information, along with the January 5 Norfolk memo, would have resulted in a change in our security posture on the Hill.

Since January 6, there have been multiple media reports regarding undercover FBI agents in the crowd outside the Capitol during the attack. And multiple media outlets have reported that FBI confidential informants, sometimes referred to as "special employees," were also in the crowd and that some may even have participated in the attack on my officers and breached the Capitol itself. While I have no specific information regarding the involvement of FBI agents or confidential informants, much media reporting has surrounded a man named Ray Epps. Epps has been shown in several videos taken in Washington, DC, on January 5, openly telling the protesters that they need to breach the Capitol Building. Epps was again videotaped on January 6, right outside my perimeter on the West Front, apparently coaching rioters seconds before they violently attacked my officers and breached the perimeter. As the former chief of the Capitol Police, I find this behavior extremely concerning. I watched the brutal attack on my officers at this perimeter, and anyone who was involved should be arrested—especially when they were seen a short time later within the restricted area. Yet, to my knowledge, Mr. Epps has not been arrested for any of his alleged crimes.

Similar allegations have surfaced regarding the FBI's involvement in other activity with far-right groups. The plot to kidnap Michigan Governor Gretchen Whitmer by militia members who were angry with her COVID-19 lockdowns is one such case. The court affidavit filed by the FBI's lead investigator in the Whitmer kidnapping case, Special Agent Richard Trask, stated that the FBI had two undercover employees and multiple confidential human sources assisting in the investigation and that one of these two attended every group planning meeting for the kidnapping plot. While I have no further information regarding these claims, taking them into consideration, along with Sanborn's testimony that the FBI was tracking suspects planning to come to DC on January 6, makes me wonder if there could be some validity to the claims of FBI informant participation. In a strange twist of events in the Whitmer kidnapping case, Trask was fired in September 2021 for allegedly assaulting his wife after participating in a swingers party. And at the conclusion of the April 2022 criminal trial of the four suspects in the Whitmer case, jurors acquitted two of the suspects and failed to convict the other two, which resulted in a mistrial. Media reports indicated that jurors felt that the actions of the FBI and their confidential employees were inexcusable and appeared to border on entrapment. (The judge did order the two to be retried, however, and both were later found guilty.)

Concern has also been raised that the FBI's ability to monitor open-source intelligence may have compromised its response to January 6.

Conflicting knowledge and interpretation of the Bureau's authority to monitor open-source information could have hindered its ability to detect the information regarding January 6. During the Senate hearings, when asked by Senator Sinema if the FBI was aware of specific conversations on social media, Assistant Director Sanborn replied no, explaining that without an already predicated investigation, the FBI was not permitted to monitor First Amendment activities.[19] But the FBI later acknowledged that it can and does look at social media information. The conflict between Sanborn's statement and the FBI's later backtracking on her comment is emblematic of the confusion that exists within the Bureau over what they are allowed to monitor online.

The FBI's reluctance to monitor open-source information is something that law enforcement in Washington has experienced in the past, especially when it came to demonstrations that were turning violent. The Bureau's authority in carrying out these investigative actions is governed by the Department of Justice and outlined in a publicly available document entitled *The Attorney General's Guidelines for Domestic FBI Operations*.[20] The "Investigations and Intelligence Gathering" section of this report outlines when the FBI can conduct investigations to detect threats to national security and prevent federal crimes. These guidelines include two sections that I believe are very relevant to the FBI's ability to conduct investigations into the joint session of Congress. The first relevant section of the guidelines that explains this investigative capability tells us the following:

> Investigations may also be undertaken for protective purposes in relation to individuals, groups, and other entities that may be targeted for criminal victimization or acquisition, or for

19. Ken Dilanian, "Why Did the FBI Miss the Threats about Jan. 6 on Social Media?" NBC News, March 8, 2021, www.nbcnews.com/politics/justice-department/fbi-official-told-congress-bureau-can-t-monitor-americans-social-n1259769.

20. Michael B. Mukasey, *The Attorney General's Guidelines for Domestic FBI Operations*, US Department of Justice, September 29, 2008, www.justice.gov/archive/opa/docs/guidelines.pdf.

terrorist attack or other depredations by the enemies of the United States. For example, the participation of the FBI in special events management, in relation to public events or other activities whose character may make them attractive targets for terrorist attack, is an authorized exercise of the authorities conveyed by these Guidelines.[21]

The second section of these guidelines that is manifestly applicable to January 6 is the development of assessments. According to the guidelines, assessments may be carried out to assist in identifying and obtaining information about potential targets or vulnerabilities to criminal activities that violate federal law or threaten national security. Conducting assessments of the United States Capitol as a target during the joint session of Congress seems a reasonable application of this policy. But the attorney general's guidelines provide additional information about the development of assessments, which even further supports the Bureau's ability to conduct proactive investigations into the online activity associated with January 6:

> Assessments, authorized by Subpart A of this Part, require an authorized purpose but not any particular factual predication. For example, to carry out its central mission of preventing the commission of terrorist acts against the United States and its people, the FBI must proactively draw on available sources of information to identify terrorist threats and activities. It cannot be content to wait for leads to come in through the actions of others, but rather must be vigilant in detecting terrorist activities to the full extent permitted by law, with an eye towards early intervention and prevention of acts of terrorism before they occur. Likewise, in the exercise of its protective functions, the FBI is not constrained to wait until information is received

---

21. Mukasey, *The Attorney General's Guidelines*, 16.

indicating that a particular event, activity, or facility has drawn the attention of those who would threaten the national security. Rather, the FBI must take the initiative to secure and protect activities and entities whose character may make them attractive targets for terrorism or espionage. The proactive investigative authority conveyed in assessments is designed for, and may be utilized by, the FBI in the discharge of these responsibilities. For example, assessments may be conducted as part of the FBI special events management activities.

More broadly, detecting and interrupting criminal activities at their early stages, and preventing crimes from occurring in the first place, is preferable to allowing criminal plots and activities to come to fruition.[22]

Reading this with the events of January 6 fresh in my memory makes me shake my head in astonishment. *All* the threat notifications we received from the FBI concerning the joint session of Congress appeared to be coming in the form of tips to the FBI and not through proactive investigations or assessments. If the FBI had been proactively conducting investigations and assessments concerning the joint session, the leaderboard would have been flashing red a long time beforehand, alerting everyone to the threat that loomed on the horizon.

THE DEPARTMENT OF HOMELAND SECURITY

Similar issues appeared to be affecting the DHS, a massive government organization that was established to protect America's domestic security following the attacks of 9/11. Despite the extensive online warning signals raising serious concerns about January 6 at fusion centers across the country, the DHS never produced a bulletin specific to the date or

22. Mukasey, *The Attorney General's Guidelines*, 17.

to the joint session of Congress. Moreover, the DHS and the FBI never produced a joint intelligence bulletin for the joint session. I find this unusual in light of all the troubling information that the DHS and the FBI were seeing about the joint session, and all the media attention the event was getting. DHS-FBI joint intelligence bulletins are often produced before a major event in the city. Why not this time?

One of the main reasons the DHS was formed was to help eliminate information silos that existed and to help "connect the dots" by evaluating information at all levels to ensure that another 9/11 never happens. In support of this information sharing, the DHS extensively supported the development of state, local, and tribal fusion centers. The fusion centers were designed to monitor information and suspicious activity at the local level and to help support the DHS Information Sharing Environment at the federal level. The DHS also operates the National Operations Center (NOC) in Washington, DC. The NOC is a 24-hours-a-day, 7-days-a-week, 365-days-a-year ops center. The NOC serves as the DHS hub for situational awareness and information sharing and provides reports derived from traditional sources and social media monitoring.

Yet even on January 5, the day before the attack, the DHS Office of Intelligence and Analysis distributed a national summary to local and federal law enforcement nationwide that read, "Nothing significant to report."[23] Although we now know that social media was flooded with calls for violence on January 6 in Washington, DC, the DHS never produced a bulletin specific to that day. The cabinet-level department tasked with protecting our national security never elevated the National Terrorism Advisory System (NTAS) level or even issued an NTAS bulletin.

Since January 6, however, the DHS has produced several NTAS bulletins about concerns regarding domestic violent extremists (DVE) and groups engaged in grievance-based violence. The DHS is the authority that designates special events as National Special Security Events (NSSE).

---

23. Rachael Levy, Dan Frosch, and Sadie Gurman, "Capitol Riot Warnings Weren't Acted On as System Failed," *Wall Street Journal*, updated February 8, 2021, www.wsj .com/articles/capitol-riot-warnings-werent-acted-on-as-system-failed-11612787596.

This NSSE designation helps bring significant planning and security resources to the table for events so designated by the secretary of the DHS.

In addition, the DHS can assign a special event assessment rating
(SEAR) to an event. The SEAR will often make recommendations on
the level of local or federal support that is necessary to secure a specific
event. But the DHS offered none of this support to the USCP for January 6. Although I realize that both the NSSE designation and the SEAR
risk assessment are often conducted at the request of the host city or
organization, if the DHS was seeing significant concerns looming over
the horizon in connection with the joint session of Congress, I would
think they should have reached out and offered this support.

The security and information-sharing policies and mandates put in
place after September 11 failed miserably on January 6. My intelligence
unit didn't share the information it had, and the FBI and DHS didn't
gather the information they should have shared. We failed miserably
to see the apparent warning signs and the danger, like a "gray rhino,"
charging right at us.[24]

In my role as chief of the Capitol Police, intelligence did me no good
if it wasn't included in the intelligence products that we were producing
or receiving. With the way security on the Hill operates, the Capitol
Police Board, Congressional leadership, and my oversight committees
expect us to provide accurate intelligence and briefings to paint a clear
picture of the threats we face. This is truly a case where words matter.
Intelligence and assessments drive *everything* we do on the Hill, and they
must be thorough and accurate.

THE CAPITOL POLICE BOARD, OVERSIGHT COMMITTEES, AND CONGRESSIONAL LEADERSHIP

Simply put, the security structure on Capitol Hill is a recipe for disaster.
The role of the Capitol Police Board and congressional leadership in the

---

24. Michele Wucker, *The Gray Rhino: How to Recognize and Act on the Obvious
Dangers We Ignore* (New York: St. Martin's Press, 2016).

management and oversight of the USCP had disastrous repercussions on January 6. The delay and denial of critical resources, contributing to the devastating effects and loss of life on that day, can be directly attributed to this security structure and the laws imposed by Congress to support it. While the structure creates a "chief of police" as a figurehead for security on the Hill, it places the chief under the authority of three politically appointed board members, two of whom—the House and Senate sergeants at arms, the "chief law enforcement officers"—are often politically opposed, especially when it comes to security matters. There are too many sheriffs in this town, and no single person is authorized to make security decisions to protect the members of Congress and the entire campus. As a result, security on the Hill is far too often looked at from a political perspective rather than from a purely security-oriented one. How security is viewed by members, staff, and even constituents should *never* be a consideration when developing security plans—especially when very few of the "sheriffs" have any law enforcement background. But this happens far too often on the Hill, pitting the chief's position against that of the sergeants at arms, who will always represent the positions and desires of their partisan leadership.

Nowhere was this situation more evident than in the denial of my request for the National Guard on January 3 and the extensive delay I faced waiting for approval to request the Guard while we were under attack on January 6. On January 3, Irving denied my initial request for the National Guard over the concern for optics. This preoccupation with "optics" arose from the House leadership's concern over the look of "storm troopers" on campus.

I was surprised at the speed with which Stenger came up with the suggestion that I call someone over at the National Guard when I went to see him that morning of January 3. I had just walked into his office and began to request the National Guard when, within seconds, he interrupted me and proposed that I call someone at the Guard. I have always felt that Stenger must have gotten a heads-up that I was coming to him to request the Guard.

On April 8, 2021, Stenger and I met for lunch at the Barrel and Bushel restaurant in Tysons Corner. During our meeting, I asked him specifically whether he'd gotten a heads-up that I was coming to see him about the Guard and how he was so quick to come up with the idea of my making a call. Stenger didn't skip a beat: he said Irving had called and told him I would be coming his way to request the Guard. According to Stenger, Irving told him, "Sund just came here requesting the National Guard. We have to come up with another idea. Pelosi is never going to go for that."

If authorization to use the support of the National Guard had been granted on Sunday, January 3, when I first made the request, it would have been immensely helpful to our security posture on January 6. The advance authorization would have allowed the USCP to coordinate with the Department of Defense and the National Guard for two full business days before January 6, allowing both agencies to coordinate formal requests and develop staffing needs, making for a much securer perimeter.

Three days later, while we were under attack on January 6, my efforts to protect the Capitol and the members of Congress were again severely hampered by congressional oversight as I faced a seventy-one-minute delay waiting for the House and Senate sergeants at arms to approve my urgent pleas for National Guard support. When I first called Irving at 12:58 p.m. to request the National Guard, he stated, "I will run it up the chain and get right back to you." The ultimate decision maker in Irving's chain of command was the Speaker of the House. Irving was seen with Pelosi in the House Chambers minutes after I first called him.

Although Irving sought her approval for everything, he would rarely reach out to her directly, instead preferring to go through Pelosi's close confidant Jamie Fleet or her chief of staff, Terri McCullough. To this day, I am perplexed and angered why it took over seventy minutes to get approval. I do not believe for a second that Irving shouldered the responsibility for the repeated delays after my multiple calls and updates. I fully suspect he was seeking leadership approval and the repeated delays were coming from above him. Not having received approval, he called the 1:50 p.m. meeting of House and Senate leadership staff in Stenger's office to finally get the green light.

What is so frustrating about the situation is that Irving didn't have to go to leadership to approve my emergency request for the National Guard on January 6. During an emergency, he had the ability to authorize the use of executive-branch agencies and the National Guard. The same was true for Stenger. Either sergeant at arms could have granted immediate approval to request the support for his chamber's side of the Capitol. But Stenger would not grant the approval until Irving concurred. Although Irving had the authority, he was afraid to grant it without the concurrence of leadership, or without at least making leadership staff aware. He was always one to want some cover in case it was viewed as a bad decision later. Stenger testified that he met with Irving sometime between 1:30 p.m. and 2:00 p.m. and that Irving was "waiting for approval from House leadership to move forward with the request."[25]

While the Senate report indicated that Irving apparently didn't fully understand the process for requesting the National Guard, I believe he sought leadership approval out of an abundance of caution to protect his behind from the mauling that would result if he were to bring the National Guard onto Capitol Hill without first notifying the Speaker. The tragedy of this delay is that if, at 12:58 p.m., the CPB had immediately approved my request, I could have officially notified General Walker much earlier, which could have resulted in additional support arriving at the Capitol sooner, preventing numerous injuries and likely saving lives. And possibly even preventing the breach of the building itself.

The confusing structure of the CPB is further evidenced by AOC Brett Blanton's accusation that I did not make the request of the board because I didn't also reach out to *him*. Not only is that grossly inaccurate, but it also exemplifies the convoluted nature of the board's structure and negates the role of the chairman of the board. The law that created the CPB provides an overview of its role:

> The Capitol Police Board oversees and supports the United States Capitol Police in its mission, and helps to advance

---

25. Peters, Portman, Klobuchar, and Blunt, *Examining the U.S. Capitol Attack*, 68.

coordination between the Department and the Sergeant at Arms of the House of Representatives and the Sergeant at Arms and Doorkeeper of the Senate, in their law enforcement capacities, and the Congress.[26]

In law enforcement matters, even the public law that formed the board recognizes the direct relationship between the department and the House and Senate sergeants at arms. It doesn't call for coordination between the department and the AOC in their law enforcement capacities because that was not the intent of the AOC's inclusion on the board. I was already going to Irving and the chairman of the CPB. This accounts for two of the three voting members of the board. Without Irving's and Stenger's support, the support of the AOC wouldn't have made a difference anyway.

Another issue that shocked the American public on January 6 involved the physical hardness of the Capitol Building itself. This concern played out on national television when a rioter appeared to break the window on the upper West Terrace of the US Capitol Building with relative ease. Brett Blanton described the window on the upper West Terrace that was broken by a protester as one of the "two-hundred-fifty-year-old windows there that can be broken with the lightest touch."[27] This was a surprise not only to those who watched it on television but also to members of Congress, their staffs, and even police officers were astonished at how easily some of the windows broke. The AOC is part of the CPB in order to help coordinate physical security initiatives with the USCP and to maintain the structure and integrity of the building. Physical security is very expensive, especially for historic buildings, but issues like the unreinforced, easily broken window, as well as the doors into the Capitol and the nonfunctioning garage doors, have existed on the Hill for decades.

26. Public Law 108–7, div. H, title I, §1014, 117 Stat. 36, February 20, 2003, https://www.uscp.gov/the-department/oversight/capitol-police-board.

27. House Committee on Appropriations, "FY 2022 Budget Hearing for Architect of the Capitol," 1:15:37.

Like the USCP, the Architect of the Capitol operates on a limited budget provided by Congress, and over half of the AOC's required projects go unfunded.[28] The increasing needs of Congress have taken away funding that was originally designated for infrastructure and physical security projects. In 2021, the AOC faced a $1.8 billion backlog of projects that needed funding. The same budgetary constraints that I faced are also placed on the AOC, who is forced to pick and choose among various physical security initiatives in order to stay within the allotted budget. This lack of budgeting could have led to a much greater tragedy on January 6.

Blanton explained he was extremely concerned that if some of the rioters had tried to light fires inside the Capitol Building, the result might have been disastrous. According to him, the building didn't even have an effective fire-suppression system. Blanton stated, "The events of the sixth really put that into a scary reality for me; it probably should be for everybody. If there was a fire in there, that would have been a terrible situation because we would not have had the resources nor the suppression system to suppress the fire."[29]

This statement by Blanton floored me. Many winter nights I would walk the quiet grounds of the Capitol, smelling the wood fires burning in the numerous fireplaces within. Now the Architect was stating that they don't have an effective fire-suppression system. Yet they allow members of Congress to have fires in their offices? Just one of the many ironies on the Hill. Capitol Police Board regulations didn't allow open flames outside the buildings, but they were allowed *inside* a building without an effective fire-suppression system. You can't make this stuff up! Again, these are safety and security issues that have existed for decades and that need funding to be addressed—funding that Congress controls.

The aftereffects of January 6 are likely to hurt the USCP for years

28. J. Brett Blanton, *Statement of J. Brett Blanton, Architect of the Capitol*, United States Senate Committee on Appropriations, April 21, 2021, 3.
29. House Committee on Appropriations, "FY 2022 Budget Hearing for Architect of the Capitol," 54:18.

to come, and some of the consequences are yet to be reckoned with. On January 8, the CPB, undoubtedly with congressional leadership's approval, made a hasty and irresponsible decision when it decided to confirm Pittman, the assistant chief of protection and intelligence operations, as acting chief of police. Not only did this decision deliver a major hit to the morale of the department—since many felt that this person bore significant responsibility for January 6—but it also hampered the department's ability to investigate the failings of January 6 in an unbiased fashion. From the very beginning, there were significant concerns that this could have been the result of an intelligence failure. By selecting the person who was in charge of intelligence and putting her in charge of the entire agency, they also put her in charge of the internal investigation and the information that would be shared with oversight and the inspector general to assist them in their investigations. Putting in charge the one person who could become a primary focus of the investigation and giving that person full authority over the department—including everything from investigations and discipline to personnel matters and promotions—creates a plethora of ethical issues for the Capitol Police Board, congressional leadership, and the department.

A better course of action would have been to consider bringing in a retired USCP executive or chief, someone who clearly had "clean hands." The CPB could also have requested to temporarily borrow an executive from another agency to help run the department while the investigation was being conducted. Instead, the CPB placed the assistant chief of intelligence in charge and gave her unencumbered authority over the agency and all the information associated with January 6.

A little over two months after being named acting chief, Pittman made twenty-three promotions of USCP personnel, including individuals whose performance on January 6 was questionable at best. Then, in June, Assistant Chief Thomas was forced to leave the department, which further advanced and focused public and media scrutiny on the USCP uniformed operations and away from its intelligence operations.

The politicization of security on the Hill continues even after January 6. On March 4, 2021, the USCP again faced delayed approval from the CPB regarding the National Guard. Acting Chief Pittman had asked the board to extend the presence of the National Guard, but she couldn't get their approval. Again, it was the division right down the center of the Capitol: in this case, Speaker Pelosi and the House side approved it immediately, but Acting Senate Sergeant at Arms Jennifer Hemingway, representing Senate leadership, wouldn't commit to a decision. When only days remained to make a decision, the acting chief decided to bypass the sergeant at arms, writing a letter to congressional leadership to force the decision.[30]

The security apparatus that exists on Capitol Hill creates a no-win situation for whoever is chief. You have the Capitol Police Board, four oversight committees, and 535 bosses plus their staffs telling you what to do. There's too much concern for optics, and the politicization of security continues to create issues. The Capitol Police Board needs to be reformed, and the USCP chief of police needs to be granted full authority to handle all security-related matters, without consideration for optics or politics. The idea of a single oversight or advisory board is not a bad idea, but the current structure is not the solution.

THE DEPARTMENT OF DEFENSE

As chief of the United States Capitol Police, I was appalled at the response I received from the Department of Defense on January 6. The US Capitol was under siege for *hours*, in one of the most violent and visible attacks that we have ever been subjected to. I was watching my officers fight for their lives to protect the members of Congress, the vice president, and his family as armed rioters fought them mercilessly, trying to breach the Capitol and stop the election process.

I had already called in federal, state, and local resources to assist, but the attack was clearly exceeding my resources. Yet even after the

---

30. Yogananda Pittman, "Read the Letter from the Acting Chief of Capitol Police on Extending National Guard Troop Presence," *New York Times*, March 4, 2021, www.nytimes .com/interactive/2021/03/04/us/national-guard-request.html.

Capitol Police Board, at 2:09 p.m., finally gave its approval to call in the National Guard, I still had to wait over *three and a half more hours* before any military assistance arrived. During that time, I repeatedly begged and pleaded with the Pentagon for assistance as I watched the onslaught against my officers continue, yet members of the DC National Guard—a unit known as the "Capital Guardians"—many of whom were positioned within eyesight of the Capitol and equipped with riot gear—never came to assist us. It now appears the military leaders at the Pentagon did not want them anywhere near the Capitol, not before the attack began and not even as the attack unfolded.

I was equally appalled when, on November 16, 2021, the Inspector General for the Department of Defense released its findings regarding the DoD's response to my requests for assistance at the Capitol on January 6. According to the Inspector General's report, "We concluded that the DoD's actions to respond to the USCP's RFA on January 6, 2021, were appropriate, supported by requirements, consistent with the DoD's roles and responsibilities for DSCA, and complied with laws, regulations, and other applicable guidance." The Inspector General went on to state, "We also determined that DoD officials did not improperly delay or obstruct the DoD's response to the USCP RFA on January 6, 2021."[31]

This was a transparent CYA attempt by the Department of Defense. To fully understand the frustration I felt at this response, just look at the days leading up to January 6, when DoD missteps first began. In addition to the FBI and DHS having significant intelligence about January 6 that failed to rise to the highest levels, it now appears that the military itself also had information that raised serious concerns in the Department of Defense. On Sunday, January 3, Secretary of Defense Miller convened a White House cabinet-level call that included Acting Attorney General Jeffrey Rosen, Secretary of the Interior David Bernhardt, Acting Secretary of DHS Chad Wolf, and National Security Advisor Charles O'Brien.[32] Miller also stated that a senior official from the operational

31. DoD Inspector General's Report, 70–71.
32. Peters, Portman, Klobuchar, and Blunt, *Examining the U.S. Capitol Attack*, 77–78.

side of DHS participated on the call, but he could not remember the name. According to Miller, the purpose of the meeting was to "coordinate and synchronize" and to discuss the request for National Guard assistance they had received from the District of Columbia.

SECDEF Miller and General Mark Milley then went to meet with President Trump. As chairman of the Joint Chiefs, General Milley is the highest-ranking, most senior military officer in the United States armed forces, as well as the principal military advisor to the president, secretary of defense, National Security Council, and Homeland Security Council. According to Miller, the purpose of the meeting was unrelated to January 6, but the topic was discussed when President Trump brought up the joint session of Congress. In the meeting, Trump concurred with activating the DC National Guard to support the existing request from the MPD. Unlike in any other jurisdiction, in Washington, DC, the president of the United States controls the National Guard. But that authority had been delegated to the secretary of defense, who had delegated it to the secretary of the army.

The very next day, however, on January 4, SECDEF Miller convened a second call with White House cabinet members to discuss rising concerns over the upcoming demonstrations on January 5 and 6.[33] The purpose of this call was for him to voice his concerns about how the demonstrations had been growing more aggressive and that it could be "a pretty dramatic day." SECDEF Miller stated that these concerns were also being raised internally within the highest levels of the DoD.

Later on the fourth, during an interagency conference call, Miller and General Milley both raised their growing concerns about violence. Specifically, they were concerned about the demonstration permits that had been issued at the US Capitol. According to Miller's testimony, their concern about the permitted groups at the Capitol was so great that both Miller and Milley inquired about the ability to revoke the permits. They must have known that was an overreach, but the mere fact they were discussing the

---

33. Peters, Portman, Klobuchar, and Blunt, *Examining the U.S. Capitol Attack*, 78.

possibility of revoking permits for First Amendment activities on Capitol grounds should give everyone pause. During the call, General Milley also suggested locking down the city to control the violence that he believed to be coming. For the highest-ranking military officer in the country to recommend locking down the nation's capital in order to control violence, they must have had some pretty damned concerning information!

According to Miller, the interagency conference call was attended by representatives from the Department of the Interior and DC city officials. If the call concerned the US Capitol and involved the secretary of defense and the chairman of the Joint Chiefs, why weren't the sergeants at arms or I on the call? The chief of the Capitol Police is the one who signs the demonstration permits—not the Department of the Interior or the DC mayor's office. They should have called me immediately to express any concerns. If the US military, the SECDEF, or General Milley was concerned about the Capitol, wouldn't they want to talk to the chief of the United States Capitol Police, as opposed to someone from the Department of the Interior or the DC city government? Several ranking members of the military have my cell number, and the number to the USCP is listed on the website, and calls are answered 24-7.

Chris Miller had been the director of the National Counterterrorism Center before being named acting secretary of defense. Thus, he was keenly aware of intelligence, the intelligence community, and concerns over domestic violent extremism.

Department of Defense organizations make up half of the intelligence community's eighteen agencies. It is now apparent that both Miller and Milley had significant concerns regarding upcoming events at the Capitol on January 6. The question that needs to be asked is, if Miller and Milley had such significant concerns, why weren't those concerns pursued or shared with the appropriate authorities? Instead, on January 4, Miller issued unprecedented restrictions on the DC National Guard, preventing it from responding to the very types of unrest he apparently was envisioning. After Miller issued the extensive restrictions, the only resource left available to General Walker was the quick reaction force (QRF).

SECRETARY OF DEFENSE
1000 DEFENSE PENTAGON
WASHINGTON, DC 20301-1000

JAN - 4 2021

MEMORANDUM FOR SECRETARY OF THE ARMY

SUBJECT: Employment Guidance for the District of Columbia National Guard

This memorandum responds to your January 4, 2021 memorandum regarding the District of Columbia request for District of Columbia National Guard (DCNG) support in response to planned demonstrations from January 5-6, 2021. You are authorized to approve the requested support, subject to my guidance below and subject to consultation with the Attorney General, as required by Executive Order 11485.

Without my subsequent, personal authorization, the DCNG is not authorized the following:

- To be issued weapons, ammunition, bayonets, batons, or ballistic protection equipment such as helmets and body armor.

- To interact physically with protestors, except when necessary in self-defense or defense of others, consistent with the DCNG Rules for the Use of Force.

- To employ any riot control agents.

- To share equipment with law enforcement agencies.

- To use Intelligence, Surveillance, and Reconnaissance (ISR) assets or to conduct ISR or Incident, Awareness, and Assessment activities.

- To employ helicopters or any other air assets.

- To conduct searches, seizures, arrests, or other similar direct law enforcement activity.

- To seek support from any non-DCNG National Guard units.

At all times, the DCNG will remain under the operational and administrative command and control of the Commanding General of the DCNG, who reports to the Secretary of Defense through the Secretary of the Army.

You may employ the DCNG Quick Reaction Force (QRF) only as a last resort and in response to a request from an appropriate civil authority. If the QRF is so employed, DCNG personnel will be clearly marked and/or distinguished from civilian law enforcement personnel, and you will notify me immediately upon your authorization.

Christopher C. Miller
Acting

OSD000020-21/CMD000059-21

Figure 4.4. Memo from SECDEF Miller

But according to Miller, Walker could deploy the QRF only as a "last resort" and in response to a request from an appropriate civil authority. In a baffling move that defies all logic, on January 5, SECARMY McCarthy further tied Walker's hands by restricting the use of the QRF without first obtaining McCarthy's express approval of a concept-of-operations plan for the use of the QRF.[34] Miller was unaware of this added restriction on the QRF because McCarthy never informed him he was going to impose additional restrictions on Walker.[35]

Equally concerning is the fact that Miller issued these restrictions *only* for January 5 and 6—the very days he and Milley had expressed such grave concerns about. This would turn out to be a tragic error. The Department of Defense is considered the backstop to federal, state, and local government agencies in the event of an emergency that exceeds their capabilities. This is exactly what I faced at the Capitol on January 6. But when the Department of Defense implemented these restrictions, it didn't advise any of its fellow stakeholders: the first-responder agencies in DC—in other words, the very people who would be relying on the Guard's emergency support.

It also doesn't appear that Miller and Milley ever shared their concerns about violence on these dates with their top two military commanders in DC: General Omar Jones, commanding general of the Military District of Washington, and General William Walker, commanding general of the DC National Guard. Both Jones and Walker were on a video call I arranged on January 5, and neither expressed any concerns about violence at the Capitol. Yet, on January 6, both generals had to spring into action due to the attack at the Capitol. I am sure they would have liked to know their DoD bosses' concerns before things started going bad. Both men are friends of mine, and I would like to believe they would have told me if they knew that trouble was brewing on the horizon.

According to the Senate report and the DoD Inspector General's report, these restrictions were put in place following the large-scale

34. Peters, Portman, Klobuchar, and Blunt, *Examining the U.S. Capitol Attack*, 7.
35. Peters, Portman, Klobuchar, and Blunt, *Examining the U.S. Capitol Attack*, 82.

protests that occurred in Washington, DC, and around the White House over the summer. During these protests the National Guard employed some questionable tactics, such as flying a Lakota UH-72 helicopter low over groups of protesters.[36] It was also at this time that Trump, on June 1, staged his photo op in front of St. John's Church in Washington, DC. During the event, Milley, the then secretary of defense Mark Esper, Attorney General William Barr, and others joined the president as he walked from the White House across Lafayette Square to St. John's Church for the famous picture.

On June 11, 2020, Milley produced a YouTube video apologizing for his participation in the Trump photo, stating that the military's participation "gave the public a perception of the military involved in domestic politics." Miller and McCarthy testified before the Senate committees that they implemented the January 5 and 6 restrictions on the National Guard as a result of the ongoing concerns about the military's involvement in protests over the summer.[37]

If that was indeed the case, this response raises some serious concerns:

1. Why not implement these changes immediately after the summer demonstrations and after Milley's apology?
2. If the use of military personnel and equipment in support of law enforcement activities was a concern, why not make this change part of the standing policy?
3. Why was the policy implemented *only* for January 5 and 6— the two days of the Trump rally—and not indefinitely?

These were unprecedented restrictions that radically altered a standing DoD policy on how the military provides support when requested by civil authorities. On January 6, a total of 340 DC National Guard

36. Mark Milley, "Nation's Top Military Officer Apologizes for Appearing at President Donald Trump Church Photo-op," CNBC, June 11, 2020, www.youtube.com/watch?v=AtXdpbzyGiQ.
37. Peters, Portman, Klobuchar, and Blunt, *Examining the U.S. Capitol Attack*, 73–74.

soldiers were activated to support the DC government and the Metropolitan Police Department under Executive Order 11485. Military support for the police department is governed through a program called the Defense Support of Civil Authorities (DSCA). The National Guard was activated in advance based on a request for assistance (RFA) from the DC government to support the MPD in directing traffic and assisting with crowd control around six Metro subway stations. They also had a small number of soldiers providing supervision and response for hazardous materials, and a forty-member quick reaction force. Since they were assisting the MPD with a law enforcement mission, the Guard soldiers were sworn in by the MPD as special police officers. They were activated in a Title 32 capacity, which means they were exempt from the provisions of the Posse Comitatus Act and were able to conduct law enforcement activities, even as US military soldiers. As I mentioned earlier, the DSCA program is codified by Department of Defense Directive 3025.18, *Defense Support of Civil Authorities*.[38]

While all the lingo and military jargon sounds complicated, the takeaway is that the Department of Defense has a process to support civil authorities such as the Capitol Police. The established process provides military support for planned events, which involves submitting formal requests for assistance, obtaining approval through the DoD, conducting a mission analysis and planning, and then providing the requested boots on the ground on the day of the event. This process was followed when the DC government submitted the request for the National Guard to support the Metropolitan Police Department with traffic and crowd control in the city on January 5 and 6.

But what is critical to understand—and highly pertinent to January 6—is that there is also a process for the military to provide an emergency response to an *unplanned* event beyond the capabilities of the civil authorities. In other words, the military can provide immediate support

---

38. US Department of Defense, Directive 3025.18, *Defense Support of Civil Authorities (DSCA)*, December 29, 2010, www.dco.uscg.mil/Portals/9/CG-5R/nsarc /DoDD%203025.18%20Defense%20Support%20of%20Civil%20Authorities.pdf.

when the police need help and "dial 911." While the Posse Comitatus Act limits the government's ability to use the military in an active law enforcement role within the United States, the DoD's emergency response statute to support authorities takes this into consideration. When civil authorities experience an emergency, the DSCA policy has two avenues to provide emergency response:

> **Immediate Response.** As authorized by the Stafford Act, and prescribed by DODD 3025.18, *Defense Support of Civil Authorities (DSCA)*, federal military commanders, heads of DOD components, and responsible DOD civilian officials have immediate response authority. In response to an RFA from a civil authority, under imminently serious conditions and if time does not permit approval from higher authority, DOD officials may provide an immediate response by temporarily employing the resources under their control, subject to any supplemental direction provided by higher headquarters, to save lives, prevent human suffering, or mitigate great property damage within the US. Immediate response authority is not an exception to the PCA nor does it permit actions that would subject civilians to the use of military power that is regulatory, prescriptive, proscriptive, or compulsory.[39]

> **Emergency Authority.** Emergency authority is a federal military commander's authority, in extraordinary emergency circumstances where prior authorization by the President is impossible and duly constituted local authorities are unable to control the situation, to engage temporarily in activities that are necessary to quell large-scale, unexpected civil disturbances because such activities are necessary to prevent significant loss

---

39. US Department of the Army, Joint Publication 3-28, *Defense Support of Civil Authorities*, October 29, 2018, II-5, www.jcs.mil/Portals/36/Documents/Doctrine/pubs /jp3_28.pdf.

of life or wanton destruction of property and are necessary to restore governmental function and public order or duly constituted federal, state, local, territorial, or tribal authorities are unable or decline to provide adequate protection for federal property or federal governmental functions. Responsible DOD officials and commanders will use all available means to seek presidential authorization through the chain of command while applying their emergency authority. Emergency authority should not be confused with immediate response authority. Federal forces acting under immediate response authority are still bound by the PCA and may not participate directly in law enforcement; whereas, emergency authority and actions taken under the Insurrection Act are exceptions to the PCA.[40]

The immediate response authority did not apply to my emergency request for assistance on January 6 because it does not provide an exemption to the Posse Comitatus Act and does not permit the military to participate in law enforcement activities. It's important to note that this authority includes a stipulation for military leaders to provide restrictions to military commanders through the included language: "*subject to any supplemental direction provided by higher headquarters.*"[41] This is the very type of supplemental direction that Miller and McCarthy provided to the DC National Guard.

But since my urgent request for assistance included the need for the National Guard to fulfill a law enforcement mission, my emergency request should have fallen under the emergency authority. The circumstances under which emergency authority can be activated read almost like a textbook description of January 6: "*to quell large-scale, unexpected civil disturbances because such activities are necessary to prevent significant loss of life or wanton destruction of property and are necessary to restore governmental function and public order . . .*"

40. US Department of the Army, Joint Publication 3-28, II-6.
41. US Department of the Army, Joint Publication 3-28, II-5.

It is also critical to note that, unlike immediate response, the emergency authority does *not* provide any language allowing higher head-quarters to impose additional restrictions on the emergency response. To make this even clearer, in an emergency authority situation, the policy does *not* permit the type of restrictions that Miller and McCarthy imposed on the National Guard. This is likely because emergency authority would be enacted only in the most egregious circumstances. I believe that the intent of this section of the policy was to give military commanders the greatest degree of authority to assist immediately in extraordinary life-and-death situations.

But somehow, the DoD Inspector General determined that the use of emergency authority did not apply to my repeated pleas for assistance on January 6, even while the lives of every member of Congress and the vice president and his family were at stake. We had shots fired inside the Capitol, fatalities inside and outside the building, and numerous critical injuries. But the Inspector General reported, "*They could not exercise emergency authority because exercising that authority requires that it be impossible to communicate through the chain of command to obtain a presidential authorization to conduct civil disturbance operations, and those circumstances did not exist on January 6, 2021.*"[42]

A significant flaw in the Inspector General's logic is that it left out one of the most important sentences of the "Emergency Authority" section: "*Responsible DOD officials and commanders will use all available means to seek Presidential authorization through the chain of command while applying their emergency authority.*" As this reads, the National Guard should have been trying to seek presidential approval while also immediately responding to my repeated requests for emergency assistance. The big question is, who did or did not seek presidential approval? Miller stated that he never spoke to Trump on January 6. Either way, there is a serious issue here.

If the DoD Inspector General is correct, *someone* was able to

---

42. DoD Inspector General's Report, 71.

communicate with the president to seek emergency authorization approval. If that is the case, who was seeking the approval, and what was the answer? Did the president deny my request? If the Inspector General is wrong and either no one tried or no one was able to communicate with the president, then where the hell was my National Guard backup under the emergency authority clause while they were trying to get an answer? It appears that the Inspector General was treating this as a standard request for assistance rather than the critical emergency request that it so clearly and unambiguously was.

The secretary of defense may argue that presidential authority pertaining to authorization of the emergency authority clause was delegated by the president to the secretary of defense when the overall management of the District of Columbia National Guard was delegated. If that were indeed the intent, then the emergency authority clause would have made the stipulation that the authority can be granted by the governor in the case of state National Guard forces and by the president in the case of the District of Columbia. But it doesn't. It specifically states presidential authorization. Therefore, it is apparent that the authority for this critical authorization was reserved specifically for the president of the United States. So I reiterate: who sought presidential approval while my women and men were fighting their asses off for over three and a half hours, while hundreds of National Guard troops within two miles of the Capitol were not being deployed to assist?

It is now becoming clear that the Department of Defense did not want the National Guard involved in the violent attack on the Hill. The DoD Inspector General's report states:

> Mr. Miller told us, "There was absolutely no way . . . I was putting U.S. military forces at the Capitol, period." He cited media stories alleging that the President's advisors were pushing him to declare martial law to invalidate the election and that Mr. Miller was an ally installed as the Acting SecDef to facilitate a coup. He also cited a January 3, 2021 open letter from 10 former Secretaries of Defense warning the DoD not to use

the military in a manner antithetical to the U.S. Constitution. Mr. Miller stated that he "made a very deliberate decision that I would not put U.S. military people . . . East of the 9th Street, northwest . . ."[43]

Miller was worried that the presence of military personnel on Capitol Hill during the certification of the Electoral College would create a true constitutional crisis. McCarthy echoed that feeling, saying he did not want to create the perception of military involvement in the electoral process.[44] This pre–January 6 aversion to the use of the National Guard anywhere near the Capitol translated into delay after delay in sending in uniformed military personnel to help protect the Capitol while it was under siege. While I pleaded for help, the DoD spent hours assessing the situation and developing a plan to respond.

The DoD Inspector General confirmed what General Walker had been saying all along: the National Guard troops on the traffic posts, the Metro stations, and the quick reaction force all had their riot gear with them.[45] According to Walker, if he had been authorized to deploy his forces immediately and had not been subject to Miller's and McCarthy's restrictions, he could have sent about 150 soldiers to the Capitol within twenty minutes. But the DoD never had them respond to assist with the riot at the Capitol, which had turned deadly. Instead, they remained on their traffic and Metro station assignments with all their riot gear, without being issued other orders.[46]

At 5:00 p.m., the National Guard soldiers who had been in the field with all their riot gear were moved from their traffic posts, many within view of the Capitol, and returned to the DC National Guard armory to complete their tour of duty. None of the approximately 150 National Guard troops who had been assisting with street closings were

43. DoD Inspector General's Report, 30.
44. DoD Inspector General's Report, 30.
45. DoD Inspector General's Report, 5.
46. DoD Inspector General's Report, 6.

deployed to assist at the Capitol. Instead, the military opted to use only the second shift, the relief shift of Guard troops, who had arrived at the armory earlier that afternoon to provide support at the Capitol.[47] The QRF and the evening National Guard troops were finally put on buses, and they left the armory at 5:15 p.m., headed to the Capitol.

As chief of the Capitol Police, I was infuriated by this response. The military leadership disregarded my repeated pleas for assistance during a deadly attack on the Capitol, electing not to reassign 150 fully outfitted soldiers who were just blocks away from the Capitol. Instead, they were allowed to remain on their traffic assignments until shortly before five, when they returned safely to the DC armory. To better understand how utterly ridiculous this is, visualize how this played out:

The National Guard armory is directly east of the Capitol, about two miles straight down East Capitol Street. The locations where some 150 fully outfitted National Guard soldiers were deployed were anywhere from about half a mile to two miles west of the Capitol. The soldiers and the armory were on precisely opposite sides of the US Capitol. To fully grasp the absurdity of the situation, picture the National Guard soldiers with all their riot gear, only blocks away, having to *drive around* the Capitol while my officers were still battling there, not being allowed to assist, only to return to the armory to be relieved—*all while the Pentagon was sending security details to protect the military leaders' homes and while the military leaders in the Pentagon were watching the attack play out on national television.*

Even the quick reaction force sat idle at Joint Base Andrews, ready to deploy, only twenty minutes from the Capitol, and was prevented from responding for over three hours.

The members of Congress, the vice president and his family, and my officers were all in peril, and this was the response I was getting. By the time the Guard troops arrived at the Capitol, were sworn in, and were deployed to the field, it was almost 6:00 p.m. The battle was over,

47. DoD Inspector General's Report, 49.

and all the National Guard ended up doing was help form a line on our perimeter. A USCP official on the scene stated that numerous National Guard soldiers were outraged, lashing out at their leadership for the repeated delays. Many soldiers felt they could have made a difference had they been allowed to respond. The USCP official told me it was heartbreaking to watch these soldiers, many on the brink of tears, frustrated that they weren't allowed to help protect their nation's Capitol.

And yet, somehow, the DoD inspector general considers this an acceptable response. I wonder whether they would feel the same if their house were being broken into and they kept calling 911, but the police first had to form a plan to respond, and then waited for the next shift to come on before responding. Oh, but wait—first they must send people to protect their *own* homes and make sure they didn't get vandalized. All while leaving you and your family to fend for yourselves. Forgive my language, but give me a fucking break. This is unacceptable, and the American people should be *livid* that this was the response we got from our military leadership.

Following the attack, there were a lot of discrepancies between the Pentagon's timeline of events and General Walker's. SECDEF Miller considered the discrepancies as the result of the "fog and friction of chaotic situations."[48] Like Miller, General McConville also felt that the "fog and friction" affected timelines, and added that the Pentagon is "an administrative headquarters" rather than a tactical "command and control headquarters that's actually fighting a battle."[49]

That is another interesting response. Why were Miller and McConville inserting themselves into the tactical response to the Capitol on January 6 in the first place? Why not let the commanders in the field make the tactical decisions? If this is how they respond to a civil riot, imagine what might happen in the "fog" of actual war. The Department of Defense's response on January 6 draws concerning parallels to the inaction in Benghazi and the lack of planning in leaving Kabul. If Miller and Milley had been so damned concerned about extensive violence

48. Peters, Portman, Klobuchar, and Blunt, *Examining the U.S. Capitol Attack*, 90.
49. Peters, Portman, Klobuchar, and Blunt, *Examining the U.S. Capitol Attack*, 90.

in the city on January 6, why didn't they develop a contingency plan?

On November 16, 2021, the Department of Defense Office of the Inspector General concluded its investigation. To no one's surprise, it found that the Pentagon responded "appropriately" and did not delay urgent requests for National Guard assistance and that Miller, McCarthy, and other senior DoD officials acted reasonably. Ultimately, the DoD Inspector General based its decision on a determination that the overall response time, from receipt of my request until the arrival of the DC National Guard, being about three and a quarter to three and a half hours, was acceptable because they *"did not identify a standard that required DoD to fulfill a DSCA RFA within a specific amount of time after receiving one."*[50]

If this isn't a load of Washington bureaucratic doublespeak, I don't know what is. Again, the Inspector General is treating this as a standard RFA and not an emergency request for life-and-death assistance. They had National Guard personnel equipped with the right gear less than half a mile from the US Capitol under siege. But rather than assist the outnumbered police, they sent these soldiers back to the DC armory and then eventually sent the evening relief personnel to the Capitol. Considering the urgency and gravity of the situation, why would they not send every available soldier to assist, instead of unnecessarily making me wait three and a half hours for assistance while the Capitol and our democracy were under attack?

I voluntarily participated in an interview with the DoD Inspector General on March 15, 2021, and provided them with all my email and phone records. Much like the USCP inspector general's various investigations, this was not an in-depth, independent review of these events, conducted to prevent this type of issue from occurring in the future. Rather, it was clearly an attempt to cover up and give the US military a pass, specifically on the Pentagon's delays in granting General Walker authorization to deploy to the Capitol. If the National Guard had the unencumbered ability to enact its emergency authority as prescribed by

---

50. DoD Inspector General's Report, 71.

Department of Defense directives, General Walker could have redeployed National Guard troops to the US Capitol *at once* and might even have had them on-site before the first window at the Capitol was smashed at 2:10 p.m.—possibly preventing the loss of two military veterans' lives.

Two weeks after the DoD Inspector General released its findings regarding the military's response, Colonel Earl G. Matthews, a decorated and highly respected combat veteran and attorney for the army who had served as the army's acting general counsel and principal deputy general counsel, wrote a blistering thirty-six-page letter rebuking the DoD Inspector General's report and indicating that the analysis was critically flawed and biased and that Lieutenant General Piatt and Lieutenant General Flynn had lied about my 2:34 p.m. call with the Pentagon.[51]

On January 6, Colonel Matthews was serving as General Walker's staff judge advocate and was listening during my call with the Pentagon. Although the DoD Inspector General's report indicated that Lieutenant Generals Piatt and Flynn had been unable to get a clear understanding of the mission that I wanted the Guard to fulfill at the Capitol, Matthews's letter said otherwise: "Sund knew exactly what mission he wanted the DCNG personnel to perform was. Sund wanted as many riot-equipped (helmets, body armor, shin guards, batons and shields) D.C. National Guard personnel as possible to report to the Capitol where they would assist USCP personnel in re-establishing the security perimeter which had been breached. Chief Sund had previously provided a link-up location where DCNG personnel should report to the USCP, the corner of New Jersey & Louisiana Avenues."

According to Matthews, the recollections of Piatt and Flynn were extremely flawed, and he described the two ranking military officials as "unmitigated liars." Much of SECARMY McCarthy's recollections of the military's response and timeline are seriously called into question by significant evidence in Matthews's letter, which raises more concerns

---

51. Earl G. Matthews, *The Harder Right: An Analysis of a Recent DoD Inspector General Investigation and Other Matters*, December 1, 2021, www.politico.com /f/?id=0000017d-8aca-dee4-a5ff-eeda79e90000.

about why the Pentagon did everything it could to stay out of the fight, and why its Inspector General is covering for it.

To sum up my grave concerns about the overall failure to provide me with the intelligence I needed before January 6, it now appears that a majority of the intelligence community—FBI, DHS, DoD—were all seeing red in the intelligence they had, but *none* of the agencies were ringing the alarm or sending up the balloon. These threats were directed at government leaders and institutions, Congress, and the vice president. What is unclear is whether any of the eighteen agencies that make up the intelligence community acted on this intelligence and initiated Duty to Warn protocols as outlined in Intelligence Community Directive 191.[52] I was involved in Duty to Warn notifications while at the USCP, and they trigger a significant internal response. Before January 6, a Duty to Warn notification would have come in to either of the two sergeants at arms or at the highest levels of the USCP. If the USCP had been contacted by an organization in the IC or, more specifically, the FBI regarding a Duty to Warn notification, it would have been a big deal—certainly not just an email to a low-level USCP intel desk. The notification would have been immediately elevated to the chief and the two sergeants at arms. But this notification never seemed to materialize. Federal agencies were receiving intelligence regarding a coordinated attack on the Capitol, fusion centers were raising significant concerns, and the Pentagon was talking about locking down Washington, DC, because the concern for violence at the Capitol was so great. Yet no one considered notifying Congress or the officers sworn to protect it.

THE UNITED STATES CAPITOL POLICE

Besides the serious failure of the USCP's intelligence division, an array of other internal USCP issues hindered the department's response on that day. Although many of the issues had been affecting the department

---

52. Office of the Director of National Intelligence, *Intelligence Community Directive 191*, July 21, 2015, www.dni.gov/files/documents/ICD/ICD_191.pdf.

for years, several operational decisions and actions clearly could have been handled better.

Since the events of January 6, I have received a lot of criticism from members of Congress and the media regarding the officers' training and equipment. Many noted that some of the USCP officers appeared to be fighting wearing only their regular street uniforms, as opposed to the helmets, shields, and padding that some of the civil disturbance unit officers were wearing. The issue of equipment for officers was something that had been plaguing this department for decades. Training was also a challenge due to available manpower and budget. Coming into January 6, the USCP was operating at a significant deficit of sworn police officers—a shortage that was well known to the Capitol Police Board and oversight and was an issue I had reiterated during my first budget hearing as chief on February 11, 2020.[53]

Immediately upon my arrival at the USCP in 2017, I began to look at our training and equipment. As the new chief of operations, I wanted to improve on several areas, including CDU equipment, less lethal capabilities, intelligence systems, and basic personal protective equipment (PPE) for every officer, including a helmet, baton, and air-purifying respirator (APR). These items were standard issue for every MPD officer, and I wanted the same for the USCP. In addition, I wanted to purchase new CDU equipment, a lot of which had not been replaced in years. I met with our budgeting and procurement personnel and included subject-matter experts from the MPD to help me develop a plan and standards for new equipment. I wanted to bring the USCP up to the same standards as the MPD. Launching new initiatives and implementing new technology was something I excelled at while at the MPD, and I looked forward to doing the same at USCP.

Like every federal agency, we were always operating from a budget

53. Steven A. Sund, *Testimony of Steven A. Sund, Chief of Police, United States Capitol Police, Before the United States House of Representatives Subcommittee on Legislative Branch, Committee on Appropriations*, February 11, 2020, www.congress.gov/116/meeting /house/110477/witnesses/HHRG-116-AP24-Wstate-SundS-20200211-U1.pdf.

that had been developed at least a year in advance, and the equipment I was planning to purchase was going to be a substantial cost. With the mandatory budget needs of the department increasing, especially with the skyrocketing threats against members of Congress, my equipment requests would be pushed off to future budget cycles. When I became the chief, I was faced with the promise of Congress to cut the budget of its own police department by tens of millions of dollars as part of the "defund the police" movement, further impacting the ability to identify funding for the equipment. Nonetheless, I continued to push for a number of other less costly initiatives, such as obtaining less lethal PepperBall systems and Tasers for the department. It wasn't until September 2020 that my CAO and CFO were able to creatively identify $300,000 to purchase new riot helmets. However, due to supply-chain issues as a result of COVID-19, the delivery of the helmets was delayed for months, and we were only able to receive a partial shipment just days before January 6.

Another issue that the Senate committees and the USCP inspector general used to denigrate the USCP response on January 6 was the lack of an operational plan for the *entire* department for January 6. It is important to understand that there was indeed a plan developed for the demonstrations and any civil disobedience that could occur on Capitol grounds. This plan was developed based on the intelligence and assessments provided by the IICD.

We should have had a plan that combined the outside and inside events on January 6. Waldow had completed the CDU plan for the exterior, but there was no corresponding plan for the joint session taking place inside the Capitol. Extensive planning and preparation go into a joint session of Congress. Becky Daugherty of the Senate sergeant at arms office and Ted Daniel of the House sergeant at arms office would coordinate meetings and walk-throughs in advance to ensure that everyone knew the required protocols and processes of the joint session. These meetings would also address such things as VIP access, USCP escort teams, the media, timelines, and evacuation plans. These walk-throughs and meetings would include the USCP, the House and Senate sergeants at arms, media galleries, and the United States Secret Service—all of which should be reflected in an operational plan. An operational plan for the joint session inside the Capitol Building on January 6 followed standard operating procedures and a template that had existed for years. The responsibility to prepare special event plans is spelled out in our departmental directives and is the responsibility of the Command and Coordination Bureau, which is tasked with preparing for and managing emergencies, planning special events, and managing multiagency responses to evolving emergency and crisis situations.[54]

When asked by the committees why no department-wide plan had been created, Pittman stated that it would have been the chief of police's responsibility to request that operational commanders prepare such a plan and that she could not explain why I chose not to do so before January 6.[55] Pittman's statement that I did not direct that a plan of action be developed for this event is not completely accurate. A plan of action is required for *all* large events at the Capitol and is standard procedure at the USCP. So I should never have had to specifically direct that a plan be developed for January 6. It should have been automatic. Both Thomas and Pittman were aware of the long-established policies and practices regarding special event planning at the USCP even before my arrival there.

Less than four months earlier, on September 16, 2020, I had issued a standing directive to Thomas, Pittman, Gallagher, and Loyd to make sure that coordinated plans were developed for *all* events at the Capitol. This had followed a security incident that occurred only the day before, involving House Minority Leader Kevin McCarthy.

Regardless, as the chief, I fault myself for not ensuring that a comprehensive operations plan had been developed and placed on my desk for review. The buck stops with me.

As the attack spread across the campus, other aspects of departmental operations began to break down. Incident management and

---

54. US Capitol Police, Directive 2000.001, *Organizational and Management Structure of the USCP*, 5.
55. Peters, Portman, Klobuchar, and Blunt, *Examining the U.S. Capitol Attack*, 54.

communications quickly became overwhelmed and ineffective, and the lack of useful operational guidance to our CDU platoons left them ill-prepared and without critical equipment. During a battle like this, officers should not have to call repeatedly over the radio for assistance or direction.

The Capitol Division commander and the CDU incident commander had both become personally engaged in the fighting on the West Front, trying to hold the line and helping defend their officers. Sergeants, lieutenants, and captains took control of the scene and helped coordinate officers battling in places like the rotunda, the Crypt, and the third floor, outside the chambers. And although their efforts helped us gain control of some of these critical sites, they would not have been necessary within a well-run incident management system.

The breakdown in incident command and the repeated unanswered calls over the radio should have been detected by those in the Command Center, including me and my two assistant chiefs. Because numerous incidents were occurring all around the campus, the Command Center should have shifted to an area command structure (in which operational control is handed off to the individual incident leaders) to ensure that the multiple events were being properly managed. I have extensive experience in this area and found myself frustrated that I did not become aware of this issue and address it sooner. My two assistant chiefs, who were in charge of all department operations and were part of the USCP Critical Incident Management Team (CIMT), should have helped me manage the event, moving to an area command structure while I was dealing with bureaucratic minutiae and calling in resources.

This lack of command-level involvement, especially from the Command Center, cascaded into further operational failures in the field—one of the biggest being the failure to direct the evacuation of the members of Congress earlier during the attack. By 1:50 p.m., almost an hour into the attack, we knew that things were really bad. The Capitol was surrounded by thousands of rioters on all sides, and we were starting to see people climb onto the upper West Terrace. Thousands of violent rioters were battling with hundreds of police officers on the West Front, and thousands more were becoming agitated on the East Front. From within the Command Center, we had a clear picture on the video screens of the threat the Capitol was facing.

Pittman and Gallagher, who oversaw member protection, were sitting to my left in the Command Center. The video screens all around us were clearly showing the increasing threat moving closer and closer to the Capitol. By now the order should have been given to evacuate the leadership and the members of Congress. This would have given us much more time to start evacuating the members before the first rioters could force their way into the Capitol. But the order wasn't given.

Although it has been reported that Loyd had locked down the Capitol earlier, Pittman ordered a lockdown of the Capitol from the Command Center at 2:00 p.m. Eight minutes later, rioters had made it all the way up and onto the upper West Terrace, having fought their way past all our barriers and police lines. Although Pittman ordered a lockdown of the entire congressional campus at 2:08 p.m., evacuation of the chambers had not yet been ordered. At 2:11 p.m., we had windows smashed on the upper West Terrace by the Senate Chamber and on the East Front by the center stairs—opposite sides of the Capitol. At 2:12 p.m., rioters were entering the Capitol from the upper West Terrace. It was at this point that Vice President Pence was escorted from the Senate Chamber and leadership began to be evacuated. It was not until the rioters had entered the Capitol that Congress would start to be evacuated, and even then there was considerable delay.

At 2:13 p.m., the Senate was gaveled into recess, followed by the House at 2:17 p.m. Rioters were now inside the Capitol and making their way up to the third floor, where the chambers are located, prompting USCP chamber officers to barricade the doors. The Capitol was being breached on both the East and West Fronts, with hundreds of rioters flooding into the rotunda at 2:19. But the House and Senate still had not been evacuated. Now, with rioters making their way through the various parts of the Capitol, the evacuations had to be delayed further while safe routes were located.

By 2:28 p.m., the Senate had been evacuated, but the House Chamber was just beginning to be evacuated. The House Chamber and galleries would not be completely evacuated until 2:57 p.m., thirteen minutes after the fatal shooting of a rioter trying to climb through a window into the Speaker's Lobby just behind the House Chamber. This was way too close a call, and we were damned lucky to get all the members evacuated without any of them being injured or worse.

Although it appears that Loyd was working to coordinate the evacuations from within the Capitol, this was a call that should have been made much earlier by command officials in the Command Center, who had the most complete situational awareness of what was occurring around the Capitol at that moment. We were amazingly lucky that no members of Congress were caught or surrounded by the mob.

A serious breakdown also occurred in the command of the civil disturbance unit platoons, beginning well before we were breached on the West Front. The designated field force commander (FFC) is responsible for providing directions to the hard platoons, such as when to report to their staging locations and when to put on their protective gear. But it appears that the FFC failed to adhere to previous AAR recommendations. CDU platoons were not deployed to their assigned locations at the beginning of their tour and were not outfitted in their hard gear. Riot shields and bottles of water were not kept in close proximity to the CDU platoons, resulting in some of them being left on a locked bus and unavailable to the officers.

During the attack, there was a lack of operational guidance from the field force commander, who appeared to be quickly overwhelmed by the situation. The USCP response would have been far more effective if the FFC had made sure the CDU platoons were prepared when the rioters arrived, and if those platoons had been able to coordinate immediately with Inspector Glover from the MPD. But this did not occur. As a result, additional CDU resources that could have been brought to bear during the height of the battle, such as more effective versions of less lethal munitions, weren't considered.

———

Since January 6, federal investigations have led to the arrests of over 850 suspects, some of whom are current or former members of the military and law enforcement. My observations of the crowd, as well as reports from my officers, indicated that some groups of rioters appeared to be well coordinated and trained.

Following the attack, many in the press and on social media were making allegations impugning the actions and motives of my officers. According to National Public Radio, "USCP officers can be seen opening barricades allowing the mob to enter the Capitol complex without resistance."[56] I have even heard allegations of USCP officials "freezing" and not taking any supervisory or assistive actions involving the officers around them, or officials electing not to respond to the attack on the Capitol at all. Before leaving the USCP, I referred several cases over to our Office of Professional Responsibility (OPR) for investigation, and since my departure, the department has initiated additional investigations involving the actions of officers and officials.

Ultimately, some forty-one allegations of misconduct involving USCP officers were referred to the Office of Professional Responsibility as a result of January 6. The misconduct included everything from conduct unbecoming a police officer to criminal allegations involving obstruction of justice.

Of those cases, the USCP was able to identify officers' involvement in only twenty-seven. Some of the alleged misconduct referred to the OPR did not contain sufficient information to identify the officers involved. In twenty cases, the OPR found no evidence of officer wrongdoing. Of the remaining seven cases, six were sustained for administrative violations, and one was referred to the US Attorney's Office regarding criminal charges. According to the department, one case involving an official being accused of unsatisfactory performance and conduct unbecoming is also still under investigation.

In my eighteen months as chief, I worked hard to develop those

---

56. H. J. Mai, "Capitol Police Suspends 6 Officers, Investigates Dozens More after Capitol Riots," NPR, February 19, 2021, www.npr.org/sections/insurrection-at-the -capitol/2021/02/19/969441904/capitol-police-suspends-6-officers-investigates-dozens -more-after-capitol-riots.

around me. My goal was to implement the strategic plan I had just published and to move the agency forward into being one of the premier law enforcement agencies in the country. At the time, I felt confident in my team's ability to handle the responsibilities of their positions. I expected my team members to provide the necessary management and oversight of their appointed parts of the organization, to ensure that proper intelligence was being cultivated and distributed, and to develop and implement effective operational plans.

Perhaps I trusted people to a fault. I should have pushed the request for the National Guard more forcefully, and I should have been more aware of what was going on in the field and what support my officers needed. From the posting and preparation of the CDU platoons to the distribution of the riot helmets, very little seemed to go as planned on January 6. While internal issues within the USCP contributed to a lack of preparedness that day, no level of internal preparedness by the USCP alone would have enabled us to prevent the breaching of the Capitol. When the rioters finally broke into the Capitol Building itself, I had about a thousand MPD officers assisting us, as well as officers from several other law enforcement agencies. No law enforcement agency in the country is prepared to fend off an attack by thousands of violent rioters without substantial assistance. The biggest obstacle I faced on January 6 was the inaccurate and incomplete intelligence that prevented us from getting the assistance that could have prevented this attack.

January 6 will forever be a blemish on our nation's history. The Capitol was mercilessly attacked, and our democracy was put at risk. In the end, I was failed by the very intelligence apparatus I had been working to build into the best in its class. This was an intelligence failure that led to a series of ill-informed decisions and poor planning. Many lives were at stake that day on the Hill, and sadly, in the end, I couldn't rely on the military to help me retake and secure the Capitol. The DC National Guard—the "Capital Guardians"—was not allowed to carry out its mission to help my officers defend the seat of our nation's democracy. Instead, I was able to accomplish this mission with the critical support of over 1,700 officers from seventeen agencies. Hardworking police officers from federal, state, and local agencies came together to defend the Capitol and the Constitution. These were some of the same people who are out there responding selflessly to 911 calls regardless of who needs assistance—the same police officers who are vilified by politicians and the media day after day.

Because of the relationships I had forged with the leadership of so many of these agencies, they knew without question that if I was asking for help, I truly needed it. They were there for me, and I will be forever grateful for their support and heroic efforts. I know many in the DC National Guard, and I appreciate and respect the work they do. It is apparent that the efforts to delay the Guard's involvement in defending the Capitol came from above General William Walker. I know that Walker would have been there immediately if he had been authorized. Although the DoD Inspector General found no fault in the military's handling of this situation, perhaps it will consider my perspective and earnestly look for ways to prevent this from ever occurring again.

The efforts of almost every single Capitol Police officer that day were heroic, and they should feel unabashed pride that when faced with an attacking mob of thousands, they fought valiantly to protect the members of Congress, the vice president, and all the staff on the Hill. They did not fail in their mission. The security apparatus on the Hill must be changed, or future leaders of the USCP will face the same issues again. It is inevitable.

Oversight of the police department by individuals who answer only to the political majority on their side of Congress is a recipe for disaster, and it creates an environment where the politicization of the police department can go unchecked. This must be changed before the security on the Hill can truly get better.

Almost two years after the events of January 6, the department is not in a better place or on a readier footing. Few people in the department feel that there is a viable plan to move the agency into a better position. Hundreds of officers have left the department since January 6, and many feel it is only going to get worse.

On December 22, 2021, President Biden signed into law a bill that had passed by unanimous vote in both House and Senate, known as the Capitol Police Emergency Assistance Act. This new law allows the chief of the Capitol Police to directly request the assistance of the National Guard and other federal law enforcement agencies in the event of an emergency like what I faced on January 6, without first being compelled to seek approval from the Capitol Police Board. For me, this cumbersome process resulted in a painful seventy-minute delay at one of the most critical points in the battle. But, perhaps unsurprisingly, the CPB and congressional leadership made sure they still had their override system in place—they made the chief's authority *revocable*.[57]

The Senate joint committee identified this as a needed reform back in February 2021, and frankly, I'm surprised it took almost a year to get it on the books. But while this bill will allow the chief to immediately request federal assistance in an emergency, it will not effectively change any restrictions or prevent hurdles and delays like those I faced from the Department of Defense.

Congress would be wise to put a single individual in charge of security at the Capitol complex, as opposed to one for each side of the campus, as exists now. It must be someone who is not subject to any partisan influence and who looks at security from a purely apolitical standpoint.

Although empowering a chief with full authority in making security decisions seems like not just a good idea, but a crucial strategy, I doubt it will ever happen. The House and Senate both want to have their say on how security is handled. No wonder CNN referred to the chief of the USCP as having "one of the hardest policing jobs in America."

---

57. Capitol Police Emergency Assistance Act of 2021, Public Law 117-77, December 22, 2021, www.congress.gov/117/plaws/publ77/PLAW-117publ77.pdf.

CHAPTER 5:
FINAL THOUGHTS, AND SOME QUESTIONS

If you do not take an interest in the affairs of your government, then you are doomed to live under the rule of fools.

—Plato

In my career, I have had the honor of meeting and protecting every living US president and numerous other world leaders. I have been involved in the planning of almost half the National Special Security Events (NSSE) in DC history. In those twenty-five years with the MPD, I also witnessed the less glamorous aspects of policing in DC. As a street cop, I responded to more life-and-death situations than I can recall. I saw some of the most tragic scenes a police officer can encounter. I ran to the aid of fellow police officers, providing assistance to several, including MPD Master Patrol Officer Brian Gibson, who was assassinated sitting in his patrol car at a stoplight solely because of the uniform he wore. I have been to numerous homicide scenes, chased and apprehended violent murder suspects, entered buildings looking for armed drug dealers, conducted foot chases in dark alleys, pulled bodies out of homes, vehicles, and the Anacostia River, and comforted abused women, traumatized children, and grieving families. The on-the-job stress of being a city cop would have been unbearable to deal with had it not been for my family and my faith. God has blessed me and kept me safe on many occasions.

During my time with the USCP, especially as chief, I felt that we accomplished a tremendous amount of good. I truly loved and cared for the men and women on the force and wanted to see the department expand its training opportunities and operational experience. I implemented a regionalization program so that the USCP would have field offices across the country, similarly to the Secret Service. We developed and published a road map and strategic plan to take the agency forward over the next five years, fine-tuning its operational and intelligence capabilities.

Perhaps my greatest accomplishments, however, were the relationships I developed with members of the workforce, and the sense of pride I watched them develop during my time with the department. I believe that my officers felt they had a chief who knew what it meant to be a cop and who always had their interests in mind. I prided myself in regularly making the time and the opportunity to talk to officers on post, finding out what their concerns and issues were, and addressing these as quickly as possible. I was fair with discipline and willing to meet with officers whenever possible. An employee satisfaction survey that was conducted while I was chief demonstrated a strong positive trend and increase in morale, with high marks for me and my executive team, and a record-breaking 44 percent of the workforce completing the survey. In previous years, the department struggled to bring survey participation up to 30 percent.

Since leaving the department, besides spending quality time with my family, I have examined what happened on January 6, writing and offering support and mentoring to the many officers and officials from the USCP and MPD who still contact me.

I have concluded that the siege of the United States Capitol on January 6 was not a single-day event or the result of a poorly planned police operation. Hearings have been held and reports written, but in true DC partisan fashion, where everything is done to promote one's party and platform, the facts have been largely ignored or glossed over.

In each case, the police are caught in the middle as both Democrats and Republicans shamelessly politicize the event.

Insurrection is now a politically charged term. There were people in the crowd who had planned and coordinated an attack on the Capitol to disrupt the certification of the Electoral College results, and this, by definition, is an insurrection. These individuals came with a mission to breach the Capitol by any means necessary. It was a classic mob attack, manipulated into a frenzy by a core group of individuals, that succeeded in breaking through our police lines due to their sheer numbers. History has many examples of mob violence. It is a powerful force.

The USCP's job was to protect life and restore order. Officers used their own bodies to block the mob from reaching the members of Congress. Their willingness to place themselves between the mob and the lawmakers should not be downplayed. It is especially shameful when some of those same lawmakers take cheap shots at the heroic actions that may well have saved their lives that day, all just to score political points.

We were not a battle-ready department, but no police department truly is. We are civil authorities entrusted to keep the peace. Anger toward law enforcement's lack of lethal force was shocking on multiple levels. The same politicians who decry police brutality were livid that we did not fire at the crowd. What they fail to understand is how law enforcement works. They need to understand that police officers do not use lethal force lightly. The decision to unholster your weapon and point it at another human does not come easily. Most officers will never resort to lethal force in their entire careers. The few high-profile cases of police shootings are exceptions, not the norm.

My goal in writing this book is to provide information in the same way that I policed—based on the facts, in a fair and apolitical fashion. I have tried to outline all the issues I believe contributed to the attack on the US Capitol, to show how those issues affected our planning for January 6, and above all, to paint a true and accurate picture of what happened on that day.

The impact of January 6 only further solidifies my desire to help support my fellow police officers. I look forward to working with several outstanding foundations that work not only to help officers and agencies through traumatic experiences but also to provide mentoring and professional guidance in career development as they move through the ranks or consider a move out of law enforcement. I believe that it takes a special person to become a police officer and that the skills and experience that person possesses can also be immensely valuable in other aspects of society besides law enforcement.

———————

Now that January 6 is behind us, many questions remain. Why didn't a single one of the intelligence agencies accurately report the intelligence they possessed? Why didn't the Department of Defense share its concerns over violence, while simultaneously taking such extraordinary actions to prevent military support from assisting me during the attack? Why did the sergeants at arms, congressional leadership, and the military all seem to obsess about optics above everything else? Why, after I had taken steps trying to secure the Capitol in advance of and on January 6, was I removed so quickly? Why are the congressional inquiries so studiously not focusing on what really went wrong? And finally, what would the death toll have been if I had not pre-positioned MPD by the Capitol and been so quick to call in all the other law enforcement support? As tragic as the death toll already was on that day, I still wake up in a cold sweat thinking how much worse it could have been.

America needs to know the answers to these questions. What I faced as the chief of police on Capitol Hill, stuck in the middle of a terrible attack that played out in front of the whole world, is only one part of the puzzle. While on the surface this battle looked like an ugly mob of violent protesters pitted against police officers, January 6 was something much bigger and representative of greater issues in America.

Americans are feeling pessimistic about the economy, their national security, rapidly rising violent crime, and the possibility of World War III on the horizon. Our confidence in our elected members of Congress hovers in the single digits, and for the executive and judicial branches of government, it isn't much higher. For a society to thrive and prosper, it needs a sense of safety and security. The American public feels that it has neither right now. The antipolice rhetoric and riots of 2020 have caused irreparable damage to law enforcement. Although many of the "defund the police" politicians have now backpedaled on their demands due to a dramatic rise in crime and violence, their shrill cries condemning our entire justice system as systemically racist have greatly undermined policing in this country. Besides the uptick in crime and violence, the 2020 social-justice protests conditioned many citizens on both ends of the political spectrum to no longer respect the law.

We are failing to see the bigger picture and focus on what is creating the divisions in our country. We need to heal and bring this nation back together. We need to see politicians ending their childish behavior and beginning to address the real concerns that are paramount to Americans: safety and security, jobs and the economy, and our education system. Right now our cultural and political differences are like a bad playground dispute, but without any levelheaded teachers who can bring the two sides together to talk out their differences.

Too many members of Congress behave like celebrities and social media influencers and have forgotten that their role is to represent their constituents and not themselves. They need to realize that holding on to power at all costs is not the most important thing—that *serving the American people* is the most important thing. Things have to change, and soon, or we may lose our great democracy forever.

The terrible events of January 6 are etched in our consciousness and cannot be forgotten. Many who were there believed they wouldn't make it out of the Capitol alive that day. It was one of the worst days in American law enforcement history.

The foundation of our country is based on the rule of law, which maintains the civility of our society by establishing a clear set of laws that apply *equally to everyone*, and which has a fair and equal process to adjudicate these laws. The rule of law was so important to the framers of our Constitution that they instituted a set of inalienable rights within it, known as the Bill of Rights. For a society based on the rule of law to succeed, everyone must abide by the laws and must be held to the same standard. From presidents, members of Congress, military leaders, and law enforcement to the public, for a sense of civility to exist, everyone must be on board. The rule of law applies to all, or it applies to none.

Lady Justice is often depicted wearing a blindfold and holding a scale and a sword. The blindfold represents a critical aspect of our rule of law: that to be fair and impartial, justice must be blind to outside influences that could tip the scales. But when a society no longer feels that the rule of law is being applied equally to everyone, people lose faith in their government and political leaders, and the social fabric begins to unravel. Our leaders have allowed their personal biases to affect the application of the law, tearing the blindfold from the lady's eyes and striking a crippling blow to justice and the rule of law.

The civility of society erodes when the individual becomes more important than the institution, and the party's rule becomes more important than society itself. Law enforcement plays an essential role in our society, but to work, it must be seen as fair and impartial in applying the law. The presence of law enforcement can bring a sense of safety, security, and justice to often chaotic and lawless situations. But when officers' actions begin to be manipulated and no longer support the rule of law, people start to lose faith in this critical institution.

We began to see this occurring in Washington, DC, over the summer of 2020 when the city's leading law enforcement agency, the Metropolitan Police Department, came under external political pressure and was not allowed to respond to the violent protests occurring at the White House. During these violent protests, many federal law enforcement officers were seriously injured, and the president of the United States and his family were forced to seek safety in the White House bunker. The MPD, an agency formed by Congress to keep the peace and protect the president and other government officials, stood by on adjacent city streets and watched members of the United States Secret Service being beaten and bloodied. We are on dangerous ground when actions like this are allowed to occur. One need only visit the United States Holocaust Memorial Museum in DC to see the dark historical precedent for what occurs when a nation's police are used to enforce the political will of its leaders.

Neither is our military immune to political pressure. On January 6, leaders in the Pentagon disregarded their oath to defend the Constitution when they ignored my repeated pleas for assistance at the United States Capitol. They refused assistance to the women and men of the USCP and our partner law enforcement agencies who were putting their lives on the line to defend the constitutionally mandated certification of the Electoral College results. Fully outfitted National Guard members stood just blocks away, unable to get approval from their leaders to deploy. Our military leaders made a conscious decision *not to respond*, and to let law enforcement deal with the violent mob on its own. In closing their eyes and ears to our pleas, they abdicated their responsibility to society, their solemn oath to the Constitution, and their adherence to the rule of law and the Uniform Code of Military Justice.

What caused the Department of Defense to implement such crippling restrictions on the use of the military? How did the intelligence community miss what *60 Minutes* called "one of the most predictable attacks in American history"? It now appears that my attempts to protect the legislative branch of government were hijacked by an internal battle within the executive branch over the limits of executive power. Following the November election, many within the Pentagon, the intelligence community, and the president's cabinet had become increasingly concerned about the peaceful transition of power on January 20, 2021. On one side of the battle line, some of the president's closest confidants and appointees to key positions were pushing for the president to consider invoking the Insurrection Act and declaring martial law, or even using the military to stop the certification of the Electoral College results. In response to this concern, members of the president's cabinet, some of his most prominent military and intelligence leaders, began to work behind the back of the commander-in-chief to prevent him from implementing martial law. One of the most important parts of their strategy was to eliminate any possibility of military personnel being deployed anywhere near the Capitol. Their concern was that President

Trump would try to use the military presence on Capitol Hill to hold on to power. Their strategy would prove to have disastrous consequences for law enforcement on the Hill.

Before January 6, significant intelligence indicated threats against the Capitol and our elected officials during the joint session of Congress. Tips were coming into the FBI about expected violence at the Capitol, the intel community was tracking possible domestic terrorist suspects, and fusion centers around the country were sounding the alarm. Yet the heads of the major DC law enforcement agencies, including me, were kept in the dark. If the intelligence had clearly indicated the threat and the level of violence expected on January 6, and if we had been made aware of that intelligence, law enforcement would have been vastly better prepared for what was to come. Accurate and complete intelligence would have provided me with tangible information to seek an emergency declaration and to demand the support of the National Guard on Capitol Hill.

At one point, Miller and Milley's concerns about violence on January 6 actually led them to discuss locking down the city and revoking demonstration permits on Capitol Hill. Only the chief of Capitol Police, not the DoD, can revoke permits on Capitol grounds, yet neither man reached out to me to discuss these concerns. Was this because they knew that if they informed me, I would immediately notify the two sergeants at arms and demand military support to protect my officers and perimeter on January 6? Milley has stated he feared that Trump was seeking a "Reichstag moment" in which he could invoke the Insurrection Act. But instead of notifying the chief on the Hill regarding the threats of violence, SECDEF Miller and SECARMY McCarthy implemented unprecedented restrictions on military assistance to law enforcement.

Was this a case of intelligence being missed? Or was it a case of intelligence leaders realizing how this information could be used and thus choosing to underreport it? Did the FBI and DHS take overt actions *not* to fully assess the threat on the Capitol during the certification of the Electoral College votes, over concerns that President Trump could use the intelligence to implement martial law? What about the president's daily brief? It, too, seems to have been conspicuously silent regarding any sort of alarm about January 6. Was the intelligence purposely watered down so the intel reports would not convey that violence was imminent, and thus not give the president the ammunition he needed to assert the Insurrection Act and deploy the military in the city and around the Capitol?

Some of the key people expressing their concerns for the president's use of the military to stay in power had once been leaders in the intelligence community. Acting Secretary of Defense Christopher Miller had been in charge of the National Counterterrorism Center just months earlier. Mike Pompeo, then secretary of state, had been the previous director of the CIA. He is the one who believed that "the crazies have taken over" Trump's inner circle, and CIA Director Gina Haspel feared a "right-wing coup."[1]

When I spoke to Paul Irving on January 3 and asked for perimeter reinforcement from the National Guard, he responded quickly with concern for the "optics" of having the military on the Hill, adding that "the intelligence doesn't support it." His quick response gave me the distinct impression that this topic was front and center in his mind and, possibly, the subject of recent discussions with congressional leadership or staffers. *Optics* was a term repeatedly used by the military, specifically regarding the deployment of National Guard troops to the Hill on January 6. I find no coincidence in the fact that Irving used this same term in his initial response to me. It was no secret that General Milley had regular conversations with lawmakers and congressional leadership—specifically, Paul Irving's boss, Nancy Pelosi. I can only suspect that congressional leaders had already been contacted by Milley, Miller, or Pentagon leadership about their concerns over deploying National Guard troops near the Capitol.

Ultimately, the Pentagon delayed the deployment of military troops

---

1. Ryan Goodman and Justin Hendrix, "Crisis of Command: The Pentagon, the President, and January 6," Just Security, December 21, 2021, www.justsecurity.org/79623/crisis-of-command-the-pentagon-the-president-and-january-6/.

to the Capitol until all the fighting was over, police had already secured and cleared the building, and Congress was getting ready to go back into session. The military leaders had succeeded in keeping the troops out of the crisis. When the Guard finally arrived, the soldiers lined up in their hard CDU gear with riot shields and took a well-orchestrated photo forming a police line with the United States Capitol in the background. These were the very optics that Lieutenant General Piatt had wanted so badly to avoid, which to me just proves that the optics were never their real concern all along. Yet, a little over a year and a half after January 6, General Milley and many of the same Pentagon leaders allowed US marines to be used as props flanking President Biden during his controversial "fascism" speech in Philadelphia. But this time there was no public apology or YouTube video from Milley over the incident, as there was in 2020. Where were their concerns for optics, or for the perception of the military involving itself in domestic politics for this event? Again, we are at a dangerous point when the military is viewed as an appendage of a political party.

In Miller's attempt to prevent one constitutional crisis, he almost created a much larger one. If I had not immediately called in law enforcement support and instead just waited those seventy minutes for the sergeants at arms to approve the request for federal resources, the violent mob would have breached the Capitol much sooner, trapping the members of Congress, the vice president, and congressional leadership (including the next three successors to the presidency) inside the chambers. This could have resulted in significant bloodshed and loss of life for both protesters and politicians. It also would have prevented the certification of the Electoral College results and plunged the United States into a far more chaotic constitutional nightmare.

Instead, thanks to law enforcement, not a single member of Congress was injured, and all of them were able to safely reconvene only hours later to certify the Electoral College votes. The nation should be forever grateful for the quick and competent response from the fine women and men of these law enforcement agencies. Every day, I am thankful for the relationships I had formed with these various agencies throughout the DC area. While the National Guard would not move without the assurance of an emergency declaration, I am thankful that my brothers and sisters in blue came to my immediate assistance even though my request for help may have been in violation of federal regulation. But as the saying goes, *I'd rather be tried by twelve than carried by six.*

In the center of Washington, not far from the Capitol and MPD headquarters, stands the National Law Enforcement Officers Memorial. The memorial was established to honor all the law enforcement officers who have died in the line of duty in the United States. As a young officer, I would spend a lot of time walking between the US Attorney's Office and the DC Superior Court and would often pause to look at the names and read the inscriptions on the memorial. My children grew up visiting the memorial and attending the annual candlelight vigils. I have always felt it is important for future generations to understand the sacrifices that officers and their families make every day. At the end of one of the walls is an inscription I have often read and reflected on. The quote, revered by police officers across the country, comes from the wife of Sergeant Christopher Eney of the United States Capitol Police.

> *It is not how these officers died that made them heroes, it is how they lived.*
>
> —Vivian Eney Cross, survivor

I could not have imagined when I first read these words that just a few decades later I would have the honor of leading this fine agency and representing the legacy of police officers like Christopher Eney and many others.

I feel I still have much to offer this profession and my fellow officers. Beyond continuing to support law enforcement through mentoring and working with various foundations, I also look forward to returning to teaching in some of the local universities and continuing to seek out the lessons to be learned from this event. But deep down, I will forever miss putting on the uniform and pinning on the badge. I will continue to think of the officers who are out there on post, patrolling the neighborhoods and roadways at night, on weekends and holidays, working to keep our communities safe, and upholding the rule of law. I will always be grateful to those who have chosen this profession and to their friends and families who support them.

The events of January 6 have been turned into a political weapon, with each side either overplaying or underplaying the significance of the day. No, January 6 was not on the scale of Pearl Harbor or 9/11 (although it certainly could have been much worse if more lethal force had been applied or if the rioters had gotten their hands on members of Congress). But neither was it an ordinary day at the Capitol, with tourists just strolling through and taking pictures. January 6 was a brutal attack of American against American, resulting in death, destruction, and serious trauma not only to my officers but to all those responding police officers and civilians working on the Hill that day. We may not agree on who is to blame or even what to call it, but there are lessons to be learned from January 6, and we will learn those lessons only if we leave our politics aside.

On July 10, 2021, the last row of security fencing came down, returning the Capitol campus to its pre–January 6 security posture. The public was once again allowed access to the East Plaza and the West Front. Within minutes of the East Plaza being opened, the first protester arrived. It was a sight that the officers had not seen in over six months. The officers stood their posts, defending democracy and the individual's constitutional right to free speech. The protester paced back and forth near the Senate steps. A lone individual, carrying a flag that read "Fuck Biden" and wearing a T-shirt that read "Fuck the Police." It appears that things are returning to normal on Capitol Hill.

CHAPTER 6:
POSTSCRIPT. THE JANUARY 6 HEARINGS

On July 27, 2021, the highly publicized and politically charged House of Representatives Select Committee to Investigate the January 6th Attack on the United States Capitol conducted a preliminary public hearing called "The Law Enforcement Experience on January 6th." It included the testimony of USCP officer Harry Dunn and Sergeant Aquilino Gonell, and MPD officers Daniel Hodges and Michael Fanone. This preliminary hearing was powerfully emotional, with the four officers recounting their personal stories from that day. As of this writing, the committee has held eight more public hearings, all televised and two of them during prime time.

While I often relive the events of January 6 from my perspective, listening to the testimony of others during these hearings was difficult for me. I had watched all of them being viciously attacked that day. But to hear their recollections in their own words only underscored the impossible situation they and their fellow officers had faced.

I listened to the testimonies and watched the images being replayed, and it made me wish all over again that I could have done much more to help them. And I am far from the only one who feels this way. I've spoken with many other USCP and MPD officers who share these feelings. Some officers have told me these hearings opened up old wounds. One officer told me outright this was a nightmare he wished would just end.

But it doesn't. The headlines continue, with new information coming out regularly. I keep getting calls from officers wanting to talk and from reporters I'm not ready to talk to. Not right now. January 6 is still a very difficult topic for me, as I am sure it is for every officer who had to do battle that day. It doesn't seem to get any easier. The emotional impact on families, loved ones, and civilian staff must not be understated.

————

On April 20, 2022, I was interviewed by the January 6 Committee. They asked me for a three-hour time commitment, which I accepted at once, nor did I object when the interview went twice as long as promised. I was willing to assist in their investigation because I want this tragedy to never happen again. But as the panel went around the room asking their questions, it became quickly and painfully obvious they were looking only for answers that supported a specific narrative. *Disappointing, but not unexpected.* Answers to questions that had long been established as true, and corroborated by many others, were now being reexamined and skewed.

During the interview, one of the investigators asked me two very peculiar questions regarding my requests for the National Guard. The investigator stated that when the committee had interviewed Irving, he informed them that on January 3, I had approached him in person with an "offer" for assistance from the National Guard, and that "the three of us [Irving, Stenger, and Sund] collectively determined that based upon the intelligence that the National Guard would not be necessary." The investigator then asked me, "How would you respond to that?"

I answered that this statement was incorrect. The conversation Irving referenced regarding an "offer" never occurred. Why would Irving direct me to ask Stenger about the request if it were an *offer*? Why would Stenger suggest I call General Walker that evening if we had already collectively decided only that morning not to pursue it?

The committee also said Irving claimed that when I first called him at 12:58 p.m. on January 6 to urgently request the Guard, he immediately gave me "full authorization." The investigator then asked me what I thought of that.

I replied, "That is incorrect. One hundred percent incorrect. My repeated calls to Irving were made in the company of at least one of my two assistant chiefs, but also my general counsel, Tad DiBiase. There is a reason why I called Irving at 12:58 p.m. and followed up repeatedly." My voice was rising in volume as I relived the frustrating events of that day, and now I hear that Irving is telling the committee he had immediately granted me approval! I continued answering the question: "Finally at 2:09 p.m., after I talked to him, I hung up the phone and I yelled across the Command Center (to the watch commander), 'Mark the time as 2:10!' I finally got approval from the Capitol Police Board for the use of the National Guard. That is categorically false what he is telling you!" Moreover, General Walker's testimony at the Senate hearing on March 3, 2021, supported my account of the events on January 3 and January 6.

There appeared to be a distinct bias on the J6 Committee to disregard my position in favor of Irving's and the CPB's. Numerous times, they took the position that since Irving did not specifically say the words, "No, you may not have the National Guard," it did not constitute a denial of my request. They seemed unable or unwilling to understand, no matter how many times I tried to explain it, that according to federal law passed by Congress, the CPB must approve an emergency declaration to authorize the National Guard. *Period.* Anything short of an emergency declaration is the same as an emphatic "NO!" This frustrating, ludicrous back-and-forth on the lack of the word *no* went on for several minutes, several times throughout my six-hour interview.

The interview then shifted to the intelligence related to January 6. The committee read summaries of some of the very concerning intelligence that IICD had in advance of January 6. This was intelligence that clearly could have played a significant role in better preparing the USCP. However, even though, on December 23, I had forwarded Pittman and Gallagher the email that MPD had sent me about the website wild-protest.com for their awareness and for inclusion in future intelligence products, none of it was included in their intelligence assessments or shared with the department leadership and operational planners.

It was evident that the J6 Committee was focused on placing the intelligence failure squarely on my shoulders since, according to them, I had "personally selected" Donohue and Farnam for the positions as the director and assistant director of IICD. I explained several times that I was originally looking only for a director, that Donohue was selected by a review panel made up of Pittman, Gallagher, and an outside assessor from the USSS, and that Farnam was hired at the recommendation and insistence of Pittman and Gallagher. But the committee didn't want to hear it. They kept returning to the fiction that since I was the chief and hence the final hiring authority, I had personally selected those who were at the center of the intelligence failure and that therefore, I alone bore that responsibility.

It was clear that the J6 Committee did not want any of the responsibility for the intelligence failure to fall outside the USCP leadership, and especially not anywhere near the CPB, my oversight, or any members of Congress. What the J6 Committee failed to understand was that both the CPB and congressional oversight played a role in staffing these positions. On several occasions, I had to brief both the CPB and my oversight, especially the Committee on House Administration (CHA), who wanted to be kept apprised on every step of the process for filling the IICD director's position. They wanted to be briefed and to have input on all aspects of the selection process, including the posting of the vacancy announcement, the makeup of the selection panel, and updates on the process at our regular meetings. One staffer on CHA even wanted a link to the final vacancy announcement so that he could possibly send it to prospective applicants. Both the CPB and oversight wanted to be briefed on who the panel had selected, *before* any notification was made to the applicant.

I cannot say that I am surprised by the committee's position on intelligence. During their frantic call with military leaders in the middle of the attack, both Pelosi and Schumer reportedly discussed the obvious intelligence failures that had occurred. Yet, two years later, their intelligence apparatus on the Hill remains intact, indicating that leadership either views the IICD as capable and successful, or is providing some sort of cover for it. The J6 Committee's position continues to shield those in charge of intelligence while allowing congressional leadership to distance itself from the issue.

———————

On July 19 and 20, 2022, I began to receive an unusual number of calls from the media. I had been watching the news for the past couple of days and was aware that the J6 Committee was eagerly waiting for the Secret Service to turn over all the text messages associated with January 6. I had also seen reports indicating that the USSS might have a "technical issue" that could prevent it from complying with the committee's request. As the rhetoric between the Secret Service and the committee heated up about the deleted or otherwise unavailable texts, I knew this was going to create an uncomfortable situation for USSS leadership and, inevitably, raise doubts in the minds of the American people.

But why was *I* now getting calls about this issue? What I didn't know was that the Secret Service had been able to comply only partially with the committee's request. Following a few days of searching, while the committee and the American public eagerly waited, the USSS finally turned over a single string of text messages associated with January 6. This string would be the texts between the former chief of the USSS Uniformed Division, Thomas Sullivan, and me, coordinating my urgent requests for critical resources only minutes after my officers were attacked on the West Front of the Capitol. This was a major surprise for me.

According to the Secret Service, the loss of all other text messages associated with January 6 occurred due to a "network data migration" issue. If this is true, then the only reason my texts with Sullivan survived the data migration may be because when Sullivan left the USSS in January 2022 and handed his phone over, it may have ended up in an IT office and so was not subject to the data migration. Either way, I'm still grateful for the assistance Sullivan offered me, and I'm glad my correspondence with him was preserved—especially since the acting head of DHS, Chad Wolf, has stated that I never asked DHS for assistance until several hours after the attack began.

In an ironic twist, it now appears that the text messages of both Chad Wolf and his acting deputy secretary, Ken Cuccinelli, from the days immediately before January 6 are also mysteriously missing. Perhaps these messages could have shed some light on the mishandling of intelligence by the DHS in the days leading up to January 6. Back at the Capitol, Pelosi's and Irving's texts and emails are reportedly sealed and off-limits to investigations. Stand by for another technical issue if they are ever unsealed.

———————

As I hope I have made clear in this book, January 6 was a genuinely horrible and tragic day for every law enforcement officer who was there fighting to retake the Capitol and protect the members of Congress, the vice president, and all the congressional community who were on the Hill that day. There were many close calls between our protectees and the advancing mob—instances in which only a few feet or a few seconds separated the two. When I finally arrived at the location where the vice president had been secured that evening, I could see the concern on the faces of the Secret Service agents and the members of the USSS Counter Assault Team gathered to protect him. It was a look I had not seen before.

Together with my USCP and SWAT team officers, the USSS agents, the vice president, his brother, and his family—none of us had ever imagined what we were facing that day was even possible. As I've said, a lot of the officers fighting outside told me later they thought they were going to die. These were not rookies, but seasoned veteran officers whom I have known for years and trust without question. I do not doubt that many standing with the vice president that evening felt the same way, so I am not surprised now to hear that some of those officers and agents were messaging their families with final goodbyes. And I suspect there were many similar messages from others in the field that day.

I can only imagine the impact that receiving such a message had on their families, who, like mine, were glued to the television, watching the mayhem at the Capitol play out before their eyes.

The more I look at the events of January 6, the more I see a convoluted puzzle. Although I hope this book has revealed much of the puzzle, there is still too much that we don't know. It feels as though something critical has yet to be discovered, perhaps because it has been purposely hidden.

If I ever have the chance to help shed more light on this puzzle, you can be sure I will do everything I can to uncover the full truth. I will do this for the sake of every police officer who put his or her life on the line on January 6, 2021. This I can promise you.

EPILOGUE

The four years I spent with the United States Capitol Police were some of the most rewarding of my nearly thirty-year law enforcement career. To be able to walk the majestic halls of Congress each day, surrounded by paintings, murals, statues, and relics from our nation's history, was at once awe-inspiring and humbling. Looking up at the Capitol Dome, the seat of democracy and one of the most iconic and recognizable buildings in the world, I felt proud to be leading the women and men protecting it. I will always hold in the highest regard the officers who are on post around the clock in all sorts of weather and the vast cadre of civilian team members who work with them behind the scenes. The officers and employees of the USCP work tirelessly to protect the members, staff, and visitors at the United States Capitol. I could not have been prouder to be part of this team.

As chief of the United States Capitol Police, I understood my responsibilities. I had to be a leader who would inspire officers to do and be their best, mentor them, and provide them with a sense of pride and security. I had to be someone who would listen to them and make them feel as if they belonged to something greater than all of us. It was my job to fight for them, to seek equipment and training opportunities, to protect them and serve them the best I could. Being a good chief isn't just about strong leadership principles. It's about doing the right thing—even small things for your officers—as often as possible and always when needed. It's about building up your officers, treating everyone with dignity and respect, and in turn earning theirs.

The physical and mental assaults my officers and our partner law enforcement agencies endured on January 6, 2021, were traumatizing and heartbreaking. What I saw that day will forever be seared into my memory. I watched officers defend multiple entrances to the Capitol for hours while being beaten, crushed, stomped, and sprayed with chemicals.

Any reports suggesting it was a quick and easy breach are categorically false and indicate a mind that isn't terribly concerned with getting at the truth. And any suggestion that the USCP treated groups differently based on demographics is equally false as well as personally and professionally offensive to me.

I could not be prouder of the efforts of the USCP and the partner agencies who came to our aid. I will forever be grateful for the rapid response to my urgent calls for assistance. When many said it would be impossible to clear the Capitol in under twenty-four hours after such a breach, we proved them all wrong. Even when outnumbered 58 to 1, with the support of our partner police agencies, the USCP was able to get Congress back in session to certify the Electoral College results within hours of the attack and without injury to a single member of Congress.

The USCP did not fail in its mission. It succeeded in protecting the members of Congress and the democratic process. The police—the same public servants that the media and nation had turned their backs on for much of 2020—were the ones who fought and bled and restored the order that allowed Congress to safely return to work and certify the election for Joe Biden.

I am devastated by what my officers faced that day. No police department should be subjected to that level of violence and hatred. And no police department should be vilified, criticized, and condemned before the facts are known. The Capitol Police, after what they went through, should have had the immediate and overwhelming support of the members of Congress, the media, and the public. Instead, we were accused of racism, double standards, complicity, and lying about our preparations. After a summer of intense antipolice rhetoric, it was an easy knee-jerk reaction to blame the police for an unprecedented mob attack.

On January 6, USCP officers were immediately painted as racist Trump sympathizers by the media, some congressional members, and a host of Monday-morning quarterbacks on social media. Antipolice pundits and politicians were quick to join in. Even the president-elect weighed in, saying how the mob would have been treated "very, very differently" had they been black.[1] Not only was that factually wrong, but it was also insulting and insensitive to police officers across the country. Officers do not go into law enforcement to terrorize any group of people, deny any group their rights, or give preferential treatment to a certain segment of society.

During the summer of 2020, cities were defunding the police, defending rioters and looters, and condemning the police for enforcing the law. This sent a clear and chilling message to law enforcement and their families that society had come to despise the police so much that they would rather live in a lawless community than tolerate the "bigots in blue" on their streets. There hasn't been a profession so maligned, and its members so publicly hated, since GIs were coming home from Vietnam.

The condemnation of the USCP on January 6 was bipartisan. "Anyone in charge of defending the Capitol failed," Senator Lindsey Graham said. "The first thing that has to happen is to hold those accountable for failing to defend the nation's Capitol while the Congress was in session."[2] Officers were maligned by the *New York Times*, which claimed they "seemed to offer little resistance and arrested only 14 people."[3] And NBC News stated that "the relatively lenient handling of the

---

1. Adam Edelman, "Biden Slams Capitol Rioters as 'Domestic Terrorists': 'Don't Dare Call Them Protesters,'" NBC News, updated January 7, 2021, www.nbcnews.com /politics/white-house/biden-slams-capitol-rioters-domestic-terrorists-don-t-dare-call -n1253335.

2. Carney, "McConnell Ousts Senate Sergeant-at-Arms."

3. Shaila Dewan, Neil MacFarquhar, Zolan Kanno-Youngs, and Ali Watkins, "Police Failures Spur Resignations and Complaints of Double Standard," *New York Times*, January 7, 2021, www.nytimes.com/2021/01/07/us/Capitol-cops-police.html.

invaders was deeply troubling."[4] The stinging criticism and misreporting of facts have had a terrible effect on the department.

Almost two years after the Capitol attack, the police force charged with protecting Congress still finds itself at a painful juncture in its nearly two-century history. The force is emotionally and physically traumatized. It is overworked, having to pull extra shifts to adjust to the shrinking numbers of officers and increasing security demands. Retirements and resignations from the department are at an all-time high, while employee morale is at an all-time low. Officers and officials are leaving the department for other agencies, and some are so fed up they are leaving without any job prospects at all. Many just want to leave the toxic environment of the Hill, while others want to get out of law enforcement altogether. Officers have had to work six days a week for most of 2021 and 2022, with many still having to pull twelve-hour shifts to cover all the additional security requirements.

Officers are being told, "If you don't like it here, leave. There will be others to fill your spot." That doesn't help officers heal, nor does it give them the impression that anyone has their back. Moreover, the workforce feels that no one is charting a clear path forward for the department after January 6.

Even as it became clear that intelligence was the biggest failure on January 6, the chiefs and directors overseeing intelligence have not been held accountable. In fact, they either were promoted or have remained in charge of these critical units. The rank and file were justifiably very upset about this. In February 2021, the union held a vote of no confidence for Pittman, Gallagher, and other members of the USCP command staff. The vote resulted in more than 80 percent of the participating officers expressing no confidence in the two officials in charge of intelligence. Yet the vote had no impact, and almost two years later, the two remain in the same positions.

4. Jon Schuppe, "Failed Response to Capitol Riot Shows Deep Divide over Police Use of Force," NBC News, January 9, 2021, www.nbcnews.com/news/us-news/failed -response-capitol-riot-shows-deep-divide-over-police-use-n1253508.

Following my resignation, Assistant Chief Thomas was forced to retire under Acting Chief Pittman in June 2021.

Inspector Kim Schneider, who was in charge of the Dignitary Protection Division on January 6 and in consideration for promotion to deputy chief, resigned from the department in an apparent objection to how the intelligence was handled and to the failure to hold the Protective Services Bureau leadership accountable.

Deputy Chief Jeffrey Pickett, who was instrumental in helping me deploy the law enforcement resources on January 6, retired early, citing the mishandling of intelligence, the department's "lack of accountability" for the officials overseeing intelligence, and frustration over "the wrong people being fired."

Deputy Chief Eric Waldow retired in December 2021 and left to work for a suburban county police department.

These are people with years of experience, training, and skills that the department desperately needs. Experience like this will take years, if not decades, to replace. The departure of both senior and rank-and-file members of the department continues to have a negative impact on those who remain.

On the Hill, the Capitol grounds are once again open to the public and to protests. Immediately after January 6, walk-through metal detectors were installed for members of Congress accessing the House Chamber, and this continues to be a significant point of contention and division along party lines. The prosecutions and arrests stemming from January 6 have continued, with more than 850 people arrested at the last count.

The USCP has become the target of conspiracy theorists following Arizona Republican Representative Paul Gosar's June 15, 2021, statement that Capitol Police were "lying in wait" to kill a Trump supporter.[5] *Lying in wait* is a specific legal term denoting an aggravating

5. Aaron Blake, "The Slow-Building Conservative Effort to Turn Ashli Babbitt into a Martyr," *Washington Post*, June 18, 2021, www.washingtonpost.com/politics/2021/06/18/slow-building-conservative-effort-turn-ashli-babbitt-into-martyr/.

circumstance in murder cases in which a murderer waits for the victim and then kills in an ambush-style attack. This type of language from a member of Congress, for whom these very officers would lay down their lives, is irresponsible and only further drives the wedge of division in the country, not to mention further sinking officers' morale. I lost officers as a result of January 6, and several sustained severe enough injuries that they have yet to return to full duty as police officers.

Acting Chief Pittman was passed over for the position, and on July 22, 2021, retired Montgomery County Police Chief Thomas Manger was hired as the new chief of the United States Capitol Police. Upon hearing of his selection, I sent him a congratulatory text message. I have known Manger for almost two decades. We met and worked side by side on a multijurisdictional police line during one of the most violent IMF/World Bank protests in DC in 2000. At the time, I was in charge of the area for the MPD, and Manger was the official in charge of the Fairfax County Police officers supporting us. It was an intense scene on the front lines, where we had to deploy gas and CDU platoons to protect the motorcades carrying delegates to the meetings. I think many of us on the line during that event bonded and earned each other's respect. I wish him the very best at the USCP.

I truly miss the USCP workforce, sworn and civilian. I think about them every day and talk to many of them regularly. I would consider it an honor to put on the uniform once again and represent the fine women and men of the USCP, but I don't think that's in the cards. Perhaps there is a more important need for me elsewhere, helping with this healing process on a larger level.

We shall see.

––––––––––

On June 27, 2022, Michael Stenger died after a prolonged illness. That afternoon, I received a call from a close family friend who told me I was on a short list of people Mike wanted to be notified. I was saddened by his passing, and my wife began to cry. She felt he was another casualty of January 6. The funeral services were to be held in his hometown in New Jersey. Out of respect for his half century of service to our country and for the position he held at the Capitol, I decided to attend the service. While quite a few former employees of the Senate sergeant at arms office attended, including former SSAA Frank Larkin, no current representatives from the SSAA or USCP came to show their respect for Mike or his family. His former counterpart in the House, Paul Irving, did not attend either. But the United States Marine Corps did send two honor-guard members and a bugler to play taps at his graveside. A fitting tribute for his service in the military and to his country.

Semper fidelis.

ACKNOWLEDGMENTS

Since January 6, 2021, I have continued to examine the events and the convoluted misinformation, disinformation, and missteps that contributed to this tragic event. I have gone through some very dark and trying times reliving that day, second-guessing my actions. The outreach from USCP members—the texts, calls, emails, letters, and postcards—has meant so much to me. Their outpouring of support has brought me great comfort. While it's impossible for me to mention them all by name, it is critical for all of them to know just how important these regular interactions and their continued support have been to me. I am purposely not naming many currently employed or recently separated from the Hill, for fear of retaliation against them. You know who you are. Thank you!

My heartfelt appreciation goes out to all the fine women and men of the USCP who fought so hard to defend our Capitol on January 6. They and all the first responders who gave me immediate assistance when we needed it most—the Metropolitan Police Department, USSS, ATF, FBI, Virginia State Police, Fairfax County Police Department, Arlington Police Department, and others—are the ones who saved Congress that day. They are true heroes.

Thanks to my friends and former colleagues from other agencies for their continued friendship and support: Murray, Sullivan, Dyson,

Miller, Sloan, and Bonus with the USSS; Colonel Gary Settle with the Virginia State Police; Contee, Carroll, Glover, Burke, Gentile, and my DSO crew with the MPD; Donnelly with DC Fire; Adamchik with the USPP; and Brito with the Rockville Police Department, to name just a few. I would also like to thank J. J., Andy, Mary, Neysha, and Wen-Ling for the regular check-ins and support.

Thank you to my family in Virginia and my extended family, from California to Hawaii, who continue to be there for me and who have motivated me to push beyond January 6. To B&B and Irene, thanks for all your guidance and support over the years. I am blessed to have in-laws who have treated me as a son and taught me the importance of family, "all pulling the same wagon together." To my sister-in-law Lana, who once proudly served with the San Francisco Police Department, thank you for always checking on Maria and me and for always encouraging us to keep pushing forward.

To my children—a father could not ask for kinder and more caring kids. I apologize for all the birthdays and family events I have been called away from by my job. I know you all understood and considered it part of the mission of a police family. Thank you for all your help getting through the difficult times and your regular applications of humor to cheer me up and keep me positive.

My brilliant and beautiful wife, Maria, has my never-ending love and appreciation. My polyglot pianist whose music and green thumb grace passersby in the neighborhood—she has been my rock, sacrificing much for my career and for our children. This book is the result of hundreds of early mornings and late nights researching, writing, and editing. Days that often ended with me falling asleep in bed with my laptop, only to wake up seeing my wife take over and polish the work into the early morning hours. You will always have my love, admiration, and coffee in bed.

To all my friends who have been there for my family and me, your immediate and continued support means more than I can express. Vera and Marc, Ingrid and Troy, Tammy and James, Dannielle and Doug, Cassandra and Joe, Wendy and James, Katie and Ryan, Tala and Kevin,

Alicia and Kent, Anya, Nat and Andrew, Serge, Katy and family, and many others—thank you for the encouragement, kind notes, and beautifully timed deliveries of food and companionship. Thank you all for helping us through a very rocky time.

Special thanks to Brad and Carol, my two law enforcement mentors and the reason I pursued a career in policing. Thank you for your guidance and for instilling in me the "prime directive" to always do right no matter how difficult. I only hope that people considering a career in law enforcement today have similar role models to help them survive in such a crazy environment.

I have been very fortunate to be part of a growing group of first responders who are associated with the Naval Postgraduate School's Center for Homeland Defense and Security. This is an outstanding program greatly enhancing the capabilities of the first-responder community. The continued support and assistance I have received from many of the professors, staff, and classmates have been priceless to me. I am especially appreciative of all the help I got from Christopher Bellavita throughout this process. While many others at CHDS played important roles, I specifically want to thank Dr. Kathleen Kiernan, Heather Hollingsworth Issvoran, and Greta Marlatt for all your assistance.

I sincerely appreciate everything the fine men and women of the US military do and the sacrifices their families make for this country. I appreciate the willingness of Major General William Walker and Colonel Earl Matthews to continue speaking the truth of this day. I know that every soldier, if given the approval, would have responded immediately to the Capitol and would have done everything they could to help me that day. I will continue to hold all our soldiers in the highest regard. However, I do not share that same opinion for the military leaders in the Pentagon, who either failed to realize or ignored the gravity of the situation and placed their concerns over the lives of my officers, the members of Congress, and the vice president and his family.

I also want to thank all the fine people at Blackstone Publishing for their commitment and dedication to this project. I also owe a debt of gratitude to Steve Hamilton and Michael Carr, who helped me edit and complete this project. Thank you for your patience and diligence!

A very special acknowledgment goes to Bryan Wittman. From the very first day I met him in his office at Disney, he has been a true friend. Bryan was one of a few who immediately reached out to check on me on January 6, and he has been an advisor and a guiding force through the ups and downs of this life-changing ordeal.

Finally, any author will tell you that a major key to their success is having a great literary agent. I have been fortunate to have the best in the business: Shane Salerno, who, besides being an agent, is also an incredibly talented author, screenwriter, director, and producer. I will be forever grateful for the support of both Shane and Ryan Coleman at the Story Factory. Ryan read and provided valuable assistance on the manuscript and other important matters throughout the writing process. They promised and delivered in having my back throughout this entire process. Thank you.

POLICE OFFICER'S PRAYER

Lord, I ask for COURAGE
Courage to face and conquer my own fears.
Courage to take me where others will not go.

I ask for STRENGTH
Strength of body to protect others
And strength of spirit to lead others.

I ask for DEDICATION
Dedication to my job, to do it well.
Dedication to my community to keep it safe.

Give me, Lord, CONCERN for others who trust me
And COMPASSION for those who need me.

And please, Lord, through it all
BE AT MY SIDE.

—Author Unknown

ABOUT THE AUTHOR

Steven Sund began his thirty-year career in law enforcement as a police officer with the Metropolitan Police Department, working in some of the most crime-ridden areas of the District of Columbia at a time when it was experiencing a record number of homicides and was plagued by the crack cocaine epidemic. He quickly rose through the ranks at the MPD, reaching the rank of deputy chief and commanding the elite Special Operations Division for five years.

Sund traveled worldwide with the United States Secret Service, studying mass demonstrations and security planning. He also taught major event management with the USSS and has been involved in twenty-nine of the major events designated by the Department of Homeland Security as National Special Security Events, including the past six presidential inaugurations. He wrote many of the special-events manuals for the District and helped shape the Department of Homeland Security's National Response Framework. He was also the on-scene incident commander at the 2009 Holocaust Museum shooting, the 2012 shooting at the Family Research Council, and the 2013 Navy Yard active-shooter incident.

In January 2017, Sund was appointed the assistant chief in charge of operations for the United States Capitol Police, just five months before a lone gunman opened fire on a baseball field filled with members of Congress practicing in Alexandria, Virginia. On January 6, 2021, Steven Sund was the chief of the United States Capitol Police when a mob of thousands of violent protesters stormed and breached the United States Capitol.

APPENDIX: LIST OF INITIALISMS

AAR	after-action report
AHOD	all hands on deck
AOC	Architect of the Capitol (on January 6, J. Brett Blanton)
APR	air-purifying respirator
BLUF	bottom line up front
CDU	civil disturbance unit
CERT	Containment and Emergency Response Team
CHA	Committee on House Administration
CPB	Capitol Police Board
CYA	cover your ass
DIR	daily intelligence report
DNC	Democratic National Committee
DNI	director of national intelligence
DODD	Department of Defense Directive
DOE	Department of Energy
DOJ	Department of Justice
DOS	Department of State
DPD	Dignitary Protection Division
DSCA	Defense Support for Civil Authorities
DSO	domestic security operations
ERT	Emergency Response Team

FAA	Federal Aviation Administration
FAMS	Federal Air Marshal Service
FFC	field force commander
HSAA	House sergeant at arms (on January 6, Paul Irving)
IC	intelligence community, incident commander
IICD	Intelligence and Interagency Coordination Division
JTTF	Joint Terrorism Task Force
MPD	Metropolitan Police Department (Washington, DC)
MWCOG	Metropolitan Washington Council of Governments
NIMS	National Incident Management System
NOC	National Operations Center
NSSE	National Special Security Event
NTAS	National Terrorism Advisory System
OSB	Operational Services Bureau
PCA	Posse Comitatus Act
PIO	public information officer
PMRD	Patrol Mobile Response Division
PPE	personal protective equipment
PSB	Protective Services Bureau
QRF	quick reaction force
RFA	request for assistance
RNC	Republican National Committee
SAA	sergeant at arms (see HSAA and SSAA)
SECARMY	secretary of the army (on January 6, Ryan McCarthy)
SSAA	Senate sergeant at arms (on January 6, Michael Stenger)
SSB	Security Services Bureau
USCP	United States Capitol Police
USPP	United States Park Police
USSS	United States Secret Service
WFO	Washington Field Office
WTO	World Trade Organization

GLOSSARY OF NAMES

ADAMS, JULIE: The thirty-third secretary of the Senate (2015–2021). She began her public service career as deputy of communications for Senator Mitch McConnell in 2003.

ANTIFA: Left-wing antipolice, antigovernment extremist group in the United States.

ANZALLO, MICHAEL: Assistant chief of the Metro Transit Police Department from 2018 to 2021. He was promoted to chief of police in 2022 and has more than thirty years of police experience.

BABBITT, ASHLI: A rioter who was fatally shot during the breach of the Capitol Building. Babbitt was shot in the shoulder by a US Capitol Police officer and later died at the hospital.

BAILEY, DAVID: USCP special agent who was injured in the shooting at the congressional baseball practice in Alexandria, Virginia, in 2017. Bailey was protecting House Majority Whip Steve Scalise when the shooting occurred.

BANKS, LISA: Founding partner of Katz, Banks and Kumin, a plaintiffs' employment law and whistleblower firm. She provided legal representation to Steven Sund.

BARR, WILLIAM: The seventy-seventh and eighty-fifth US attorney general under Presidents George H. W. Bush (1991–1993) and Donald Trump (2019–2020).

BARRETT, AMY CONEY: Associate justice of the Supreme Court. She served as a circuit judge on the US Court of Appeals for the Seventh Circuit from 2017 to 2020 and was nominated in 2020 to succeed Ruth Bader Ginsburg.

BARRETT, BARBARA: Secretary of the air force from 2019 to 2021. Before her appointment, Barrett was the US ambassador to Finland and the senior advisor to the US Mission to the United Nations.

BENEDICT, ASHAN: Special agent in charge of the Bureau of Alcohol, Tobacco, Firearms and Explosives (ATF) Washington Field Office from 2016 to 2021. He began his career in ATF in 1998 with the High Intensity Drug Trafficking Area (HIDTA) Task Force in Washington, DC.

BERNHARDT, DAVID: Secretary of the interior from 2019 to 2021. He began working for the US Department of the Interior in 2001.

BERRET, EMILY: Director of operations for Nancy Pelosi at the time of the January 6 attack. She was named deputy chief of staff for Pelosi in July 2021.

BEUTLER, JAIME HERRERA: US congresswoman representing Washington's Third District (2011–present). She is the first Hispanic to represent Washington State on the federal level.

BIDEN, JOSEPH R.: The forty-sixth president of the United States. He served as the forty-seventh vice president under Barack Obama from 2009 to 2017. Biden also served as a US senator from Delaware from 1973 to 2009.

BLACK, BARRY: The sixty-second chaplain of the US Senate. Black served in the US Navy for more than twenty-seven years before beginning his chaplain career in the Senate in 2003.

BLANTON, J. BRETT: The twelfth Architect of the Capitol (AOC). The AOC is responsible for operation, maintenance, preservation, and development of the US Capitol Complex.

BLODGETT, TIMOTHY: Deputy sergeant at arms (2009–2021) and then acting sergeant at arms (January 12, 2021–April 21, 2021) of the US House of Representatives. He provided testimony as part of the January 6 investigation.

BLUNT, ROY: Republican US senator representing the state of Missouri since 2011. Blunt previously served in the US House of Representatives from 1997 to 2011. On January 6, he was serving as a teller for the 2021 Electoral College vote certification.

BOEBERT, LAUREN: Congresswoman representing Colorado since 2021. Boebert is known for her gun rights advocacy and became communications chair of the right-wing Freedom Caucus in January 2022.

BOGGS, SCOTT: Director of the Metropolitan Washington Council of Governments (MWCOG) Department of Homeland Security and Public Safety.

BOOGALOO BOYS: A loosely organized far-right, antigovernment movement in the United States. One of its stated aims is to instigate a second civil war or American revolution.

BOWDICH, DAVID: Deputy director of the FBI (2018–2021).

BOWSER, MURIEL: Mayor of the District of Columbia since 2015. Before being elected mayor, Bowser was a member of the Council of the District of Columbia from 2007 to 2015.

BRADDOCK, RICHARD: Chief administrative officer for the USCP.

BROOKS, GARTH: A multiplatinum country music singer and recording artist. Brooks is one of the world's bestselling music artists and was inducted into the Country Music Hall of Fame in 2012.

BROWN, MICHAEL: Eighteen-year-old who was shot and killed by a police officer in Ferguson, Missouri, in 2014. Following his shooting, protests and unrest ignited in Ferguson, sparking awareness of police officer–related shootings.

BUSH, GEORGE W.: The forty-third president of the United States (2001–2009). Bush was president during the terrorist attacks on September 11, 2001. He led the country through the recovery process and created the Department of Homeland Security.

CAMPBELL, KIM: Assistant House sergeant at arms at the time of the January 6 attack.

CARROLL, JEFF: Assistant chief of the Metropolitan Police Department and manager of the Homeland Security Bureau (HSB). Before taking this role, Carroll was the commander of the Special Operations Division (SOD).

CERNOVICH, MIKE: Alt-right political commentator.

CHESTNUT, JACOB: USCP officer who was killed in the line of duty during the 1998 US Capitol shooting and became the first African American to lie in honor at the Capitol.

CHESTNUT, WEN-LING: Wife of USCP Officer Jacob Chestnut, who was killed in the line of duty during the 1998 US Capitol shooting.

CLYBURN, JAMES: Congressman representing South Carolina. He has served as the House majority whip since 2019. He also served in this position from 2007 to 2011 and was the House assistant minority leader from 2011 to 2019.

CONTEE, ROBERT: Chief of the Metropolitan Police Department. He joined the department as a cadet in 1989 and was sworn in as an officer in 1992. Contee was promoted to captain in 2004 and held many other leadership positions before his promotion to chief in 2021.

COOK, JAMES: Assistant chief of the Amtrak Police since 2020.

CORBIN, CAROL: Program director at the US Department of Defense.

CROSS, VIVIAN ENEY: Wife of Sergeant Christopher Eney, who was fatally shot during a USCP training exercise. Vivian became an advocate for police survivors and is quoted on the Law Enforcement Officers Memorial.

CUCCINELLI, KEN: Acting deputy secretary of homeland security from 2019 to 2021. He previously served as the attorney general of Virginia (2010–2014) and as a state senator in Virginia (2002–2010).

D'ANTUONO, STEVEN: Assistant director in charge of the FBI's Washington Field Office. He was involved in the arrests and investigation of the January 6 attack at the Capitol.

DANIEL, TED: Assistant sergeant at arms for the US House of Representatives at the time of the attack on the Capitol. He provided coordination and leadership for the joint session of Congress.

DAUGHERTY, BECKY: Protocol officer for the Senate sergeant at arms office at the time of the attack on the Capitol. She provided coordination and leadership for the joint session of Congress.

DAVIS, RODNEY: Republican congressman who has represented Illinois's thirteenth congressional district since 2013.

DAWSON, JIM: Special agent who has served with the FBI for more than twenty-three years. He was the special agent in charge of the Washington Field Office at the time of the January 6 attack.

DIBIASE, THOMAS "TAD": USCP general counsel. His job was to provide legal advice to the operational and administrative elements of the USCP.

DOHR, ROBERT "BOB": Chief operating officer for the House sergeant at arms since 2017.

DONOHUE, JOHN "JACK": Director of the Capitol Police's Intelligence and Interagency Coordination Division (IICD).

DOTSON, SAMUEL: Chief of the Amtrak Police Department (2020–present). Previously, he was chief of the St. Louis Metropolitan Police Department.

DUNN, HARRY: USCP officer for about fifteen years. He provided testimony regarding the January 6 insurrection.

DYSON, ALFONSO: Assistant chief of the United States Secret Service Uniformed Division during the time of the January 6 attack. He began his career with the Secret Service in 1990 and became chief of the Uniformed Division in 2022.

EDWARDS, CAROLINE: USCP officer who was knocked unconscious during the battle on the West Front. Edwards provided testimony regarding the January 6 insurrection. She began her career in law enforcement in 2017.

ELDER, FITZHUGH: Staff director for the Senate Rules Committee from 2018 to 2021, and staff director for the Joint Congressional Committee on Inaugural Ceremonies from June 2020 to July 2021.

ENEY, CHRISTOPHER: USCP sergeant who lost his life in the line of duty during a 1984 training accident.

EPPS, RAY: Participant in the events on January 6 at the US Capitol.

EPSHTEYN, BORIS: Strategic advisor for Donald Trump's 2020 presidential campaign. He also served as a senior advisor to Trump's 2016 campaign. Epshteyn is an investment banker and lawyer.

ERICKSON, JOHN: Inspector for the United States Capitol Police.

ESPER, MARK: Secretary of defense from 2019 to 2020. Esper's public service dates back to 2006 following more than twenty years in the US Army and National Guard.

EVANS, WILLIAM "BILLY": USCP officer who was killed on April 2, 2021, after a man rammed a car into him and another officer outside the Capitol Building. Evans had been with the Capitol Police for eighteen years.

FADO, KELLY: Democratic liaison to the Senate sergeant at arms under Senator Chuck Schumer. Fado previously served as the staff director for the Senate Rules Committee. She became the deputy sergeant at arms of the Senate in March 2021.

FALCICCHIO, JOHN: Chief of staff for Mayor Muriel Bowser (2014–present). He also serves as the deputy mayor for planning and economic development in the District of Columbia.

FANONE, MICHAEL: MPD officer who was beaten and threatened during the January 6 insurrection. He was knocked unconscious and suffered a heart attack during the encounter. Fanone provided testimony to the January 6 Committee.

FARNAM, JULIE: Assistant director for the USCP Intelligence and Interagency Coordination Division (IICD) at the time of the January 6 attack at the Capitol.

FIELDS, JAMES ALEX, JR.: A Nazi sympathizer who drove his car into a group of counterprotesters near a Unite the Right rally in Charlottesville, Virginia.

FLAKE, JEFF: Current US ambassador to Turkey. Flake served as a congressman representing Arizona from 2001 to 2013 and as a US senator from 2013 to 2019.

FLEET, JAMIE: Staff director for the US House of Representatives (2015–present). He has also served on the Committee on House Administration.

FLOYD, GEORGE: A forty-six-year-old African American man who was murdered by a police officer in Minneapolis, Minnesota, in 2020. Floyd's death sparked protests and outrage against police brutality.

FLYNN, CHARLES: Commander of the United States Army Pacific since 2021. Flynn has an extensive military background including several deployments, leadership positions, and a promotion to general in 2020.

FLYNN, MICHAEL: Retired US Army lieutenant general who was the national security advisor in the Trump administration.

FUENTES, NICK: Attendee and speaker at far-right events before the January 6 insurrection. Fuentes is a far-right political commentator.

GAINER, TERRANCE: Former USCP chief as well as the Senate sergeant at arms. During his tenure as USCP chief, Gainer recommended that a fence be built around the US Capitol.

GALLAGHER, SEAN: Deputy chief in charge of the Protective Services Bureau for the USCP during the time of the January 6 attack.

GERI, MOSES: A man who was arrested in Arlington, Virginia, for discharging a weapon in a public place, only a few days before the attack on the Capitol. He was found in possession of weapons and a large quantity of ammunition, and evidence suggests Geri was planning to attend the January 6 protests.

GIBSON, BRIAN: MPD officer who was killed in the line of duty in 1997 during an ambush and shooting while sitting in his police car.

GIBSON, JOHN: USCP officer who was killed in the line of duty during the 1998 US Capitol shooting. He had been with the agency for eighteen years.

GIEBELS, TIM: Secret Service special agent who was serving as the lead for the vice president's security detail during the January 6 attack.

GLOVER, ROBERT: MPD Special Operations Division commander. He began his career with MPD in 1994 and received many promotions. Glover worked as an incident commander during the events on January 6. He retired in 2022.

GOHMERT, LOUIE: Republican congressman who has represented Texas since 2005. Gohmert was appointed chief justice on Texas's 12th Court of Appeals in 2003.

GONELL, AQUILINO: US Capitol Police officer. Gonell provided testimony to the January 6 Committee.

GOOD, ROBERT "BOB": Republican congressman representing Virginia's Fifth Congressional District. He assumed office in January 2021.

GOODMAN, EUGENE: USCP officer who encountered a mob of rioters inside the Capitol Building on January 6 and diverted them away from the Senate Chamber. He received the Congressional Gold Medal in 2021.

GORKA, SEBASTIAN: Deputy assistant to Donald Trump in 2017. Gorka was a speaker at the Freedom Plaza on January 6.

GOSAR, PAUL: Republican congressman representing Arizona since 2013.

GRAHAM, LINDSEY: US senator representing South Carolina since 2003. Graham chaired the Senate Judiciary Committee from 2019 to 2021 and has held many leadership positions during his tenure in public service.

GRASSLEY, CHARLES "CHUCK": US senator representing Iowa since 1981. He previously served eight terms in the Iowa House of Representatives (1959–1975) and three terms in the US House of Representatives (1975–1981).

GRAY, FREDDIE: An African American man who was arrested by the Baltimore Police Department in 2015. Gray sustained injuries while being transported and died seven days later.

GREEN, NOAH: A twenty-five-year-old Black nationalist who attacked US Capitol Police on April 2, 2021, by crashing into a barricade and running at officers with a knife. One USCP officer died in the attack, and another was hospitalized.

GREENE, MARJORIE TAYLOR: Republican congresswoman representing Georgia since 2021.

GRINER, CRYSTAL: Dignitary Protection Division (DPD) agent for the USCP. Griner was seriously wounded in a shooting at a Republican congressional baseball practice.

GRZELAK, CHRIS: Virginia state trooper who offered medical assistance to Officer Brian Sicknick during the January 6 attack at the Capitol.

GIULIANI, RUDY: Former mayor of New York City (1994–2001) and former US associate attorney general (1981–1983). In 2018, Giuliani joined Donald Trump's personal legal team.

GUTZWILLER, DAMON: Santa Cruz County Sheriff's deputy sergeant who was killed in the line of duty by a far-right extremist in 2020.

HARRIS, KAMALA: The forty-ninth vice president of the United States. Harris is the first female vice president as well as the first African American and first Asian American vice president. She was the attorney general of California from 2011 to 2017 and a US senator from 2017 to 2021.

HASPEL, GINA: Director of the CIA from 2018 to 2021. She was the first woman to hold this position.

HAWRYLAK, EGON: Deputy commander for the Joint Task Force National Capital Region and the US Army Military District of Washington.

HEBRON, STEVEN: Officer in MPD'S Special Operations Division who responded to the January 6 attack at the Capitol.

HEMINGWAY, JENNIFER: Deputy Senate sergeant at arms during the January 6 attack. She was named the acting SSAA following the resignation of Michael Stenger. Her public service began in 1999 when she became the deputy staff director of the US House Committee on Oversight and Reform.

HODGES, DANIEL: MPD officer who provided testimony following the January 6 insurrection. Hodges was trapped and crushed defending the lower West Terrace door.

HODGKINSON, JAMES: Shooter who fired on members of the Republican congressional baseball team in 2017.

HONORÉ, RUSSEL: Retired lieutenant general who provided leadership to Task Force 1-6. His previous leadership included serving as commander of Joint Task Force Katrina.

HYDE-SMITH, CINDY: US senator from Mississippi since 2018. She previously served as Mississippi commissioner of agriculture and commerce and as a Mississippi state senator.

HYMAN, AMY: USCP inspector and commander of the Senate Division on January 6, 2021.

IRVING, PAUL: House sergeant at arms from 2012 to 2021, when he resigned following the January 6 attack. Irving also held various positions within the Secret Service from 1983 to 2008.

JOHNSON, MICAH XAVIER: Shooter who opened fire on police in Dallas, Texas, in 2016 during a Black Lives Matter protest, killing five police officers and wounding nine others.

JONES, ALEX: Alt-right radio show host and conspiracy theorist. Jones is known for the website InfoWars, *The Alex Jones Show*, and the Sandy Hook shooting litigation.

JONES, VERNON: Congressman in the Georgia House of Representatives from 1993 to 2001 and 2017 to 2021. He was a speaker at the Freedom Plaza on January 6.

KANE, MORGAN: MPD commander on January 6. As of April 2022, Kane serves as assistant chief of police for Patrol Services North (PSN). She has served with the Metropolitan Police Department since 1998.

KAREM, ROBERT: National security and defense advisor for Senator Mitch McConnell at the time of the January 6 attack. Karem previously served as the assistant secretary of defense for international security affairs from 2017 to 2018.

KAVANAUGH, BRETT: Associate justice of the Supreme Court. He was nominated by President Donald Trump in 2018. Kavanaugh was a US Circuit Court judge before his nomination.

KELLY, MIKE: Congressman representing Pennsylvania since 2011.

KING, AVIS: Former detective for the MPD who recommended that Sund contact the law firm Katz, Banks and Kumin.

KLOBUCHAR, AMY: Democratic US senator from Minnesota since 2007. She campaigned for the Democratic nomination for the president of the United States in 2020.

LANIER, CATHY: Chief of police for MPD from 2007 to 2016. She began her career with the department in 1990, serving in various roles and responsibilities before retiring in 2016.

LARKIN, FRANK: Senate sergeant at arms from 2015 to 2018. Larkin has served in the US Navy, the Secret Service, and the Department of Defense.

LEIBOVITZ, ANNIE: Photographer famous for her portraits of celebrities.

LEONNIG, CAROL: Investigative journalist and staff writer for the *Washington Post*. Leonnig has received several awards, including two Pulitzer Prizes for national reporting.

LEVINSON, MOLLY: Founder and CEO of the Levinson Group. Levinson is a communication specialist who served on Steven Sund's legal and media team.

LIEBENGOOD, HOWARD: USCP officer who took his own life shortly after the January 6 insurrection. Liebengood had been an officer guarding the Capitol since 2005.

LOFGREN, ZOE: Congresswoman representing California since 1995. She has chaired the House Administration Committee since 2019.

LOYD, THOMAS: USCP inspector who served as the commander of the Capitol Division, in charge of all events inside the Capitol, during the January 6 attack.

MADIGAN, TOM: USCP civilian director of facilities and logistics who oversaw the Property Asset Management Division at the time of the January 6 attack.

MALECKI, EVA: USCP's public information officer at the time of the January 6 attack.

MANGER, THOMAS: Former Montgomery County police chief who was hired as the chief of the USCP in July 2021. Manger also served as the official in charge of the Fairfax County Police during the IMF/World Bank protests in 2000.

MARCHESE, STEVE: A high-level staffer for the House Appropriations Subcommittee at the time of the January 6 attack.

MARTIN, TRAYVON: A seventeen-year-old African American male who was fatally shot in Sanford, Florida, by George Zimmerman in 2012. Martin's death resulted in protests and marches across the United States.

MATTHEWS, EARL G.: Veteran and attorney who was serving as General Walker's staff judge advocate on January 6. Matthews was the acting general counsel of the Department of the Army from 2017 to 2018.

MAYBO, ANDY: United States Capitol Police K9 officer during the January 6 attack.

MCCARTHY, KEVIN: Republican congressman representing California who was House minority leader during the January 6 attack. McCarthy has been serving as a representative since 2007.

MCCARTHY, RYAN: Secretary of the army from 2019 to 2021. McCarthy was formerly an army ranger serving in Afghanistan and has served in many leadership positions in both the public and private sectors.

MCCONNELL, MITCH: US senator from Kentucky since 1985. On January 6, he was the Senate majority leader.

MCCONVILLE, JAMES: General who has served as the US Army chief of staff since 2019. McConville has received many awards and decorations for his military service.

MCCULLOUGH, TERRI: Chief of staff to Speaker Nancy Pelosi since 2019. McCullough also served as chief of staff for the US House of Representatives from 2003 to 2011.

MENDOZA, NEYSHA: USCP captain who has been a member of the Capitol Police for twenty years. Mendoza sustained injuries during the January 6 insurrection and provided testimony regarding the event.

MIKA, MATT: Lobbyist who was injured in the shooting attack on members of the Republican congressional baseball team in 2017.

MILLER, CHRISTOPHER: Retired US Army Special Forces colonel who was the acting secretary of defense on January 6. Miller previously commanded the Fifth Special Forces Group in Iraq and Afghanistan.

MILLER, MATTHEW "MATT": US Secret Service agent who was director of the Washington Field Office at the time of the January 6 attack. He served as the assistant director for the office of protective operations in the USSS before retiring at the end of June 2022.

MILLEY, MARK: US Army general and chairman of the Joint Chiefs of Staff. Milley has held multiple command positions within the army and was appointed chief of staff of the army in 2015.

MILTON, PAT: Senior producer of the CBS News Investigative Unit. Milton previously worked with the Associated Press for more than twenty years.

MITCHELL, JEANITA: USCP captain during the January 6 attack. She was promoted to inspector in 2021.

MONAHAN, TIM: Deputy staff director for Representative Rodney Davis at the time of the January 6 attack. Monahan was promoted to staff director in April 2021.

MORENO, EDUARDO: Train engineer who tried to attack the United States Navy hospital ship *Mercy* in 2020.

NAGIEL, SCOTT: Supervisor in the Security Services Bureau, a unit within the United States Capitol Police. Nagiel has more than thirty years of experience in law enforcement.

NEWSHAM, PETER: Chief of the MPD in DC from 2017 to 2020. Newsham is currently the chief of the Prince William County Police Department in Virginia.

O'BRIEN, ROBERT CHARLES, JR.: National security advisor at the time of the January 6 attack.

OATH KEEPERS: A far-right antigovernment militia.

PATTON, SEAN: USCP captain who has served for more than twenty years. Patton worked to protect senators during the January 6 attack at the Capitol.

PAVLIK, RON: Chief of the Metro Transit Police at the time of the January 6 attack. Pavlik served for twenty-five years with the department and retired in 2021.

PELOSI, NANCY: Speaker of the United States House of Representatives. Pelosi has represented the state of California since 1987. She is the first woman to be elected Speaker.

PENCE, GREG: Congressman from Indiana since 2019. He served in the Marines and is the older brother of former Vice President Mike Pence.

PENCE, KAREN: Second Lady of the United States from 2017 to 2021. She is married to Mike Pence.

PENCE, MIKE: Vice president of the United States from 2017 to 2021. Pence was the governor of Indiana from 2013 to 2017 and a member of the US House of Representatives from 2001 to 2013.

PENNY, JODIE: USCP officer and a member of the executive board of the Police Labor Union.

PEZZOLA, DOMINIC: Rioter during the January 6 insurrection who stole a Capitol Police riot shield and used it to break a window in the Capitol Building.

PIATT, WALTER: Lieutenant general of the US Army who serves as the director of army staff. He enlisted in 1979 and has held many leadership positions within the army.

PICKETT, JEFFREY "J. J.": USCP deputy chief during the January 6 attack. Pickett joined the USCP in 1990 and retired in 2021.

PICKETT, KATHLEEN: USCP captain who served as the commander of the Hazardous Incident Response Division during the January 6 attack.

PITTMAN, YOGANANDA: USCP Assistant chief in charge of Protective and Intelligence Operations on January 6. She became acting chief when Sund resigned.

POTAPOV, SERGE: Assistant supervisory air marshal in charge of the Federal Air Marshal Service (FAMS) Washington Field Office on January 6.

PRESLER, SCOTT: Political activist and Trump supporter.

PROUD BOYS: Right-wing extremist group.

RODRIGUEZ, CHRISTOPHER: Director of the DC Homeland Security and Emergency Management Agency (HSEMA).

ROESSLER, ED: Fairfax County Police chief at the time of the January 6 attack. He served for more than thirty years in the department. Roessler retired in 2021.

ROHRER, DAVE: Fairfax County deputy executive at the time of the January 6 attack.

ROMNEY, MITT: US senator from Utah since 2019. He served as governor of Massachusetts from 2003 to 2007 and was the Republican nominee for president of the United States in 2012.

ROSEN, JEFFREY: Acting attorney general from December 2020 through January 2021. Previously, Rosen served as the deputy secretary of transportation from 2017 to 2019.

ROY, CHIP: Congressman representing Texas since 2019. He previously served as the chief of staff for Senator Ted Cruz.

RUMSFELD, DONALD: Secretary of defense from 1975 to 1977 and 2001 to 2006. Rumsfeld held many public service leadership positions including as a US congressman representing Illinois (1963–1969). He died on June 29, 2021.

RYAN, TIM: Congressman representing Ohio since 2003. At the time of January 6, he was the chairman of the Legislative Branch Appropriations Subcommittee.

SANBORN, JILL: Assistant director of the FBI Counterterrorism Division at the time of the January 6 attack. She became the executive assistant director of the National Security Branch of the FBI in May 2021.

SAYOC, CESAR A., JR.: Supporter of President Trump who manufactured and mailed improvised explosive devices in 2018 to people he identified as opposing Trump.

SCALISE, STEPHEN "STEVE": Congressman representing Louisiana since 2008. In 2017, he was shot and seriously wounded during a congressional baseball practice.

SCHNEIDER, KIMBERLY: USCP inspector and head of the Dignitary Protection Division (DPD) at the time of the January 6 attack.

SCHROEDER, RACHELLE: Deputy Republican staff director of the Senate Rules Committee at the time of the January 6 attack. She was promoted to Republican staff director of the Rules Committee in June 2021.

SCHUMER, CHUCK: US senator from New York since 1999. He became the Senate majority leader on January 20, 2021.

SETTLE, GARY: Head of the Virginia State Police at the time of the January 6 attack. He has been a member of the Virginia State Police for more than thirty years.

SHAFFER, MICHAEL: USCP inspector and commander of the Office of Professional Responsibility.

SHAVER, KEN: USCP officer who was injured after a man rammed a car into him and another officer outside the Capitol Building in 2021.

SICKNICK, BRIAN: USCP officer who collapsed following the January 6 attack at the Capitol. Sicknick later died at a local hospital.

SMITH, PAMELA: Acting chief of the US Park Police during the January 6 attack. She was promoted to chief in February 2021. She retired in April 2022 after twenty-four years of service.

STENGER, MICHAEL: Senate sergeant at arms from 2018 to 2021. He served thirty-five years in the Secret Service and held various leadership positions in public service. Stenger passed away on June 27, 2022.

STEWART, RONDA: Deputy Senate sergeant at arms on January 6.

SULLIVAN, THOMAS "TOM": Chief of the US Secret Service Uniformed Division from 2018 to 2022.

TARRIO, ENRIQUE: Proud Boys leader who was indicted in 2022 for his alleged role in the January 6 insurrection.

TAYLOR, BREONNA: A twenty-six-year-old African American woman who was fatally shot in her home in Kentucky in 2020. Her death led to numerous protests against police brutality across the United States.

THOMAS, CHAD: Assistant chief of the USCP in charge of Uniformed Operations at the time of the January 6 attack. He had been with the department since 1996.

THREE PERCENTERS: American and Canadian far-right, antigovernment militia.

TRASK, RICHARD: FBI special agent who was the lead investigator in the kidnapping conspiracy case involving Governor Gretchen Whitmer.

TRUMP, DONALD: The forty-fifth president of the United States, from 2017 to 2021.

TRUMP, MELANIA: First Lady of the United States, from 2017 to 2021. She is married to Donald Trump.

TYLER, TIMOTHY "TIM": Deputy chief of the Metropolitan Washington Airports Authority on January 6. He provided a leadership role following the congressional baseball practice shooting.

VERDERESE, BRIAN: USCP captain who worked to swear in and deploy special police officers during the January 6 attack at the Capitol.

VERDEROSA, MATTHEW "MATT": USCP chief who retired in 2019 following thirty-four years in law enforcement and three years as the chief of police.

VICKERS, RANDY: Chief information security officer for the House of Representatives on January 6.

WALDOW, ERIC: USCP deputy chief who was the exterior incident commander during the January 6 attack at the Capitol. Waldow retired in 2021.

WALKER, WILLIAM: Commanding general of the DC National Guard on January 6. He became the House sergeant at arms in April 2021.

WATERS, MAXINE: Congresswoman representing California since 1991. Waters became the chair of the House Financial Services Committee in 2019.

WEIGHT, MICHAEL: Lieutenant for the United States Capitol Police.

WELCH, EDGAR MADDISON: Shooter who fired into the Comet pizzeria in Washington, DC, in 2016.

WHITAKER, BILL: Television journalist for *60 Minutes*. He started his career in journalism in 1979 and began working for CBS News in 1984.

WHITMER, GRETCHEN: Governor of Michigan since 2019. In 2020, the FBI stopped a plot to kidnap Whitmer.

WISHAM, JOHN: USCP lieutenant who was assigned as the watch commander in the Command Center on January 6. He was previously a sergeant with the bomb squad.

WITTMAN, BRYAN: Personal friend of Steven Sund and former vice president of the Walt Disney company in Orlando, Florida.

WOLF, CHAD: Acting secretary of homeland security from 2019 to 2021. Wolf served in many positions within the Department of Homeland Security and was a lobbyist from 2005 to 2016.

WOLVERINE WATCHMEN: Far-right militia group that plotted to kidnap Governor Whitmer.

WOOD, SALLEY: USCP chief of staff to Steven Sund.

WOODARD, STEVE: US Secret Service special agent. Woodard began his career with the Secret Service in 1987. He passed away on June 29, 2022.

ZAKARIA, FAREED: Journalist, political commentator, and host of *Fareed Zakaria GPS* on CNN.

INDEX